The Heretic's Guide to Best Practices

The Heretic's Guide to Best Practices

The *Reality* of Managing Complex Problems in Organisations

Paul Culmsee and Kailash Awati

iUniverse, Inc.
Bloomington

The Heretic's Guide to Best Practices
The *Reality* of Managing Complex Problems in Organisations

iUniverse Star
an iUniverse, Inc. imprint

iUniverse books may be ordered through booksellers or by contacting:

iUniverse
1663 Liberty Drive
Bloomington, IN 47403
www.iuniverse.com
1-800-Authors (1-800-288-4677)

ISBN: 978-1-9389-0840-8 (sc)
ISBN: 978-1-9389-0841-5 (e)

Library of Congress Control Number: 2013906173

Printed in the United States of America

iUniverse rev. date: 5/21/2013

Dedication

Paul:

To Terrie, Ashlee and Liam. This is for you.

Kailash:

To Arati, Rohan and Vikram—for everything.

Contents

Foreword to "Heretics Guide"

It is said that you don't really understand a subject until you've taught it. Hmm—I would agree that trying to explain something new or complex will expose a lot of inconsistencies and gaps in your own understanding of the subject, so you might gain an understanding of what you don't understand, if you follow me.

But as it turns out, the truth is that you don't really understand a subject until someone has *successfully* learned it from you. After all, a lot of what passes for teaching fails to foster actual learning on the other end. And by "learning" I mean that the student is actually changed by the learning process. But that kind of learning is relatively rare. Most students are satisfied to have temporarily acquired some new conceptual baggage, hoping that when the need arises they will be able to locate and unlock said baggage.

Paul Culmsee is one of those rare students who allows himself to be used by learning, so that it rearranges all of his baggage and sends him off in a new direction. Paul (who lives in Perth, Australia) was in a web course on the basics "issue mapping" that I was teaching a few years ago. I had presented the Question Types module to the class, exhorting them to go beyond merely learning the Question Types to *becoming* them. Paul called me a few days later and said that he was struggling with the homework because he wasn't clear about the difference between "deontic" and "instrumental" questions. I listened patiently, encouraged him that it was really quite simple, and reminded him of the definitions: deontic questions ask which direction to go in, while instrumental questions ask for the best way to move in a given direction. Paul started posing example questions and asking about their types, and after twenty minutes of stumbling explanation I conceded that the distinction was more complex than I had realized. Another half an hour of wrangling with linguistic subtleties and we arrived at a new understanding, which I incorporated into the course. From that moment I've never been sure which of us has the clearer understanding of the deontic/instrumental distinction, nor even who between us the real teacher is.

About a month later, halfway through the basics course, I got a call from a guy in Perth named Mike Kapitola who had read my book and wondered if there were any dialogue mappers in Australia who could help his organization with a wicked problem they were working on. (To put my wonder about this caller in perspective, I have never gotten such an inquiry from New York, Los Angeles, or London!) I explained that we didn't have any certified mappers in Australia, but that it just so happened that I had a promising student who lived right there in Perth, and the rest fell in place as if it had been preordained. Paul wrote a blog about his experience of that first professional Dialogue Mapping session—mostly terror, as I recall—but in his blog we get a glimpse of deep learning, the kind when your molecules get rearranged and you get sent off in a new direction.

Paul's new direction has led to more well-written blogs about the mapping approach, and to clients who rave about his Dialogue Mapping work (". . . most satisfying piece of work in my career . . ."), even when he's mapping for a group in a subject area that is completely new to him. He is also teaching classes in issue mapping, and has the nerve to send me raving comments from the students in his classes.

Paul's success is incredibly gratifying to me. It's tempting to suggest that you don't *really* understand a subject until you have a student who has written a book that surpasses your knowledge of it. Of course, if I were a lot younger and had an Australian accent I could have done all these things too . . . but I guess that wasn't preordained.

My connection with Kailash is another Internet love story . . . intellectually speaking, of course. Even though we've never met in person I have immense respect for how clearly he understands the shifting organizational landscape—the tremors as industrial age thinking topples from its own weight, and the growing light of a fundamentally more human way of doing work. In my experience he's simply a very smart guy.

In Paul and Kailash I have found kindred spirits who understand how messed up most organizations are, and how urgent it is that organizations discover what Buddhists call "expedient means"—not more "best practices" or better change management for the enterprise, but transparent methods and theories that are simple to learn and apply, and that foster organizational intelligence as a natural expression of individual intelligence. This book is a bold step forward on that path, and it has the wonderful quality, like a walk at dawn through a beautiful park, of presenting profound insights with humor, precision, and clarity.

Jeff Conklin
Napa, California
Fall 2011

Preface

It is usual in a preface to talk about the authors' motivations for writing a book. It is also standard fare to convey why authors are uniquely qualified to write on the subject matter they choose. What authors are not supposed to say however, is that their book was anything but a meticulously planned and executed affair. Yet anyone who has undertaken a creative endeavour, such as writing a book, knows full well that reality does not always follow this ideal. The idea of two very different people with a keen shared interest, putting fingers to keyboard and seeing what would come out the other end strikes fear into many a book editor because an emergent writing project is simply "not the way it is done." Yet challenging the "way things are done" is one of the reasons we wrote this book.

In truth, this book is an emergent output of two years of collaboration. What you hold now was not meticulously planned from start to finish. Whilst we had a very clear idea on our chosen topic and felt suitably qualified to write it, the very act of putting fingers to keyboard and assembling our diverse thoughts was just as much of a learning process as the experiences that shaped our motivations for writing it.

Now, before we go anywhere further, we also need to say a few words about our intended audience and writing style. In short, this book is designed to be engaging, rigorous and informative. We believe this book contains actionable advice for people who sit anywhere within the organisational hierarchy—there is stuff here both for frontline employees and senior executives. As far as our writing style is concerned, it is deliberately conversational, with lots of anecdotes and references to pop-culture. Although our message is serious, our writing style is not. We believe this makes for a more accessible and readable book. We sincerely hope that by the time you have made your way through to the end, you will agree.

That said, the tale behind the creation of this book is a strange one and will need to be told from two perspectives.

Paul:

This all started with a question someone asked me some years back. The situation was a gone-off-the-rails IT project aimed at deploying Microsoft's SharePoint product. While not all readers will likely have heard of SharePoint, most are likely to be familiar with haywire projects, IT or otherwise. SharePoint, for what it's worth, can be thought of as a fancy intranet that is used for organisational collaboration.

This particular project had lots of different stakeholders with vastly different world views and as a result had lots of money spent for questionable results, resulting in a tense situation with lots of finger pointing and butt-covering. One day, around halfway through implementation, I was drinking a coffee with the sponsor of the project—the guy who signed the cheques. He asked me the following question:

> "Paul, can you tell me the difference between SharePoint and Skype?"

Now, both Kailash and I can understand readers may not necessarily know what SharePoint is, but we are pretty sure that most people know what Skype is. Comparing Skype (software for making phone calls over the internet), to SharePoint (software that powers many internet sites and corporate intranet portals), makes no sense at all. It is like asking the difference between a bus and a slice of pizza.

So, after recovering from choking on my latte, I asked this person to elaborate on his strange question.

"Well," he explained, "I can collaborate with anybody in the world using Skype for free and even call regular land lines very cheaply. Why should I pay half-a-million bucks for SharePoint to collaborate?"

That project is now long gone—as is that organisation for that matter that chased the false-goal of "improved collaboration." But the SharePoint vs. Skype question for me was a career defining moment. From it, I developed a keen interest in the area of sensemaking and dedicated myself to acquiring skills to help groups deal with really complex problems. My original intent was to use this to augment my IT skills, but people seemed to like the methods and I ended up working in areas miles away from my IT roots. In the process, I have been involved with some really interesting projects and benefited hugely from the professional and personal learning that came with it. As a result, I have made considerable study of, and gained much practice in, various techniques for collaborative project delivery and problem solving. I don't remember when I came across Kailash's amazing blog, but I soon became a huge fan and started to comment on his posts. Kailash writes with the sort of rigour that I aspire to and will never achieve. The subject matter and depth of discussion on his blog was exactly what I was looking for and I was always impressed at the research and effort that he put into his writing.

From my recollection, Kailash started reading my blog and enjoyed an old series of mine called "The One Best Practice To Rule Them All." He subsequently built upon that work with a series of brilliant posts, drawing on some really fascinating yet obscure research. After a number of long discussions on Skype (he knew the difference between Skype and SharePoint!), he suggested we write a book together.

Kailash is definitely the brains of the collaboration between us. With two PhDs and an academic former life, he comes in really handy when it comes to reading boring academic texts. He can read a paper first, give me the "Kailash version" and then I can read the paper for myself and have to expend far less brain effort to make sense of it all.

I am somewhat known around the place for my writings on SharePoint. For anybody picking up this book expecting SharePoint content, you will be disappointed. In fact, SharePoint gets no further mention from here on.

My sensemaking work has not only given me a new career; it has opened my eyes. I have been fortunate enough through this work to be in rooms with incredibly clever people, working on often very complex problems. The learning for me has been immense, and I wanted to capture that learning into a book. Besides which, there are a gazillion SharePoint books out there, but not so many like this one.

Kailash:

This book is the result of an unlikely collaboration. As Paul has mentioned, we stumbled on each other's blogs a few years ago. Soon after, we started a fitful correspondence via email and Skype. At that time, I had been blogging for a year or so, mostly on topics in and around project management and organisational theory. My experience of a decade or so of using process-oriented management techniques, often sold under the banner of *best practices*, had left me somewhat disillusioned about their utility. Quite naturally, some of my posts reflected this.

When I read Paul's posts on Dialogue Mapping, a technique that we discuss at length in the book, I realised that it addressed a key factor that mainstream management ignores: that organisations consist of people, and that the smooth functioning of organisations depends critically on the commitments that people make to each other. It was obvious to both of us that people will genuinely commit only to things they truly believe in. Consequently, they have to be convinced of what they are committing to. At the heart of this book lies the notion that dialogue between all affected organisational stakeholders is the best way to elicit such commitments. Anyway, there is much more about that in the book. For now, let me get back to the story of the collaboration.

In late 2009, I suggested to Paul that we collaborate on writing a book. Paul's instant reply was "Yes, let's do it." We knew what we wanted to write about but lacked a common thread to hold it all together. Inspiration finally came to Paul when he was laid up with a bad back and the flu. He wrote to me saying that he had got it: we should do a book on *holding environments*. Not having heard about the term before, I zipped off to Google and looked it up. I'll refrain from elaborating on the term here as there is much more about it in the book. Although I saw what he was getting at, I had no idea of how we would get there; neither did he.

Nevertheless, we started writing. As I recall, Chapter 4 was the first one we did, followed closely by Chapter 3 (correct me if I'm wrong, Paul). Writing was slow because of our day jobs, but by the end of 2010 we had a fair bit done. The book was slowly starting to take shape. We had a definite first part where we outlined existing problems and had a reasonably clear vision about how we would continue. Part 2 would outline solutions and Part 3 would outline examples based on case-studies from Paul's practice. It was then a matter of finding the time to write it out.

It's taken about two years from start to finish. In the process I have learnt a lot from Paul. He has said some incredibly kind things about me, but don't let him fool you for a minute: this book would not be what it is without his keen intelligence and practical knowledge. Moreover, he is not daunted by degrees or academic papers. I have come out of the wrong side of arguments with him countless times over the last two years. He is one of those rare practitioners who can smell manure a mile way. Thanks mate, it's been a pleasure working with you.

Much of the book is based on our experiences supplemented with a broad (if somewhat eclectic) reading of research papers in general management, project management and organisational theory. At a personal level, the process of writing and thinking about the book has been a very rewarding experience. Among other things, I'm more certain than ever that things in organisations do not have to remain the way they are simply because "that's the way things are done around here." There is a better way, and I hope this book will convey a sense of why I think so.

Acknowledgements

Paul:

There are a number of people who I would particularly like to acknowledge as playing an instrumental part of the journey that has culminated in this book.

First of all, to Jeff Conklin: as a teacher and mentor, you gave me answers that I never knew I was looking for. The elegant brilliance of your "Wicked Problems and Social Complexity" paper that started it all is still, in my opinion, the seminal work in this area.

To Mike Kapitola: for giving me an opportunity at Stirling—the shared learning since then has been immense. This book would not exist if it was not for your vision, innovation and wisdom, and I think that the best is yet to come.

Similarly, to Darryl Whiteley: an innovator, pioneer and mentor. I hope that this book might play a small part in the recognition that you richly deserve.

To Neil Preston: for insight and an amazing case study that never made it to the book (next time mate), as well as clever anecdotes that I blatantly steal to this day.

To John Robertson: for being a kindred spirit who opened doors and introduced me to many brilliant people; Daniel Heymans and Marie Verschuer for Precinct 5; Ed Nieman for introducing me to Heifetz.

All my SharePoint chums, particularly; Ruven Gotz, Joel Oleson, Andrew Woodward, Ant Clay, Erica Toelle, Debbie Ireland, Chan Kulathilake.

Also Peter Chow, Chris Tomich and Daniel Wale at Seven Sigma where we practice what we preach.

To my father, Mike Culmsee, who in return for free IT technical support and the odd single malt whiskey, spent countless hours reviewing this book.

Finally and most importantly of all: To my wife Teresa, my daughter Ashlee and son Liam, who not only have to put up with me gallivanting around the world but had put up with me locked away night after night getting this done. We finally got there!

Kailash:

There are many people who have influenced and helped me in many different ways and have thus contributed to this book directly or indirectly.

I'm indebted to Mario Techera, friend and colleague, for a route out of the cloistered world of academia and for teaching me much of what I know about management and consulting.

Jeff Conklin's book and papers on Dialogue and Issue Mapping have greatly influenced my thinking over the last few years. Jeff, I am honoured by the interest you have shown in my articles on Dialogue and Issue Mapping and am deeply grateful for all that I have learnt from your writings.

To my workmates and friends: Nick Leverett, Nick Webb, Matt Pinch and Anh Vu—many thanks for coffee and chats about matters ranging from the mundane to the philosophical. Guys, I think you may recognise echoes of some of our conversations in this book. Anh, thanks too for your help (at very short notice!) with a couple of the figures in the book.

A huge "Thanks mate!" to my good friend and colleague, Jason Rankin for making it possible for me to try out some of my crazy ideas in live situations and for connecting me with interesting work opportunities.

I am grateful to all those who have commented on various pieces on my blog. In particular, I would like to thank Glen Alleman, Craig Brown, Mike Clayton, Jeff Conklin, Tim Van Gelder, Ruven Gotz, David Green, Richard Harbridge, Robert Higgins, Narendra Khanna, Shim Marom, Bill Nichols, Martin Price, Al Selvin, Simon Shum, Prakash Vaidhyanathan and Tony Waisanen for their insights and encouraging comments.

Thanks to Tony Howes and Michael Mackay for interesting research opportunities, some of which are mentioned in this book.

A hat tip to Ben Sommerville and Ross Black for a brief but very instructive stint in an Agile software development environment.

I'm grateful to Joe Helo and Adrian Anderson for creating an environment in which some of my ideas could be developed and tested.

My thanks go out to Vlado Bokan for encouragement during the early stages of this effort and for interesting conversations about many of the topics discussed in these pages.

I'm deeply grateful to Sandeep and Pooja Chugh for their friendship and support over so many years.

A heartfelt thanks and so much more to Shubhangi and Mukund Apte, and Vishakha Pande for helping out in so many different ways.

My appreciation and love go out to: Mum and Dad; Kedar, Simrita and Siddharth; Swatee, Shrichand and Priya, for being there through ups and downs, and for their unstinting support.

To my boys, Rohan and Vikram: a big hug for putting up with my mental absences when I was writing. I love you both more than you can possibly know.

Finally, my deepest appreciation and biggest thanks go out to my lovely wife for doing all the things that made it possible for me to write this book and for so much more. Arati, you know I appreciate all that you do—and now I can state it in print.

Paul and Kailash

Our deepest appreciation and thanks to Teresa Culmsee, Mike Culmsee, Arati Apte, Christian Buckley, Andrew Jolly, Andrew Woodward, Lee Horn, Ant Clay, Chris Chapman, Craig Brown and Jim Underwood for being prepared to read the book in manuscript form and help us make it better.

THE HERETIC'S GUIDE
TO BEST PRACTICES

PART 1
Why they don't work . . .

Introduction:

Losing our Marbles

In the beginning was the plan
And then came the assumptions
And the assumptions were without form
And the plan was completely without substance
And darkness was upon the faces of the workers
And they spake unto their marketing managers, saying "it is a pot of manure, and it stinketh"
And the marketing managers went unto the strategists and saith,
"It is a pile of dung, and none may abide the odor thereof"
And the strategists went unto the business managers and saith
"It is a container of excrement, and it is very strong and such that none may abide by it"
And the business managers went unto the director and saith,
"It is a vessel of fertilizer, and none may abide its strength"
And the director went to the vice president and saith,
"It contains that which aids plant growth and it is very strong"
And the vice president went unto the senior vice president and saith,
"It promoteth growth, and it is powerful"
And the senior vice president went unto the president and saith,
"This powerful new plan will actively promote growth and efficiency of the company and the business in general"
And the president looked upon the plan and saw that it was good
And the plan became policy.

"The plan"—(David H. H. Diamond)

Have you ever noticed that infomercials trying to sell you the latest ab-sculpting, fat burning, home fitness device with three easy credit card payments, always start with questions designed in such a way that the answer is invariably "Yes"? We have too, so as a tribute to these infomercials, we are starting this book with some seriously loaded questions.

- Have you ever had the feeling that something is not quite right in your workplace, yet you cannot articulate why?
- Are you required to perform tasks that you instinctively feel are of questionable value?
- Have you ever questioned an approach only to be told that it is a best practice and therefore cannot be questioned?
- Have you ever sighed and blamed the ills of your organisation on "culture" or "that's just the way things are done here"?
- Have you ever lamented to others that "If only we got ourselves organised" we would stop chasing our tails and being so reactive?

If you answered "No" to these questions, then seriously, you are holding the wrong book. What's more, if you manage staff and you answered "No" to these questions, chances are your staff gave you this book to read in the hope that you might learn a few home truths.

For those who said a hopefully emphatic "Yes!"—and we are hoping that's a fair chunk of our readers—this book might offer you some answers, and put some names to some of the things that make your organisational "spider senses" tingle. Bear in mind, you are not going to get any glib "Seven Steps to Organisational Nirvana" type stuff here. Instead, you are about to undertake a varied and, at times, heretical journey into the fun-filled world of organisational problem solving. Not only will this book provide you with some juicy ammunition in relation to organisational debates about the validity of best practices, but the practical tools and approaches that we cover might also give you some insights into how to improve things.

Of dreams and Dilbert

The fact that we laugh at Dilbert cartoons is proof enough of the "bizarro" world of organisations, the people who make them and the things they do in the name of best practices. We simply wouldn't laugh at Dilbert-type cartoons if we couldn't relate them to our own experiences, and realise that much of the humour comes from the fact that it is all so true. Yet, to understand why Dilbert is bitingly funny, we don't have to look far. Our own subconscious makes it pretty easy.

Most people have woken up, heart pounding, from one of those dreams where they are in a public place without any pants on, freaking out, trying to work out how to get back to the sanctuary of home where they are free to roam in their underwear without fear of embarrassment and ridicule. Similarly, it is common to have the "running but not getting anywhere" dream, like being late for some critical appointment. Your subconscious puts up all sorts of surreal barriers that prevent you from reaching your goal. Another variant of this theme is when you dream you have to perform a task that you have no skill for, such as play an instrument or a sport that you have no prior experience with, yet you are thrust into the limelight and expected to perform.

In all of these kinds of dreams, your first reaction when you wake up is an overwhelming sense of relief. You think "Phew, I'm glad *that* was just a dream." Being caught with one's proverbial pants down or having to jump into unfamiliar territory can obviously be an unpleasant and stressful experience at times. So, why does our subconscious like to mess with us like this?

A developmental psychologist might point to attachment theory as a possible reason. Attachment theory is the idea that a child needs to feel safe in order to explore the world. Without this sense of security a child will not explore.

Here lies a paradox though—safety is required for us to take risks and perhaps in the process, find new paths and make new discoveries. We fear the unknown but have to act despite it. This is as true in day-to-day life as it is in our work lives, which brings us to one of the key themes of this book. *Those who manage organisations have to provide an environment in which people can explore without fear of the consequences of failure.* Without psychological safety we will not venture our opinions, articulate our thoughts or explore new ideas.

This desire to avoid the stress of being caught with our pants down is a basic, fundamental desire. We like some equilibrium or certainty in our lives and over time, we grow accustom to what our own certainty *feels* like—a feeling best summed up by the word *wellbeing*.

Keeping our marbles

We all have a certain degree of control over our personal wellbeing and take the steps we feel necessary to achieve our goals. The old fashioned wooden labyrinth game (or new iPhone game depending on your age) is a good metaphor for this. The challenge of the game is to navigate a marble through a maze while avoiding the hazards (holes) along the way, much in the way we work towards goals.

In the game, we have to continually adjust the board by tilting it, thereby causing the marble to roll in our desired direction. Sometimes, the positions of the hazards require us to exercise a high degree of control and precision by using subtle movements of the board. Adjust too far one way, the marble will fall in a hole and the game will be over. Make no adjustment at all, the marble will avoid hazards but will not get anywhere.

We instinctively know that we do not live in a predictable world and as a result we are constantly making adjustments, similar to the way in which we would adjust the marble board. The duration and angle of the tilt we apply depends on where we are in the maze and the hazards that we see ahead of us.

Sometimes we will not see a hazard and the marble of our wellbeing will fall into a hole. At the bottom of the hole, things are stressful and chaotic and we want to get the hell out of there. Other times, we might see a potential hazard in front of us and concentrate so hard on avoiding it that we fail to see hazards beyond it. Occasionally, we realise that the tilt we have made was not the right one. We then take a step back, realign our sights and start over. Those who started a college or university course and switched majors midway, realising the original choice was not for them, may be able to relate to this.

Losing our marbles

The metaphor suggests that since we are the ones tilting the board, we have complete control over our own destiny. Yet, the reality is that there are forces beyond our control that affect us. There are many different hands on the board, all tilting it in different directions at different times, forcing us to compensate by adjusting our own moves.

For example, things like the odd global economic crisis have a tendency to cause many people to face the sudden risk of losing their jobs. Such a jolt of the board may completely change how we steer our marbles towards our sense of wellbeing. More important, it may also force us to re-evaluate what that sense of wellbeing actually is.

Sometimes there is a more insidious way that we can lose our proverbial marbles. This happens when we do not even realise that the board has been tilted in a particular manner until it is too late. Then at the last minute we realise that we are heading straight for a big hole in the board, but it's too late to take corrective action.

While this is a book about organisations, shared understanding and why best practices are sometimes not best, the marble game metaphor is useful to illustrate that it *all starts with us.*

To understand why frameworks or best practices are not the answer to chaos and dysfunction in organisations, one has to understand this basic human requirement for wellbeing because it drives a lot of what we do. Our sense of wellbeing frames our reality, how we react to it and, by implication, how we collaborate with others. This is sometimes called the "What's in it for me?" factor.

This chapter started with "The plan" by David H. H. Diamond. It takes a humorous look at how a message is warped as it passes up the food chain from those on the coal face to the hallowed heights of executive suites. Thomas Keating (2009) said that we all have three instinctual needs: (1) safety and security; (2) approval and esteem; and (3) power and control. If you think about it, it is these desires that cause behaviour that others find irrational. They create a filter that censors the exchange of information between people. Examples of the filter at work include:

- "If I say this will I lose my job?"
- "If I say this will I be taken seriously?"
- "If I say this will I be laughed at?"

Perhaps the marketing manager in "The plan" felt that raising the issue the way it was put to him would upset his superiors. His desire for approval and esteem may have influenced what he said. The vice president, even less willing to risk his position, filtered the message further—essentially because his desire for power and control overrode the need for the right (but painful) message to be conveyed. Pretty soon, something that was little better then sewage magically turned into a great idea.

Now don't be scared. This is not a book on the human condition or psychology, and we aren't going to get much deeper than this. But we will be exploring some facets of how we perceive the world and the effect it has on our sense of personal wellbeing. Ultimately though, this book is about how to keep your *group or organisational marbles on the board* and moving in productive directions.

Organisational marbles and the status quo

When we talk about organisations, the wooden labyrinth game metaphor becomes much more complicated and interesting. Imagine the wooden labyrinth board with a bigger and much more complex maze. Consider this to be a board that represents an organisation. Then imagine that there are a number of individual marble games superposed on the organisational board—one for every employee. Thus, we have a number of personal games that run concurrently with an organisational game.

In this set-up, the organisational game has a significant influence on the direction that the individual (employee) marbles take. The point is this: a *tilt in one direction for an organisation may result in an individual moving towards a hazard on their personal marble board.*

Since we have many individual mazes coupled to the broader organisational marble maze, a tilt that benefits some stakeholders may steer another group straight towards what they perceive to be a hazard. This threatens their fundamental sense of wellbeing. Quite naturally, these employees want to tilt the underlying board in a different direction. This dissonance between employees and the organisation results in mistrust and ultimately, conflict. Of course, conflict is no good for anyone. Unhappy employees are likely to be unproductive employees.

Given this, it is in the organisation's interest to avoid board tilts that are going to upset the majority of employees. How can organisations handle this situation? There are two obvious ways:

- Do nothing. This is the classic approach perhaps because it involves the least effort. A variant of this is to institute a superficial change management process that makes the change anyway and tells employees how things are going to be.

8

- Involve employees in decisions on how the board should be tilted.

Many organisations choose the first option, then wonder why employees do everything they can to counter the moves of the organisation. The reason is this: stakeholders want to tilt in a direction that results in their wellbeing, but if they cannot have that, they would rather the *marble be in a known place*. From a personal viewpoint, the "known" is attractive because it offers certainty. From an organisational viewpoint it is less attractive because it represents a loss of flexibility and lack of adaptability to change. Our marble board cannot be tilted if two people are turning it in opposite directions at the same time, and the "tug of war" between the hands tilting the board means that there is a stasis or "status quo" effect. The organisation becomes slow moving or even paralysed.

Extending our metaphor, it can be imagined that if the board is kept static for a long time, key parts will begin to rust. Once this happens, a greater force is required to make a tilt because resistance to movement has increased. The problem here is that the *greater the force required, the less certain we are about where the marbles are going to end up*. The board, when it finally moves, does so with a jerk. When that happens, individual marbles scatter helter-skelter and the outcome is anybody's guess.

Then there is the second option of involving employees in organisational decision making. This can scare the hell out people, especially those who have suffered through organisational chaos before. So, how can one involve sceptical or cynical employees in organisational decision making? In brief, our claim is that this can be done through *dialogue*, or more specifically, *rational dialogue*. This will be covered in detail later in the book. For now, we simply note that such dialogue must:

- Involve the stakeholders who are affected by the decision. In terms of the metaphor, the dialogue should include all those whose marbles may be set rolling in unexpected, and possibly uncomfortable, directions.
- Enable stakeholders to offer their preferred options and their reasons for and against each other's options.

In short: the dialogue must involve collective *reasoning*, hence the adjective "rational." Further, such group reasoning cannot occur in environments that are not conducive to it. It can only flourish if certain conditions are met. Later in the book, we discuss rational dialogue and the environment needed to sustain it. For now, let us turn back to the conflict on our organisational marble board . . .

Changing states and ritual responses to them

An organisation can be thought of as a *system*, a collection of interdependent and interacting entities acting as a coherent whole. Systems occasionally undergo sudden sharp changes from one state to another. Often, such changes start out slowly in a barely noticeable manner and accumulate over a long period of time.

While we could go on at length about Enron, WorldCom or the global financial crisis, we will keep it simple with the parable of the unfortunate skier who happened to sneeze in the wrong place, triggering an avalanche that buried him. That avalanche represents a sharp and sudden change to the environment, stemming from a long period in which tiny incremental changes pushed the system ever closer to the edge. Snowflake by snowflake, season after season, the environment slowly changed. Snow fell onto a ledge, and during the warmer months, some of it melted, soaking through porous stone, washing away sand, grain by grain. Over the seasons, the combined weight of the snow and the inexorable but imperceptible melting ensured that our poor skier would be at considerable risk.

Finally, the system reached a point where the gentlest stimulus caused a sudden and devastating change from a safe state to one that was fatal. Yet, there was no overt sign of danger; there was no way to tell just by looking at the system that an avalanche was imminent. Our point is that the relationship between cause and effect is not always obvious.

There is an old saying that few things are certain, aside from death and taxes (even death may be questionable if you believe in cryogenic suspension[1]). Yet, in organisational life, we use elaborate "rituals" in the guise of management strategies, best practices, methodologies and frameworks to give us the illusion of predictability. This is a natural reaction to an inherently uncertain and unpredictable world. Moreover,

---

[1] Cryogenic suspension is the idea that people are literally put on ice when they die and maintained indefinitely until future technology allows them to be revived.

we convince ourselves, or allow ourselves to be convinced, that these rituals are rational; that they are based on sound premises and logical thought. Nevertheless, the inconvenient truth is that organisational practices are human responses to highly contingent and unpredictable environments. They are specific to particular organisations and their unique situations. Moreover, they are not necessarily rational because human judgement is subjective and often involves a healthy dose of self-interest.

Looking ahead

In the end the marble board, like all metaphors, has its limits. Organisational life has a richness and complexity that cannot be captured by a simple mechanical device. That said, it serves to illustrate a paradox of organisations; organisational actions are often counter to the wellbeing of individuals who make up organisations. That, by itself, is not a bad thing since organisational wellbeing may not coincide with the wellbeing of every individual in it. However, it helps us understand why there is resistance to organisational actions, especially those that lead to radical change. Any organisational change that threatens employee wellbeing is not going to be well received. Individual marbles will not head the way the board intends them to (and here we use the word in the sense of the organisation's board of directors too).

Management is aware of this and so employs a range of techniques to "herd marbles," to get them to roll the way organisation wants them to. These all go under the banner of change management. One of the key techniques recommended by virtually all change management practices is *communication*. Unfortunately, most change-related communication ends up achieving the opposite of what it is intended to do. This alienates employees further. In the next chapter, we look at why this happens. Among other things, we analyse why those vision statements that are supposed to get us all singing from the same sheet, get us singing *out of tune* instead.

Following this, in the remainder of Part 1, we look at some of the reasons for the disconnect between individual and organisational wellbeing. We look at the way things are in present day organisations, drawing from disciplines ranging from cognitive science to organisational theory. Our aim is not comprehensive coverage of the ills of present day organisations. That would take many long (and boring) volumes. Instead, we take our readers through a whirlwind tour of some interesting research, which suggests that all is not well in organisation-land. A lot of this work has languished, largely unread, in academic journals. We think it deserves better.

Part 2 of the book is where we describe solutions: techniques to align individual and organisational aims. The methods we describe are not new—well, not entirely new, at any rate. However, many of them are not so well known. One of the reasons these techniques have not gained mainstream recognition is that they are often seen as impractical and hard to use. We discuss why this is so and what can be done about it. Our approach is entirely practical. Accordingly, in Part 3, we discuss a few case studies that illustrate how these techniques were used to solve complex problems faced by real-life organisations. In all these, the gap between individual wellbeing and organisational aims was significant. Nevertheless, through the use of these techniques, it was possible to align individual wellbeing with that of the organisation to the point where progress could be made on tackling the underlying issues.

So, get set for an interesting and varied ride.

1

Platitudes:
Empty Words that Make the Most Noise

Market churn has set us adrift.
What we need is a paradigm shift.
Get our ducks in a row,
push the envelope,
to keep us from going o'er the cliff.

The boss says, "Let's touch base.
Make game-plans for the next phase.
We'll have meetings and talks.
Think outside the box,
to ensure we're still in the race."

But the elephant in the room
refuses to sing to our tune,
or dance to our beat,
sing from the same sheet
—even once in a blue moon.

From "A cliché-ridden corporate crisis in five limericks" (Kailash Awati)

We are an elite team . . .

What better way to start a book that takes a critical look at all the messed up stuff going on in organisations than with the cult movie "Mystery Men," starring Ben Stiller, Hank Azaria and William H. Macey.

In this movie, the fate of Champion City rests in the hands of seven self-declared superheroes. The reality is that our intrepid "heroes" are fairly inept. Among them, we have the perpetually angry "Mr Furious," the fork flinging "Blue Raja," "The Shoveler" and the mysterious "Sphinx." Despite their individual failings, which they are oblivious to, they somehow band together to triumph against the evil "Casanova Frankenstein."

The Sphinx character is our favourite. He is a master of quasi-philosophical, Zen-like utterances that have no meaning whatsoever. Consider the following classic Sphinxisms:

> "To learn my teachings, I must first teach you how to learn."
> "You must lash out with every limb, like the octopus who plays the drums."
> "He who questions training only trains himself at asking questions."

At one point, Mr Furious grows tired of these teachings, and this following dialogue ensues:

MR FURIOUS: Okay, am I the only one who finds these sayings just a little bit formulaic? (Mimicking the sphinx) If you want to push something down, you have to pull it up. If you want to go left, you have to go right. It's . . .

SPHINX: Your temper is very quick, my friend. But until you learn to master your rage . . .

MR FURIOUS: Your rage will become your master? That's what you were going to say. Right? Right?

SPHINX: . . . Not necessarily

This exchange is a classic illustration of a platitude: a meaningless statement that is presented as if it were significant and original. The word is derived from *plat*, the French word for *flat*. Platitudes are exceedingly common in management and consulting circles. In a paper, Barabba, Pourdenhad and Ackoff (2002) stated that:

> ". . . consultants are of two types: self-promoting gurus and educators. Gurus that pontificate and promote their proprietary problem solving techniques do not educate their clients. They promote maxims that define rules of behaviour but do not increase the competence of managers. They promote their proprietary solution as a fix for all problems instead of trying to increase managerial understanding of a particular corporate puzzle. They provide maxims that are really platitudes and panaceas without proof of effectiveness . . ."

Of course, one person's profundity may be another's platitude; whether or not a particular statement is platitudinous is indeed subjective. Nevertheless, the term is often used in a pejorative sense to describe seemingly profound statements that a *particular* person views as unoriginal or shallow. In this chapter we'll examine platitudes, some blatant, others a little more subtle, to see just how insidious they are and what they can tell you about the culture and maturity of organisations.

Mission and vision statements—too easy

The first and most obvious fertile hunting ground for platitudes that our friend, the Sphinx, would be proud of would have to be organisational mission and vision statements.

"The mission and vision statement maketh the organisation," says the CEO. But does it really? Will those couple of sentences in large font, proudly hanging on the wall behind reception, serve as the rudder used by management to guide the organisation to greatness?

For many reasons we think not, but we are not the first to be cynical. This topic has been done to death elsewhere, so we will simply touch on it here before we get to our main point.

For a start, the phrase "mission statement" is not the latest, nor is it the first term to be used to describe organisational aims and objectives. Nowadays though, many organisations do not label their aims and objectives as a mission statement.

So, why does a term like "mission statement" go out of fashion? Typically, this happens when everyone starts using it at every opportunity. Soon, the term loses its original intent, impact and import. The first people to notice this loss of meaning are those on the receiving end of the platitude; employees who have to translate the mission statement into reality. For these folks, Mission Impossible and Simpsonesque farce come to mind: "Your mission, should you choose to accept it, is to make this organisation Number One in Excellence . . ."

Nevertheless, executives are fascinated by platitudinous aphorisms. Legions of management consultants have figured this out. Moreover, getting in on the act is surprisingly simple. All you need to do is watch for incipient buzzwords and use them before your competitors do. For example, to be *really* cool and up to speed on the latest in high platitude fashion, you need only to appreciate that "mission statement" is like . . . so 20th century. Now, if you want to be seen or heard, you need a "Noble purpose"[1]. No one takes mission statements seriously anymore, but a noble purpose will positively have employees jumping for joy. Remember where you heard it first people—right here in this book. No royalty necessary for use of this term, an acknowledgement will do.☺

The more popular things get, the more commonplace they become. Then, regardless of the original noble intentions behind them, they are overused and ultimately depleted. Like a stock market rally, by the time everyone has caught on, the smart money has moved on. Eventually, it becomes a ritual, something that has lost its original meaning rather than an action with a purpose. In short, the mission and vision statement is done because it is what you are *supposed to do*. After all, a document with a mission and a vision statement is so much more . . . "professional," right? So, not only will we do it, but we'll hire $5000 a day consultants to help us create one. After all, who better than a rank outsider to tell us what we're supposed to be doing?

Yes, this perverse logic is all too common. We'll venture an explanation for this phenomenon in Chapter 3. For now, let's move on with our discussion of platitudes.

Over the years we have developed finely honed radars for platitudes. One particularly easy way to spot them is via the "excellence test." In the final episode of series three of The Simpsons, the TV show, Homer was rendered infertile due to years of radiation exposure. Fearing a lawsuit,

---

[1]   If we ever print a second edition we promise to change this to the coolest new term.

the nuclear power plant created an award called the "Outstanding Achievement in the Field of Excellence" and awarded it to Homer. As far as platitudes go, this award is sheer genius and is the yardstick that we will be using when rating organisational mission statements. Thus, from the very beginning, the example below was doomed to fail:

> "Our mission is to conduct all of our businesses, both energy and financial related, with four key values in mind: respect, integrity, communication and excellence. All business dealings must be conducted in an environment that is open and fair."

You see? As soon as the word excellence is there, we know that there is trouble. This was allegedly[2] the mission statement of a little company called Enron, (yeah . . . *that* Enron!), whose scandalous downfall was the largest bankruptcy in American history at the time, taking out the accounting and audit firm Arthur Andersen with it and being part of the reason for the Sarbanes Oxley regime currently operating in the USA.

Of course, our "excellence" platitude detection test lacks rigour because it misses out on an infinite number of platitudes that do not contain the word excellence. A better option is to follow the philosophy of Russell Ackoff (1987). Ackoff believed that an organisation's or group's mission statement must not state the obvious. The reason is simple: A mission statement that merely restates the obvious does not say anything that is truly aspirational. To quote from Ackoff:

> "They (groups and organisations) often formulate necessities as objectives: For example, 'to achieve sufficient profit.' This is like a person saying his mission is to breathe sufficiently."

One of Ackoff's criteria to judge the quality of a mission statement is to see if the inverse of the statement makes logical sense. If you cannot reasonably disagree with this negative, then the original statement is a platitude. Here are two examples:

---

2   Allegedly as per the following link: http://www.bbc.co.uk/dna/h2g2/ A38083494

". . . our mission and values are to help people and businesses throughout the world realize their full potential." (Microsoft 2011)

So, our inverse here is working to hinder people and businesses to realise their full potential. Hmm, after the Windows Vista experience, some people would consider Microsoft's mission statement more of an oxymoron! The next statement is attributed to General Motors[3] (King, Case and Premo 2010):

". . . a multinational corporation engaged in socially responsible operations, worldwide. It is dedicated to provide products and services of such quality that our customers will receive superior value while our employees and business partners will share in our success and our stock-holders will receive a sustained superior return on their investment."

So, the inverse of this is a socially irresponsible company that produces overpriced goods of poor quality and treats employees, partners and shareholders like crap . . . Speaking of the fast food industry, here is a mission statement attributed to more than one player in that space:

"We will prepare and sell quick service food to fulfil our guests' needs more accurately, quickly, courteously, and in a cleaner environment than our competitors. We will conduct all our business affairs ethically, and with the best employees in the mid-south. We will continue to grow profitably and responsibly, and provide career advancement opportunities for every willing member of our organisation."

This is actually the best mission statement so far. The aspirations are very clear and easily measurable. What about this?

---

[3] Although this is attributed to General Motors, it is important to note that GM, at the time of writing, does not appear to have an explicitly labelled mission statement

"We are dedicated to ensuring a long-term commitment to stakeholder value from performance and improved returns at all levels."

That one was a trick assessment. We generated it from a website[4] where you can generate your very own mission statement. It works like a poker machine. Just pull the lever and within a few seconds, a random assortment of small quotes are mashed together to create a mission statement. If you enter your company name into it, you can even print a certificate.

Figure 1.1: Sample computer generated mission statement

Finally for now, we wonder if you can guess whose organisational mission this is:

"To produce high-quality, low cost, easy to use products that incorporate high technology for the individual. We are proving that high technology does not have to be intimidating for non-computer experts."

The inverse implies that we produce low quality, high cost and hard to use products. But the second sentence redeems the statement because it is measurable. We like the notion of any mission statement starting with "we are proving" because for the next part of the sentence to make sense, it really has to be measurable. In case you didn't guess it, this is attributed to Apple in 1984[5]. Given their market success with anything with the lowercase letter "i" in front of it, we have to concede that they really have achieved that particular mission.

---

4   See http://www.netinsight.co.uk/portfolio/mission/missgen_intro.asp

5   See   http://www.kieranlevis.com/workshop-for-imperial-mba-students-3-march-2011/apple/

Just because you say it, doesn't mean it's true

In a paper entitled "Silenced by a Mission Statement: An Organisation's Cloak of Ambiguity," Gina Rathbun (2007) described her experiences in a company which had a ritual of chanting the company mission statement from a laminated card at the start of every monthly staff meeting. As you read Rathbun's quote below, try and keep in mind the characters from the "Mystery Men," all dressed up in their costumes, starting their day of crime-fighting in a similar manner.

> "Before the meeting commenced, we were instructed to "take out" our cards, which contained the vague metaphorical language . . . The mission statement's chant began:
>
> *We are an elite team of inter-dependent professionals, who are experts at creating upscale living environments. We cultivate situational awareness and act with professionalism and integrity. We are proud. We are a team."*

Rathbun noted that the mission statement recited during these meetings said nothing of where the organisation was going. A little later in the paper, she said:

> ". . . Even the platitudes "elite" and "proud" ascribed a banality that didn't provide much direction toward describing any real behaviour. Isn't any company that takes the time to formulate its values collectively, proud? What values exactly was the President endorsing?"

The point about the mission statement saying nothing about where the organisation was headed actually points to the way to get past platitudes. It may come as a surprise to readers that trying to define them is not the way.

Definitions and bywords

One thing that we all tend to get suckered into doing at times is classifying and defining the objects and ideas we work with. Granted, this is often unavoidable, especially in the world of academia where definitions are needed in order to ensure that everyone understands what's being discussed. Once you read a few papers however, you begin to notice a pattern. Many papers, particularly in the social sciences, start out with a ten page examination of all the past definitions of things that are being examined in the paper. This is followed by an equally tedious discussion of why those definitions are inadequate or incomplete, thereby paving the way for a new set of definitions. The remainder of the paper will be a detailed justification as to why the new, improved definitions are better than their predecessors.

Defining stuff is a time consuming and tiring exercise. Since we live in a world of constant change there will always be new influences which shape and frame perceptions. Therefore, a definition that an author lovingly spends so much effort on coming up with is always subject to being redefined by the next academic, blogger or marketing person who follows a similar path. This cycle plays out in a few ways:

- The new definition becomes more verbose. There are a couple of reasons for this:
    o The definition is expanded to incorporate new aspects of the topic space. In an organisational setting, this creates confusion because the definitions of multiple disciplines can often seemingly contradict each other and thus, careful "wordsmithing" is required to navigate a path through it.
    o New qualifications or exceptional situations have to be excluded. This leads to more new terms being used in the definition.
- A broader, *fundamental* definition is developed. The broader definition encompasses more and so is prone to platitudinous leanings. Further, such definitions also run the risk of being interpreted in ways other than the one intended by the author.
- A new word is used or an existing word is used in a new context to try and convey the new meanings or concepts proposed by the author. If the author gets lucky, it catches on. The metamorphosis from "mission statement" to "noble purpose" is an example of this point.

While it might seem that we are arguing against definitions, be assured we aren't. What we wish to point out is that the tendency to "definitionise" has crept into organisational settings where it is wholly inappropriate. Bywords (and their definitions) are fertile ground for a dangerous kind of platitude which can doom projects before they even begin.

"How do you measure quality, then?"

A common characteristic of a platitude is that it has no meaning until it is applied to a particular situation. Words in this category include quality, security, flexibility, innovation, effectiveness and Paul's personal favourite, governance. These words have plenty written about them and, accordingly, have many definitions. The mistake is to try and lock down a definition in an attempt to provide context to a situation or problem. This creates a very sneaky and dangerous platitude; one that deludes people into thinking that there is more shared understanding between people than there actually is.

Many years ago during a job interview, Paul suggested that many more things were quantifiable than people thought. His interviewer fired back "Well, how do you measure quality, then?" Such a question should set all platitude warning bells ringing at their highest rating. The Q word will have a particular resonance for many project managers because it represents an unconscious use of a platitude. It is often devoid of meaning when used in projects, or at least has several different and even contradictory meanings. How the term is understood can tell you a lot about how projects are tackled within an organisation. This, in turn, is a very good indicator as to whether a project may be a success or not.

Here is why this question makes no sense. An initiative of any kind takes time and effort. You could easily continue on the "business as usual" path and invest that time and effort elsewhere, such as in hiring a new staff member or buying a decent coffee machine. The latter is almost guaranteed to have an improvement on morale for relatively little cost.

Thus, you are only spending time and effort on this thing called "quality" because you believe it will make a *positive difference* in some way. If not, you would be wasting your time and resources on a pointless initiative. Your money would be better spent elsewhere.

Therefore, in relation to measuring quality, it is the *difference made* by quality that you should be measuring to see if you have succeeded or not.

Quality in this context is a *means to an end* and the definition of quality is going to be coloured by whatever that particular end is. In other words, asking if one can measure "quality" without knowing or understanding the objective, makes as much sense as asking if one can measure "innovation" or "flexibility." The question that needs to be answered first is "What difference would more quality make?" Asking "How do you measure quality?" without answering this question suggests that the means have been confused with the ends.

This point can be illustrated quite nicely via a picture. Figure 1.2 represents our present state of affairs. Given that we have undertaken a quality initiative, we obviously have some desirable future state that we want to achieve. This is because we have recognised that our present state is lacking in some way.

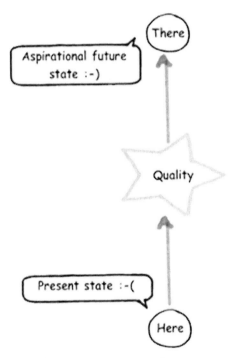

Figure 1.2: Quality as a means to an end

All projects are undertaken because of the perceived gap between these two states. In our quality example, we have determined that to get to this future state, we have to undertake an initiative under the banner of "quality." Quality is, therefore, the *means* by which you will achieve the end of getting to the aspirational future state represented in Figure 1.2.

Given that quality is the means to the end of achieving this desirable future state, asking the question "How do you measure quality?" implies that "more or better quality" is the end state as shown in Figure 1.3.

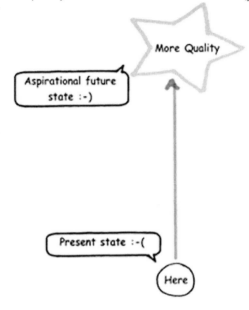

Figure 1.3: Quality as an end

What do you notice about the end state here? It is a textbook example of a platitude, an empty word that makes a lot of noise. In fact it is only a slightly less pointless goal than "more excellence." It conveys nothing and can be interpreted differently by various stakeholders. Moreover, it is unmeasurable and will fail our patented excellence test and Ackoff's inversion test. If our friend, the Sphinx, was a co-author of this book, he would probably offer some lame sort of pseudo-Confucian wisdom like:

"Ah, to seek more quality my friend, one has to master the quality of what you seek."

Hey! That one is actually pretty good! There might actually be some wisdom in those words, so let's templatise it for re-use. Here is our easier to digest version: "To seek [insert platitude word here] one has to understand what [insert platitude word here] looks like."

- To seek "quality," one has to understand what "quality" looks like
- To seek "governance," one has to understand what "governance" looks like
- To seek "innovation," one has to understand what "innovation" looks like

Now that your platitude radar has been honed a little, you will start to notice how easily platitudes sneak into the workplace. A platitude is a mental shortcut we take, a deceptively quick way to cut through uncertainty. We clump our unclear, unarticulated aspirations in a bunch of platitudes. It is easy to do, and it gives us a sense of achievement. But it is a mirage because the objective is not clear, and we cannot define sensible measurements of success if the goal is fuzzy. It never fails to amaze us that many organisational endeavours are given the go-ahead on the basis of platitudinous goals. Mind-boggling, isn't it?

. . . the quality of what we seek

Platitudes, like mirages are seductive but their beauty is as illusory as that of the oasis that isn't there. Many have been entranced by some nice sounding desirable future state incorporating some superlative. "Improved quality," "Best practice collaboration" and "Innovative solutions" are typical examples. Since the platitude becomes a sort of proxy for the end in mind rather than the *real* end, we have no *shared understanding* of where we want to get to. Empty words preclude a shared understanding because they mean nothing at all.

Figure 1.4 illustrates the *effect* of a platitude being confused with the end state, as opposed to the means to a deeper end. We do not have an aspirational future state at all. Instead, we have many possible, fuzzily-defined future states.

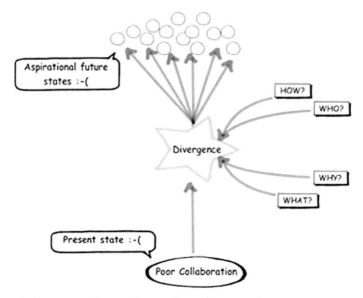

Figure 1.4: Divergence of views due to platitudinous goals

This divergence of views on what the end state is usually spells doom for many projects. However, this is very rarely foreseen in the early stages of a project because people are not talking about tangible end states but platitudinous superlative states. Another reason that platitudes aren't seen for what they are is the push to get things done. In most organisations, people feel pressured to get on with it and solve problems quickly. This minimises the time spent in reflection and diagnosis. Platitudes, thus, remain undetected until it is much too late. In fact, more reflection and diagnosis occurs at the coffee machine and the bar on Fridays than it ever does in meeting rooms during the working week.

The visible symptoms of a project with a divergent understanding among participants are well documented. For example, the infamous Chaos Report by Standish Group (1995) lists the following symptoms of a project that is headed for a world of hurt:

- Lack of user input
- Incomplete requirements & specifications
- Changing requirements & assumptions
- Lack of executive support
- Technology incompetence
- Lack of resources

- Unrealistic expectations
- Unclear objectives
- Unrealistic timeframes
- New technology

Scope creep and vague requirements mean that the project will start to unravel, yet the platitude-driven journey towards the mirage will continue. The project will lurch from crisis to crisis, with scope blowing out, tensions and frustrations rising. This is accompanied by classic blame-shift or hind-covering moves that people make when they realise that their ship's taking water.

In Part 3 of this book we will highlight a case study of an organisation that chased the platitude of "knowledge management" for three years without ever unpacking it. Due to chasing the platitude of knowledge management, the project stumbled along, being restructured and restaffed without any tangible result except a lot of budget burn and many of the visible symptoms outlined in the aforementioned Chaos Report.

The great irony is that people continue to implement platitude-based projects whilst being able to point out others' platitudinous initiatives rather easily. The source of this bias seems to stem from the role one plays on a project. As a project team member, one has to engage stakeholders and get their buy in via tools, such as the communications plan or the stakeholder engagement plan. It is easy to make the mistake of doing this via a platitudinous slogan on a coffee mug or a pretty page on the intranet.

Yet, at the same time, as employees of the organisation, or even members of the broader community, we also play the other role; that of the uninterested and cynical user, disparaging attempts to "buy us in" to initiatives that are clearly wrong-headed. Whether it is our immediate reaction to a new policy by government or the direction favoured by management of our organisations, we see through platitudes rather easily. However, that does not stop us from using the same old jaded marketing techniques to sell the benefits of the initiatives that we're pushing.

We examine why this happens in detail in the next chapter on cognitive bias, but for now, we will explore the long term damage that can be wrought by platitudinous initiatives.

TIM TAMS and the quest for "more innovation"

In the mid-nineties, when Paul was young, green and idealistic, he experienced his first company retreat, complete with the open space style circular seating, flip charts, marker pens with head spinning fumes, a glib facilitator and morale-destroying team building exercises. He was working in a small regional office of a huge mining company that was operating in a turbulent time. A combination of low commodity prices, high overheads and more nimble competition had placed significant pressure on the group. The office in which Paul worked was rumoured to be headed for closure.

Local management had reacted by initiating a strategic review, of which this retreat was a part. Accordingly, all staff brainstormed *innovative ways* in which they could reduce costs and *improve efficiencies.* Participants enjoyed the change of scene. They felt more comfortable than usual because they were having a jolly good venting session, but ultimately there were no major breakthroughs.

Once everyone was back at the office, it did not take long for the quest for "improved efficiency" to take a back seat to the more mundane aspects of work. The only tangible step taken by management was to watch costs more closely than ever, while extravagant spending continued at the rarefied executive level. This smacked of a double standard; one to which the employees weren't blind. Nevertheless, employees rationalised their situation by saying the usual "It happens everywhere."

Then one seemingly insignificant event ignited employees' collective sense of outrage: local management had the audacity to cut out Tim Tams. Now as an aside, readers outside of Australia and New Zealand may not understand the deep significance of removing Tim Tams from the lunch room. Tim Tams are a treat made up of two cracker-like biscuits with a soft chocolate filling, all covered in a hard chocolate coating. Tim Tams and the associated "Tim Tam Slam" (drinking a hot beverage using a Tim Tam as a straw) are a cultural tradition Down Under. Removing them evokes reactions akin to US citizens giving up their second amendment right to bear arms. It should come as no surprise that cutting Tim Tams had the effect of creating even more cynicism amongst mid and lower level employees in the organisation.

On that note, in Chapter 4, you will read about an organisation where creative work was impeded by a well-meant but misguided initiative.

The net effect of the process was a culture of alienated compliance and often humorous subversion. The same thing happened at the company Paul worked for. One example was when management offered a prize for employees to come up with a "slogan" that epitomised the "innovation drive" process that had begun with the retreat. Although Paul forgets the prize and the winning slogan, he remembers vividly all the politically incorrect slogans that traversed the corporate underground. A few of the printable ones included:

- MAGGOT (Management And Geologists Go Off Target)
- WANKIE (Weeding out A New Knowledge In Exploration)
- TIM TAMS (Trouble in Management, Terminate All Munchies)
- TOSS (Total Outsource of Support Staff)
- TOSSER (Total Outsource of Support Staff: Eastern Region)—Paul's office was the western region

In the end, the office was closed, confirming suspicions that employees had all along. Fast forward to the present, and Paul has gone from young, green and idealistic to grizzled veteran who has suffered through a couple more facilitated retreats with different organisations. Both initiatives suffered a similar fate to the first one, leaving him evermore cynical.

This highlights another unintended consequence of trying to motivate people towards a platitudinous goal: people see through it. As a result of his exposure to platitudes, Paul now has a propensity to come up with politically incorrect versions of *any* company catchcry, product or acronym. His finest achievement in this regard was the product name SWIFTCLIC, which was a finalist name for a new, admittedly very good product that his employer at the time was about to launch. Despite SWIFTCLIC making the shortlist on its own merits, its real meaning was actually:

Some **W**eird **I**nterface **F**or **T**he **C**lient **L**oaded **I**n **C**ash

Although Paul is justifiably proud of his small encyclopaedia of dodgy acronyms, we both humbly bow to the US military for coming up with the best one of all; one which epitomises Paul's penchant for "acronymisation" and illustrates perfectly how damaging it can be to build strategies based on platitudes.

BOHICAN Rhapsody

Coming up with a fancy name for a new initiative usually has the opposite effect to the one intended. As illustrated in the previous section, employees see this as an attempt to gain buy-in for an idea that is essentially wrong-headed. However, employees are typically in no position to affect the course of such initiatives so they resort to sarcasm and let events sweep them towards outcomes that seem predetermined.

This cynicism and apathy to any new management initiative is what the US military so eloquently calls BOHICA: Bend Over, Here It Comes Again. The BOHICA effect comes into play when organisations choose to implement a best practice methodology or framework and use platitudes, such as "innovation" or "quality," to promote the initiative.

The BOHICA Syndrome was examined in a paper by Julia Connell and Peter Waring (2002). The paper reported on three case studies that examined the relationship between organisational change initiatives and employee cynicism and the effect of the latter on the long term sustainability of such initiatives. The case studies relate to the "Australian Best Practice Demonstration Program" (ABPP), an initiative launched by the government of the Australian state of New South Wales in the 1990s. The rationale for the program is best summed up in the authors' own words:

> "The primary aim of the ABPP was to encourage organisations to improve their performance levels. This was to be achieved through the adoption of what were claimed by the architects of the program to be 'leading-edge' workplace practices that were identified from various national and international reports, a government-sponsored international study mission on Best Practice and some of the 'Best Practice' organisations."

We note that the combination of the superlatives of "leading-edge" and "best practices" is an oxymoron given that "leading edge" implies a practice that is new and, therefore, cannot be "best" since there's nothing to compare it to!

So, what were these "leading edge" practices to bring about the performance improvement? They included:

- Closer links with customers and suppliers
- More effective use of technology
- Flatter and more responsive organisational structures
- Human resource policies to promote cooperation, flexibility and employee involvement (bottom up decision making)

Connell and Waring interviewed a cross section of employees and managers from three organisations that participated in these programs. They conducted these interviews a year after the ABPP implementation and again in 2001, some six years later. Each organisation was in a different industry sector and had no direct relation with any of the others. Employees also had a long average tenure time (ranging from eleven to sixteen years) which meant most were still around at the six year mark.

The results were clear. All three organisations had largely given up on the ABPP change initiative by 2001.

> "By 2001 however these organisations had all but discarded the ABPP and moved on to adopt other change initiatives. The successive adoption and subsequent abandonment of change initiatives produced a growing cynicism among employees, not only towards management, but also towards any further change proposals."

The last of the Bohicans

When delving into each case study, it became clear that there were different reasons for the failures. Two of the organisations never managed to get to the "bottom up" decision making model and actually went back to the command and control management model that was in place originally. As a result, employees who had bought into the original change initiative felt let down. They lost faith in management's commitment, and the BOHICA syndrome was thus entrenched.

The third organisation ultimately beat BOHICA but not without pain. Senior management took the ABPP best practice of bottom up decision making model so literally that they made most of the middle management and supervisors redundant with no warning! (Talk about being go-getters).

31

This led to a serious slump in productivity because employees had no clue how such a bottom up, team-based model was supposed to work. Not surprisingly, the original change initiative fizzled out, leaving a strong Bohican legacy.

The saving grace for this organisation was that four years later the company was taken over, and significant investments were made into employee training and equipment. Employees had six months of training for a collaborative system which allowed them to identify problems, measure and predict productivity themselves. This finally gave employees what the ABPP had promised: empowerment and control over their destiny. Consequently, in the 2001 interviews, there was no evidence of BOHICA, and morale was reported to be higher than it was before the program began.

The flight to safety

To harken back to the theme of wellbeing in the introduction, most of us are trying to avoid losing our marbles, tilting the board in ways that will ensure that our sense of wellbeing is not compromised. We do not like to be out of our comfort zones, so our first reaction is to look for ways to find our equilibrium again.

Organisational change, by definition, is a tilt to the organisational marble board. This has a knock on effect on the individual marble boards of every employee. Without a shared understanding about the rationale for the change, it is only natural that there will be resistance and pushback or pullback, depending on which way the board's tilting.

Figure 1.4 illustrated that when the vision for change is platitudinous, there will be a divergence of understanding among those who have to commit to making it succeed. Why? Since platitudes have little meaning, they can be taken to mean anything or nothing at all, depending on one's viewpoint. The fate of the initial ABPP in all three organisations suggests that this was the case. When digging deeper, Connell and Waring noted a certain pattern among the change management practitioners who were engaged by the organisations.

> "One criticism to the approach was that consultants would often advocate and utilize their own model for organisational

change, regardless of the unique problems or issues faced by individual organisations."

The consultants clearly missed the irony of being inflexible whilst calling for flexibility from others. Yet, such so called "proven" models espoused by the change practitioners—and more broadly, hawked by big name consultancies—imbue executives with a sense of control; a sense that something is "being done" to tackle difficult problems. The feeling of "moving to action" offers short term satisfaction because of the initial momentum. However, it does not take long for platitudes to undermine it.

The BOHICA syndrome sometimes manifests itself when management reasserts control as a reaction to divergence in understanding. However, it can just as easily catch on even when management does *not* assert adequate control.

The third organisation that ultimately beat BOHICA initially made the mistake of selling employees the platitude of "bottom up decision making." This resulted in initial employee buy-in but wrong-side up because employees were unprepared for the void left by the sudden loss of supervisors and middle management. Thus, the seeds of BOHICA were sowed just as much by management over-exuberance as by management pullback and the assertion of command and control.

Two other lessons learned were noted from this study. Firstly, it is important for business leaders to establish credibility by clarifying their rationale for change. If they do not do this, they risk the perception that change may be seen as being arbitrary—change for the sake of change. Secondly, they recommend to "start from where people are" and proceed incrementally. Extremely radical change is likely to be beyond the capacity of the affected parties, leaving uncertainty, confusion and ultimately resistance and pullback. Quoting from the paper:

> "Emergent organisational change strategies are more likely to be understood when employees have been involved in their development and may also be associated with increased levels of commitment to change. [. . .] where this study is concerned this means demonstrating the credibility and logic of managerial action and allowing for the incremental change where possible"

What's in it for whom?

The ABPP story holds another, less obvious lesson: practices that have worked well for an organisation or even a number of organisations will generally not work well for others without extensive adaptation. Consultants who hawk best practices rarely make enough effort to understand context, which includes the organisation's working environment and idiosyncrasies. The context in which a practice operates is as important as the content and intent of the practice. This is too important a point to be left to consultants or outside experts. The onus is on the client to ensure that context is taken into account when designing or implementing a process based on best practice. The client has to understand the implications of the best practice for the organisation. Consultants will come and go; the client has to live with the consequences.

Some best practice evangelists tend to have an all-or-nothing attitude to the methods that they preach. Connell and Waring noted this pattern in the ABPP study. It is common to hear consultants of this ilk suggest that the only way to use their approach "correctly" is to change organisational processes to fit the approach rather than adapting the approach to suit the organisation. One implication of statements like this is that failure should be expected if you tailor the method or apply it piecemeal; the only way to do it right is to "embed" it in your organisation.

> "But what if it doesn't work?" asks the client, a tad hesitantly.
> (The consultant is an expert, after all).
> "Oh, don't worry. It will work. It is a best practice," is the reply.

It seems to us that the beneficiaries of such a purist approach are consultants and "authorised training organisations" that have an assured supply of training fodder to keep the tills ringing. What's in it for the consultant is pretty clear. However, the question that matters is: what's in it for the client? This often unanswered (or wrongly answered) question is the reason we wrote this book.

Coda: A cliché ridden corporate crisis

Organisational initiatives fail when there is no shared understanding of what is being done and why it is being done. At one level, most managers recognise this, hence the hoo-hah about communicating organisational strategies to the rank and file. On the other hand, most corporate communications are—you guessed it—platitudes.

One of us recalls a long and painful corporate overhaul which played out over several years. During this period no one seemed to have a clue as to what was going to happen and why and how. About six months after the initiative was announced, a three page memo from the board was sent to every employee in the company. After much uncertainty, the long-awaited memo was supposed to *finally* explain the rationale behind the sweeping organisational changes that were portended. The memo contained heart-warming phrases "our people are our most valuable asset," "engagement," "commitment" and the like, but no genuine explanation as to what was going on and why. Unsurprisingly, the net effect was just the opposite of what management had intended: fear, uncertainty and doubt (FUD) levels went through the roof.

What's crystal clear at the board level is far from obvious at the grassroots. However, hard and tricky it may be to explain, it remains the task of management to try and make rationale clear to everyone in the organisation. Why? The answer is simple: in the process of articulating the objectives, the "town-hall pitch" to the masses so to speak, employees might (or should we say, will?) find gaps in management reasoning: things they overlooked from their 50,000 foot view of the organisation—the gap between the fertiliser and the excrement of the grand plan[6].

The end state that most senior executives imagine is an ideal that exists only in the *mythology* of best practice. The "real world" examples that form the basis of these practices are but sanitised, airbrushed case studies that are interred in the pages of management journals and texts. They gloss over difficulties and seldom, if ever, apply in *your* specific situation.

We admit simple solutions are seductive. The best practitioner says "Do this and you will reap the benefits." It is so tempting to suspend thought . . . to just believe and follow. But, those who outsource their thinking will lurch from one crisis to another.

---

[6]   Refers to "The Plan" from the Introduction

We think it is appropriate to end this chapter where we started, with the observation that in times of crisis, managers, like the Sphinx, tend to lapse into cliché-speak. So, we reckon it's no surprise that things go from bad to verse . . . as in the ditty at the start of this chapter.

With platitudes and clichés done to death, it is now time to look at why decision-makers end up choosing incorrect, overly simplistic solutions to tackle organisational problems. There are two reasons for this. One relates to our tendency as humans to make ill-considered decisions and the other to the fact that ideas that gain currency aren't necessarily correct. We look at these points in the following chapters.

2

A Mind Field of Errors

"If you were an American walking around in 2005, you had a one in 10,010 chance of dying from falling off a ladder. Your chances of dying in a terrorist attack were one in 88,000. Why, then, are we not plunged into the depths of panic whenever we see a ladder? The big fat answer is that ladders aren't scary . . ."
(Josh Clark) http://blogs.howstuffworks.com/2009/10/05/cognitive-bias-or-why-humans-stink-at-assessing-threats/

Lessons from "Ben 10"

Paul's five year old boy, Liam, is a huge fan of Ben 10[1]. If you have not heard of Ben 10, you obviously do not have a five year old boy. It is the latest in a long line of cartoons that have captured the hearts and minds of kids. Like most fictional characters that kids can relate to, Ben 10 is backed up by a marketing machine that turns a mundane object into something desirable simply because it has Ben 10 written on it.

Like Teenage Mutant Ninja Turtles before it and Masters of the Universe before that, Ben 10 now appears everywhere. To date, Liam owns Ben 10 DVDs, a bag, hat, t-shirts, pants, jackets, mug, bowl, watch, shoes, water pistol, scooter, sunglasses, pencils, pyjamas and even underwear. When the family ventures out in public, Liam is a walking, talking Ben 10 advertisement.

Liam does not just walk when he is in Ben 10 mode—he struts around the place like a peacock, feeling very, very cool indeed. While his parents might think he looks a teeny bit over the top, he thinks he is the coolest kid around. Paul also remembers that around thirty five years ago, he was a huge fan of superman. His mother allowed him to wear an additional pair of underpants on the outside of his clothes and a dish towel pinned around his neck as his suit. Paul would wear this proudly wherever he went. Kailash, in typical project manager fashion, refuses to confirm or deny such childhood leanings.

Imagine how much Liam thought his Christmases had come at once when, at a fair, he came across a Ben 10 "show-bag" full of those cheap, plastic trinkets that seem to invariably end up being found down the back of a couch some months later. But hey, these were Ben 10 cheap, plastic trinkets and were therefore absolutely brilliant; they had to be purchased and used.

Unsurprisingly, most of the contents of the show-bag did end up down the back of the couch with the crumbs, loose change, candy and the TV remote. A cheap plastic toy is ultimately a cheap plastic toy, once you look past the logo on it.

---

[1]   If you are reading this book at a point in time where Ben 10 has been relegated by the next five year old cartoon fad, simply substitute Ben 10 with whatever is currently the big hit. Failing that use Spiderman—he never goes out of date.

It only takes one "Inspector Gadget"

Although the picture painted of Paul's little boy might seem cute but the reality is that, as adults, when interacting with other adults in groups or organisations, we also strut around displaying our own versions of the walking talking Ben 10 show-bag.

While we might not be wearing dish-cloths around our necks, we nonetheless demonstrate our various biases constantly. These biases affect our values and judgements and consequently, our perception of others and their perceptions of us. Most important, they affect decisions made by us and others in the organisations that we work in. In time, they lead to certain patterns of organisational decision-making and behaviour. These patterns are an *emergent* consequence of values that have been distorted by bias: emergent because they cannot be easily foreseen from individual instances of bias. In the end, these dysfunctional patterns of organisational behaviour contribute to, and often dominate, the culture of the organisation.

Perhaps an example or two would help illustrate what we mean. The small screen characters Maxwell Smart[2] and Inspector Gadget[3] have two things in common. Firstly, both are voiced by the late, great Don Adams and secondly, both characters are seemingly oblivious to their incompetence and the trail of destruction they leave in their wake. More recently, the gong for such a character in organisational life would have to go to Steve Carrell for his portrayal of Michael Scott in the Mocumentary series "The Office" (Carrell, funnily enough, also played Maxwell Smart on the big screen in 2008). Michael Scott holds inflated views of himself and is seriously lacking in self-awareness. While he describes himself as "a friend first, a boss man second, and probably an entertainer third," the reality is most of his subordinates think of him as being inept.

Consider a version of Michael Scott or Inspector Gadget in the form of a project manager who overrates his own abilities. In honour of our aforementioned small screen luminaries, we will henceforth refer to him as

---

[2]   Maxwell Smart is the central character of the TV Series "Get Smart" that ran from 1965 to 1970

[3]   Inspector Gadget is the central character of the cartoon of the same name that ran from 1983-1986

Gadget. We are pretty sure many readers can think of one or two Gadgets they have had to work with.

Gadget is a nice guy in all respects except that, because of these biases, he does not always take on board the opinions of his team. Thus, when a project sponsor asks "How long and how much?" our manager makes an optimistic estimate (cue Don Adams voice saying as Maxwell Smart "It will be *that* much") and then imposes it upon his team, who then are saddled with delivering an output in a hopelessly optimistic timeframe.

The effect is that, apart from Gadget no longer being invited to the pub with the team on Friday afternoons, the team is required to perform superhuman feats. However, these will often be in vain because the result will likely not meet expectations. The team will drink their Friday beers, have a venting session where they shake their heads and come to the conclusion that their manager's behaviour and resulting project chaos is simply a reflection of "the way things are done around here."

For those who do not know the cartoon, Inspector Gadget is always bailed out by his niece, Penny, and her dog, Brain, who do the real work while Gadget bumbles his way to the right place at the right time and gets all the credit for it.

Over time, as a result of being in this kind of environment, team members get used to the idea that it is normal that heroic efforts are needed to deliver a project. Then, when they get to the position occupied by Gadget, they start to behave in exactly the same way with their subordinates. Thus, a certain dysfunctional behaviour gets institutionalised and becomes part of the cultural fabric of the organisation.

Understanding Gadget

As the example illustrates, dysfunctional behaviour seeps into the culture of the organisation and influences how initiatives are planned and managed within the organisation. The long term effects of this include chronic problems with budget and time overruns, low morale, high staff turnover and unmet client expectations.

Sadly, our poor project team has to play with the hand they have been dealt. However, the visible effects mentioned above are the symptoms, not the cause. Although this is a social and behavioural dysfunction, management will often attempt to address it by imposing methodology—i.e. by imposing processes and procedures rather than getting to the root cause of the problem.

There are two views of project management and indeed, of management in general: the rational view and the behavioural or social view. The rational view focuses on management tools, processes and techniques, such as those espoused by frameworks and methodologies. The social/behavioural view, on the other hand, examines the softer aspects of projects; how people behave and interact in the context of a project and the wider organisation. Among other things, it recognises that people are *boundedly rational*—a term coined by Herbert Simon (1977) to refer to the notion that human decision-making can never be wholly rational—because of the following factors:

- **Incomplete information**: one can never know everything that has a bearing on a decision
- **Cognitive limitations**: as Inspector Gadget, and Dilbert cartoons aptly show, thought processes of humans are not entirely rational
- **Insufficient time:** there is never enough time to analyse all the options exhaustively

Earlier in this chapter, we discussed examples of human tendencies to make errors in judgement or reasoning based on incorrect perceptions. These errors, referred to as *cognitive biases,* are examples of the second point.

Going back to the two views, the rational view looks at how projects should be managed via prescribed tools, techniques and practices. It provides a "utility belt" of ways and means to deal with the visible symptoms of dysfunction. The social/behavioural view looks at what actually happens on projects. It focuses on how people interact and how decisions are made. When seen through the lens of bounded rationality, the difference between the rational and social/behavioural view of project management—or any aspect of managing people—starts to make sense. It tells us why there is a gap between theory and practice. The problem then boils down to asking what can be done about the gap.

A large part of this book is dedicated to answering that question. For now, we'll just note that the gap between the rational and social/behavioural viewpoints can spell the difference between project success and failure. In many failed projects, the failure can be traced back to poor decisions and the decisions themselves to cognitive biases similar to the Inspector Gadget effect.

There is no such thing as "unbiased"

We have used the term cognitive bias for a few paragraphs without explaining its background and providing some examples. It is time to rectify this. As mentioned earlier, the term refers to the tendency for people to make systematic errors of judgement (Kahneman and Tversky 1974). Daniel Kahneman is a giant of this field and ultimately went on to win the Nobel Prize in economics for this and related work.

Cognitive bias explains many mysteries of human behaviour, such as why people would actually pay to see a Steven Segal movie or buy Britney Spears CDs. It even explains why Tom Cruise has any fans whatsoever. More pertinent to this book, it also explains why people deal with uncertainty and risk in such different ways and why they make decisions that seem irrational.

Fast forward from 1974 . . . the ideas behind cognitive biases are now a part of popular literature (see Ariely 2008, for example). Wikipedia has a page listing a huge range of cognitive biases[4]. Once a person is familiar with the concept, he or she may see cognitive biases popping up in some unlikely places. For example, if we were to contribute our wisdom (or bias!) to the Wikipedia list, we might add the following:

- **Teenybopper bias**: the tendency of teenagers to display appalling taste in fashion and music
- **Fuddy duddy bias**: the tendency for adults to look back at their teenage years and cringe at their appalling choices of music and fashion taste
- **Beer goggle bias**: the illusion that people appear to be much more physically attractive as you consume more beer
- **Metrosexual bias**: the tendency to choose the more expensive t-shirt based on the name on the tag, from an otherwise identical pair

---

[4] http://en.wikipedia.org/wiki/List_of_cognitive_biases

- **Steve Jobs bias:** the tendency for Apple computer owners to be unable to bring themselves to say that a PC has any redeeming qualities whatsoever

While the examples above are a bit of fun, the fact that there is a bit of truth in them serves to illustrate that humanity is but a seething mass of cognitive bias. One wonders how we ever manage to get anything done!

The thing about estimating . . .

Dealing with uncertainty invariably involves (informed or uninformed) guesswork, which is politely termed estimation. Projects are rife with estimates of all kinds: duration, cost and effort being the most common ones. Here's a story that may be familiar to some of our readers.

Some time ago, a sales manager barged into Kailash's office. To protect the innocent, we will call her Jane.

"I'm sorry for the short notice," Jane said, "but you'll need to make some modifications to the consolidated sales report by tomorrow evening."

Kailash could see she was stressed and wanted to help, but there was an obvious question that needed to be asked. "What do you need done? I'll have to get some details before I can tell you if it can be done within the time," he replied.

Jane pulled up a chair and proceeded to explain what was needed. Within a minute or two, Kailash knew there was no way he could get it finished by the next day. He told her so, and it was not what Jane wanted to hear.

"Oh, no . . . This is really important. How long will it take?"

He thought about it for a minute or so, then said, "OK, how about I try to get it to you by the day after?"

"Tomorrow would be better, but I can wait till day after," came the reply.

Jane didn't look very happy about it though. "Thanks," she said and rushed away, not giving Kailash a chance to reconsider his off-the-cuff estimate.

After Jane left, Kailash had a closer look at what needed to be done. Fairly quickly he realised it would take him at least twice as long if he wanted to do it right. As it was, he'd have to work late to get it done in the agreed time and may even have to cut a corner or two (or three) in the process.

So, why was Kailash so wide off the mark?

Anchoring bias

Kailash had been railroaded into giving Jane an unrealistic estimate without even realising it. When Jane quoted her timeline, his subconscious latched on to it as an initial value for his estimate. Although he revised the initial estimate upwards, he was pressured—albeit unknowingly—into quoting an estimate that was biased towards the timeline Jane had mentioned. Kailash was a victim of what psychologists call "anchoring bias"—a human tendency *to base judgements on a single piece of information or data, ignoring all other relevant factors.* In arriving at his estimate, Kailash had focused on one piece of data (Jane's timeline) to the exclusion of all other potentially significant information such as the complexity of the task and other things on his plate at the time.

Anchoring bias was first described by Amos Tversky and Daniel Kahneman (1974) in one of their pioneering papers. They found that people often make quick judgements based on initial (or anchor) values that are suggested to them.

As the incident above illustrates, the anchor value (Jane's timeline) may have nothing to do with the point in question (how long it would actually take to do the work). To be sure, folks generally adjust the anchor values based on other information but these adjustments are generally inadequate. The final estimates arrived at are incorrect because they remain biased towards the initial value. As Tversky and Kahneman (1974) stated:

> "In many situations, people make estimates by starting from an initial value that is adjusted to yield the final answer. The initial value, or starting point, may be suggested by the formulation of the problem, or it may be the result of a partial computation. In either case, adjustments are typically insufficient. That is, different starting points yield different estimates, which are biased toward the initial values. We call this phenomenon anchoring."

Although the above quote may sound somewhat academic, be assured that anchoring is very real. It affects even day-to-day decisions that people make. For example, Neil Stewart (2009) presented evidence that credit card holders repay their debt more slowly when their statements suggest a minimum payment. In other words, the minimum payment works as an anchor, causing the card holder to pay a smaller amount than they would have been prepared to in the absence of an anchor.

"Catastrophic" overconfidence

Anchoring, however, is only part of the story. Things get much worse for complex tasks because other biases come into play. Tversky and Kahneman (1974) found that *subjects tended to be over optimistic when asked to make predictions regarding complex matters.*

> "Biases in the evaluation of compound events are particularly significant in the context of planning. The successful completion of an undertaking, such as the development of a new product, typically has a conjunctive character: for the undertaking to succeed, each of a series of events must occur. Even when each of these events is very likely, the overall probability of success can be quite low if the number of events is large. The general tendency to overestimate the probability of conjunctive events leads to unwarranted optimism in the evaluation of the likelihood that a plan will succeed or that a project will be completed on time."

The title of this section, "Catastrophic Overconfidence," is a quotation from a similarly named section in Douglas Hubbard's book entitled "The Failure of Risk Management." Hubbard (2009) quoted Kahneman as stating that overconfidence is the standout bias as far as risks being overlooked are concerned.

> "They will underestimate real risk systematically. The work we did showed the direction of the bias but it is the degree of the bias that is really catastrophic"

More on judgement related cognitive bias

Anchoring and overconfidence are prime examples of *judgement-related* cognitive biases commonly presented in project management. Other judgement-related biases include:

> **Availability:** The tendency to base decisions on information that can be easily recalled, neglecting potentially more important information. As an example, a project manager might give undue weight to his or her most recent professional experiences when analysing project risks, creating a barrier to an objective consideration of risks that are not immediately apparent. This particular example of availability is an illustration of the *recency effect,* which refers to the fact that people often make judgements based on recent events rather than those in the more distant past.

> **Confirmation bias:** The tendency of people to favour (or selectively seek) information that confirms their opinions. Another manifestation of this bias is when people interpret information in a way that supports their opinions. This is also related to availability bias in that information that confirms one's viewpoints is more easily recalled.

> **Illusion of control:** The tendency of people to overestimate their ability to influence events and outcomes that they actually have no control over. This is closely related to overconfidence (which we discussed earlier) and *optimism bias*—the belief that things will work out in one's favour, despite there being no evidence to support that belief.

> **Representativeness:** The tendency to make judgements based on seemingly representative, known samples. For example, a project team member might base a task estimate based on another (seemingly) similar task, ignoring important differences between the two.

Selective perception: The tendency to give undue importance to data that supports one's own views. Selective perception is a bias that we're all subject to—we hear what we want to hear, see what we choose to see and remain deaf and blind to the rest.

Loss Aversion: The tendency to give preference to avoiding losses (even small losses) over making gains. A particularly common manifestation of loss aversion in project environments is the *sunk cost* bias of throwing good money at a project that is clearly a lost cause.

Information bias: The tendency for people to seek as much data as they can lay their hands on prior to making a decision. As a result, they are swamped by too much irrelevant information.

Since the pioneering work of Tversky and Kahneman, these biases have been widely studied by psychologists. It is important to note that these biases come into play whenever quick and dirty judgements are involved. While this might be unsurprising, they also occur when subjects are *motivated to make accurate judgements*. As Tversky and Kahneman stated towards the end of their paper:

> "These biases are not attributable to motivational effects such as wishful thinking or the distortion of judgments by payoffs and penalties. Indeed, several of the severe errors of judgment reported earlier *(in the paper)* occurred despite the fact that subjects were encouraged to be accurate and were rewarded for the correct answers."

This is important—and also rather scary. Even when the system has been "gamed" to incentivise accurate and correct answers, severe errors of judgement were still encountered.

Given the difficulty of overcoming judgement-related cognitive bias, it is worth taking a quick peek into their inner workings.

The effect of intuition and rational thought

In a book called "The Happiness Hypothesis," Jonathan Haidt (2005) used an "elephant and rider" metaphor to describe aspects of human behaviour. Our rational brain (the rider) sits atop a large elephant, which represents our emotional brain. The rider holds the reins of the elephant but control is precarious because the rider is a lot smaller than the elephant. While our rider might make a resolution to eat at Subway for lunch, our elephant sometimes often begs to differ, especially when a Kentucky Fried Chicken outlet is conveniently located nearby. The rider sometimes finds it hard to control the urges of the hungry elephant.

Regardless of the metaphor that's used, elephant/rider or left brain/right brain, research in psychology has established that the various metaphorical wheels, pulleys and rubber bands that underpin human cognition works through two distinct processes (Kahneman 2003):

- System 1, which corresponds to intuitive thought (our elephants)
- System 2, which corresponds to rational thought (our riders)

In his Nobel Prize lecture, Daniel Kahneman (2002) had this to say about the two systems:

> "The operations of System 1 are fast, automatic, effortless, associative, and often emotionally charged; they are also governed by habit, and are therefore difficult to control or modify. The operations of System 2 are slower, serial, effortful, and deliberately controlled; they are also relatively flexible and potentially rule-governed."

Given the aforementioned severe errors of judgement, you might think that System 2 processes never get a look in. The surprise is that judgements *always involve System 2 processes*. In Kahneman's words:

> ". . . the perceptual system and the intuitive operations of System 1 generate impressions of the attributes of objects of perception and thought. These impressions are not voluntary and need not be verbally explicit. In contrast, *judgments* are

always explicit and intentional, whether or not they are overtly expressed. Thus, System 2 is involved in all judgments, whether they originate in impressions or in deliberate reasoning."

So, all judgements, whether intuitive or rational, are monitored by our riders of System 2. However—and this is the key point—Kahneman suggested that this monitoring can be *very cursory*, thus, allowing System 1 impressions to be expressed directly, whether they are right or not. Seen in this light, cognitive biases are lightly edited expressions of incorrect impressions. In other words, *we have a poorly calibrated System 2 filter*, allowing our elephants to run amok.

Attribute substitution: The underlying mechanism?

This notion of System 2 being always involved in judgements suggests that we can improve our decision making by "recalibrating" our System 2 filters. If we are to understand how to better calibrate our System 2 filters and make less biased judgements, then we must understand why our filters are poorly calibrated in the first place.

In a paper entitled "Representativeness Revisited," Kahneman and Fredrick (2002) suggested that the psychological process of *attribute substitution* is the mechanism that underlies many cognitive biases. Attribute substitution is the tendency of people to answer a difficult decision-making question *by interpreting it as a simpler (but related) one.*

Marketing people actually rely on attribute substitution a fair bit. Kahneman described an instance of this which involved "Save the Children" type charity programmes. These often focus their marketing on an individual child rather than many children because the story of a single child evokes a more emotional response and, as a result, a larger contribution. To quote Kahneman (2007):

"People are almost completely insensitive to amount in system one. Once you involve system two and systematic thinking, then they'll act differently ... Attribute substitution boils down to making judgements based on specific, known instances of events or issues under consideration. The idea that when you're asked a question, you don't answer that question, you answer another question that comes more readily to mind"

Kahneman (2002) summed it up nicely in a line in his Nobel lecture:

"The essence of attribute substitution is that respondents offer a reasonable answer to a question that they have not been asked. "

Foreshadowing a point we elaborate on later in the book: attribute substitution is the reason why people tend to give simplistic answers to complex questions, why organisations apply "silver bullet" best practices without bothering to adapt them to the specific context of the organisation. The basic point is that, when confronted with complex phenomena, humans try to understand them in *simple terms that they can relate to.*

System 2 to the rescue, but . . .

The discussion of the previous section tells us that people often base judgements on *specific instances* that come to mind, *ignoring the range of all possible instances.* They do this because specific instances—usually concrete instances that have been experienced—come to mind more easily than the abstract "universe of possibilities."

Those who make erroneous judgements will correct them only if they become aware of factors that they did not take into account when making the judgement, or when they realise that their conclusions are not logical. This can only happen through deliberation and rational analysis, which is possible only through a deliberate invocation of System 2 thinking. But System 2 needs to be calibrated so that our mental filters make more appropriate attribute substitutions. Some of the ways in which System 2 can be helped along are:

- By reframing the question or issue in terms that forces us to consider the range of possible instances. A common problem with estimates (or numerical judgements of any kind) is that people tend to fixate on a number rather than a range. A common manifestation of this is when people base their decisions on averages rather than considering the range of possible conditions that might occur, an assumption that Professor Sam Savage (2009) called the "flaw of averages."

- By requiring people to come up with pros and cons for any decision they make. This forces them to consider possibilities they may not have taken into account when making the original decision.
- By basing decisions on relevant empirical or historical data instead of relying on intuitive impressions.
- By making people aware of their propensity to be overconfident (or under-confident) by evaluating their *probability calibration.* Calibration generally involves asking people to answer a series of trivia questions with confidence estimates for each of their answers (i.e. their self-estimated probability of being right). Their confidence estimates are then compared to the fraction of questions correctly answered. A well calibrated individual's confidence estimates should be close to the percentage of correct answers. There is some evidence to suggest that analysts can be trained to improve their calibration through cycles of testing and feedback (Wilson 1994). However, it is still an open question as to whether improved calibration through feedback and repeated tests carries over to judgements in real-life situations.

Each of the above options forces analysts to consider instances other than the ones that readily come to mind. That said, they aren't a sure cure for the problem because System 2 thinking does not guarantee correctness. Kahneman discussed several reasons why this is so:

- It has been found that education and training in decision-related disciplines (like statistics) does not eliminate incorrect intuitions. It only reduces them in *favourable circumstances* such as when the question is reframed to make statistical cues obvious.
- Kahneman noted that System 2 thinking is easily derailed: research has shown that the efficiency of System 2 is impaired by time pressure (Finucane et al 2000). (Managers who put their teams under time pressure should take note!)
- Initial guesses based on System 1 (elephant) thinking can be way off mark. Unfortunately, corrections based on System 2 thinking are generally too small to fix this: people tend to be conservative when

making corrections. As a result their corrected estimates remain close to their (incorrect) initial guesses. In other words, their final estimates tend to remain anchored around their initial guess.

- System 2 thinking is of no use if it is based on incorrect assumptions: as a colleague of Kailash once said "Logic doesn't get you anywhere if your premise is wrong." This is true of reductionist thinking in general in that deductions are founded on assumptions and if the assumptions are shaky, the logical edifice built on them comes crashing down.

A calibration example (and a cool pub trick)

As a relief from the relatively deep dive exploration we have just taken into cognitive bias, a little respite is in order. The great thing about learning about your cognitive biases and the methods for mitigating them is that they can be practised in fairly creative ways and, as a result, you can use them in the pub, too. While we don't recommend it as a method for picking up members of the opposite sex, what we present below is a pretty cool icebreaker.

Imagine this mythical pub conversation. Pete is on his third beer and we ask this question:

US:	How many Project Managers worldwide own a yellow car?
PETE:	What the . . . I haven't the faintest idea!
US:	Well, we can understand that, so let's do an estimate. Give me a range that the answer could fall in, that you are 90% confident with." [Note: A 90% confidence means that the estimator believes that the correct answer will lie within the quoted range 90 times out of 100—or equivalently, 9 times out of 10]
PETE:	I still can't give you an estimate. I can't possibly know something like that.
US:	Well, could there be fifty million Project Managers who own yellow cars?
PETE:	Don't be ridiculous, there would be nowhere near fifty million Project Managers, period.

US:	So, you do have an upper bound then, less than fifty million. Remember this is not about the exact answer, we want a range that you would be 90% confident with.
PETE:	Okay, I get it. I think it is somewhere between three hundred and fifty thousand.

Note that at this point, we have already made the initial breakthrough. At first, Pete found it impossible to make an estimate, yet when we related the problem to something he had a fair idea of (the thought of fifty million people), he made some mental associations and blammo, he realised he had some idea about what might be reasonable after all.

Thus, by presenting him with a better frame of reference that he could use to approach the problem, Pete was able to move from "I have no idea" to a range of possible values, albeit a wide one. The width of the range reflects the degree of uncertainty about the answer. The more the level of uncertainty, the wider the range of possible answers offered.

Some project managers hate being given a ranged value because it really mucks up their task estimates and resulting Gantt charts. While we understand why this happens, these managers are forgetting that an estimate is uncertain *by definition*. The obvious way to express uncertainty is via a range of values! So, asking someone for an estimate and then complaining that the estimate is not accurate enough actually makes no sense at all. While someone might not like the "width" of the range, they shouldn't force the estimator to reduce their level of uncertainty just because it doesn't fit the plan. Any "improvement" that is achieved through coercion is illusory.

However, as the reader has likely gathered, a ranged estimate by itself is not enough. One also has to account for cognitive biases. So, without further ado, we present a calibration technique that accounts for some forms of judgement bias. Let's continue the bar conversation.

US:	Okay, so you are 90% sure that there are between 300 and 50000 Project Managers in the world with a yellow car?
PETE:	Yes
US:	So, let's make this like the game show "Deal or no Deal." If you are right and the answer is within your range, you will win $10000. BUT you have an alternative . . .
PETE:	Ok . . .

US: What if I was to present you with a bag containing 9 red marbles and 1 black marble and offer you $10000 if you pull out a red marble. Pull the one black marble and you miss out on the money. Do you want to stick to your estimate or do you want to draw a marble?

Readers should pause at this point and think about this choice before continuing. Go ahead and make a ranged estimate of the number of Project Managers worldwide who drive a yellow car, as per the conversation this far. Then, decide whether you want to stick to your estimate or take your chances with the marbles.

So, have you decided what to do? Now, be honest and see how you went against the possible outcomes. Here are the possible answers in order of likelihood . . .

- You choose to pull from the bag of marbles rather than your ranged estimate. (This is the predominant answer, accounting for 70-75% of all responses).
- You choose to use your estimate over the bag of marbles. (Perhaps 25% of people have answered with this option).
- Upon hearing the bag option, you want to change your original ranged estimate. (This has happened to Paul only once).
- You do not care which method you use.

So, which is the right answer to this question? (Drum roll, please!) Let's tackle the possible answers in order of likelihood.

"Take the marble! Take the maaaaaarble!"

For the 70 odd percent who opted to take your chances with the bag of marbles . . . BZZT! You lose!

Our suggestion is to double check your estimates in future because you have demonstrated that you are over-confident. In other words, you are suffering from optimism bias. To explain why, think about the original question carefully.

We asked originally for a ranged estimate that you were 90% confident with. We then presented an alternative option that has a very clear nine out of ten chance of success—also 90%. Although we did not explicitly state that there is a 90% chance of success, we didn't need to. Your subconscious recognised the option, in effect performing a simple and obvious attribute substitution. Your preference for the bag, however, shows that you are *less* than 90% confident about the attribute substitution you made in the yellow car problem.

From a purely rational, statistical point of view, you ought to be completely neutral as to which option to choose. This may be why you are under pressure at work. You might be making estimates that make your life harder! Either that or you are simply far too nice. When your manager looks at you with those big, sad manager eyes, your heart melts and you agree to whatever is being asked of you.

It is very interesting to see people's faces, as they understand the logic behind the choice, suddenly realise just how poor some of their past estimates have been as a result. The consolation, if it is any consolation at all, is that around four out of five people do exactly the same as you and take the marble option.

"No deal, I will stick with my estimate" (wuss)

To the smaller group who decide that their estimate is preferred: you also lose. In this case, the reason why you lose should be pretty obvious. You are so paranoid about getting things wrong, that you have made an estimate that is more like 95% or even 99% confident. Why? Your estimated range is far too wide for 90% because, when presented with a choice between your estimate and a clear nine out of ten chance of success you preferred your estimate.

While that may sound like you are confident and a better estimator than the majority who went with the bag of marbles, the reality is you are actually a bit of a wuss and your estimates are overly conservative. We think it's time you hardened up!

Honorary mention: "I want to change my estimate"

This answer has happened just once in Paul's use of this pub trick. The respondent was a strategic management consultant from an IT consultancy practice out of Washington DC. His response, we think, deserves an honorary mention for being the closest yet to winning this game.

In this case, the example used was provided by Douglas Hubbard (2007) in his excellent book "How To Measure Anything." The subject was asked to estimate the width of a Boeing 747 in feet from wingtip to wingtip. It became apparent fairly quickly that this guy had experience with estimating because he immediately started the process of calibrating the System 2 side of his brain. He went through the following chain of the logic to determine his ranged estimate.

> "Hmm, well an aircraft seat is maybe one and a half feet, and there will be ten seats in the cabin, with two passages that are probably two feet in width . . . so that adds up to . . ."

Did you notice what he did? Straight away, he related the wingspan of an aircraft (a clear unknown) to something he could make a reasonable estimate of (the width of an aircraft seat). After all, we have all sat in an aircraft seat in sardine (economy) class and know how cramped it is. He knew there were three rows of seats with a likely configuration of three, four and three seats for each row. He then used this, along with an estimate of the width of the gap between the rows to get to the width of the cabin. From there, he mentally related the cabin size to the size of each wing itself. Deducing that the wing might be 4 to 6 times the width of the cabin, he was able to make a very good ranged estimate of the overall wingspan of the plane.

Although the subject was impressive in how he arrived at his estimate, he didn't succeed. As soon as he was presented with the bag of marbles alternative, without missing a beat he said "I want to change my estimate." It took only a split second of presenting a clear 90% probability to make him realise that his estimate was still not 90%, and that he was still a little overconfident. That said, this method of relating something known in order to get a handle on the unknown is truly impressive for pub estimation!

The right answer

Okay, so as you may have guessed by now, the right answer is to shrug your shoulders and say "I don't care" or wave your hand at us and say

"Pfft, whatever." (This is one of the few times saying you couldn't care less is the right answer). By doing so, you indicate that your confidence in your estimate is indeed 90%.

The take-away from this exercise is that when asked to estimate something you are uncertain about, do the following. Begin with an initial estimate (which may be a wild guess). Then, pretend you are in a game show where you have to pick between this estimate and the bag of marbles. If you feel that you would take the marbles over your estimate, increase the width of your range until you get to the point where the two options seem equally attractive. Conversely, if you are one of the wimps who consistently understate their confidence levels, then reduce the width of your range until you feel that you get to the point of neutrality.

This pub trick demonstrates the importance of calibrating our System 2 processes when making an estimate. The main benefit is that it forces us to slow down and think rationally about the intuitive (System 1) estimates that we are so quick to come up with. Basically, a reflective approach seeks to eliminate bias by reducing the effect of intuitive judgements. This is why project management texts advise us, among other things, to:

- Base estimates on historical data for similar tasks
- Draft independent experts to do the estimation
- Use multipoint estimates (best and worst case scenarios)

Our best advice to you when asked to provide an off the cuff estimate is to reply "Let me think about it" before anything else. That window of time will give you time to "collect your thoughts" and calibrate your System 2 filter.

. . . and we complete projects how? (meta risks)

We now turn to the question of how our thought processes and cognitive biases affect our perception and management of *risk* in projects. We have established that biases are part and parcel of the mental makeup of humans and have also demonstrated their effect on estimation in the face of uncertainty. Clearly risk analysis, which involves human judgment, is also subject to the same bias. To put it in another way, when analysing *any* risk, you have to be aware of your own bias-distorted perceptions of that risk. As such then, cognitive biases may be thought of as *meta-risks*: risks that affect risk analysis. Dealing with these meta-risks involves an insight into the thought processes that govern decision-making, as opposed to the decision-making itself.

The publicly available research and professional literature on meta-risks in business and organisational contexts is sparse (is that in itself a risk?). A relevant paper by Jack Gray (2000) stated:

> "Meta-risks are qualitative, implicit risks that pass beyond the scope of explicit risks. Most are born out of the complex interaction between the *behaviour pattern of individuals and those of organisational structures*"

Although he didn't use the phrase, Gray seemed to be referring to cognitive biases when he wrote about behaviour patterns, at least in part. This is confirmed by a reading of the paper. It described, among other things, *hubris* (which roughly corresponds to the illusion of control) and *discounting evidence that conflicts with one's views* (which corresponds to confirmation bias) as meta-risks.

A paper entitled "Systematic Biases and Culture in Project Failure" by Barry Shore (2009) suggested that cognitive biases may have played a role in some high profile project failures. Shore contended that the failures examined in his paper were caused by poor decisions which could be traced back to specific biases. In the next few sections we explore one of the initiatives examined in his paper: NASA's $327 million Mars Climate Orbiter project.

A number of seemingly unrelated events

We chose the Mars Climate Orbiter project for two reasons. The first reason is because of the eventual root cause and the second, because NASA is also responsible for pulling off stunning scientific achievements involving feats of extraordinary precision.

To launch a deep space probe, such as the Cassini mission, requires hundreds of individual projects within a huge program of work, to all come together in the right way to achieve a hugely ambitious one-of-a-kind mission. Such a program of work can run over several years, even decades.

The story of the Mars Climate Orbiter project is a salutary reminder that even organisations with successful track records can be prone to errors that can be traced back to cognitive bias. The chronology of events is simple enough. The craft was successfully launched and reached Mars in six months. On September 23, 1999 it began an orbital insertion burn, during which the craft was supposed to pass behind Mars and re-establish contact 10 minutes later. Contact was never re-established and no further communication from the craft was ever received.

Was it a technical fault that caused the problem? Did one of the many components of the craft fail at a critical moment?

In the end, the root cause of the problem with the spacecraft was human error. However, it was an error that was a consequence of another failed project, one that Americans have been having a crack at solving off and on for more than two hundred years.

The root cause of the Mars Climate Orbiter disaster lay in the failure to convert between metric and British units! Apparently, the contractor, Lockheed, had used imperial units in the engine design but NASA scientists, who were responsible for operations and flight, assumed the data was in metric units and never tested that assumption. As a result, the computer-controlled thrusters on the spacecraft, which were intended to control its trajectory, were given incorrect instructions that caused the spacecraft to miss its intended altitude target of 140-150 km above Mars during orbit insertion. Instead, it entered the Martian atmosphere at about 57 km, where, atmospheric friction destroyed the craft.

Schoolchildren are taught about the need to use proper conversion factor when working with different unit systems. How could something so elementary be overlooked? To understand this, we need to get the story from those involved in the project.

The perspective of those involved

There are several papers that analyse reasons for the failure but one in particular caught our eye. It was presented at the 24th annual American Astronautical Society's "Guidance and Control Conference" (which we are sure was an absolute rock and roll style riot). The paper documented a more intimate, inside view on the causes of the failed mission. This first hand, intimate perspective presents us with an opportunity to examine the biases that occurred (Euler et al 2001).

The imperial to metric conversion issue was tracked down to a computer file with the cool name of "Angular Momentum Desaturation File" (AMDF). Without getting into scary detail, spacecraft would regularly download measurements related to trajectory of the craft to mission control. Special software would process this data and create the resultant AMDF that the navigation team used to make calculations for course adjustments. Interestingly, the Mars Climate Orbiter craft had the capability to make the correct calculations on its own but the software that processed these AMDFs performed its own calculations regardless. This was a historical artefact of the software being used on a previous Mars mission.

This is important to note: the software that processed the spacecraft flight data to produce the AMDFs was reused from a previous mission. Now, if you think that the flaw was in the old software, you would be mistaken. In fact, the old software *did not* contain the flaw and its handling of unit conversion was correct. What actually happened was the old software was upgraded for this new mission, and it was *the upgrade that contained the unit conversion flaw*. To quote from the paper:

> "As luck would have it, the 4.45 conversion factor, although correctly included in the [Mars Global Surveyor] equation by the previous development team, was not immediately identifiable by [code] inspection (being buried in the equation) or commented in the code in an obvious way that the [Mars Climate Orbiter] team recognized it. Thus,[. . .] the new thruster equation was inserted in place of the [Mars Global Surveyor] equation—without the conversion factor"

The reason cited above is that it was not clear from the old code that the unit conversion was in fact required. Further, the conversion factor itself was not obvious—it was "buried in the equation." This suggests that confirmation bias was at work. The group assumed the old code was written in a way that complied with the way they thought it should work.

There's more: consider this quotation from the lessons learned section of the paper.

"... More often than not, assumptions of 'heritage' can cloud crucial issues. For example, the Lockheed Martin development/ flight team's most recent experience base was with symmetrical and/or slowly rotating spacecraft that did not generate significant unbalanced small forces [unlike the climate orbiter]. This created a group 'mind set' that worked against mission success in this crucial area . . ."

The resultant group "mind set" reference is a textbook case of *groupthink*: the tendency of members of a group to think alike because of peer pressure and insulation from external opinions. Groupthink may be thought of as a cognitive bias that operates at the collective level. As the paper suggested later, it can be countered by ensuring that the group includes people with diverse viewpoints.

Two other lessons learned from this paper, "Unhealthy Flight Team Distractions Due to In-flight Anomalies" and "Test-Like-You-Fly (TLYF) Extension Into Mission Operations," offer further nuggets of insight into cognition.

"[in addition to] a general misunderstanding of how the navigation process was using [flight] data . . . this was an overwhelmed team. In addition to increasing subsystem staffing levels, the recommendation is to always include senior systems personnel with extensive flight experience that keep a 'sideways glance' on all data and information on the health of the spacecraft."

Back in our examination of instinctive and reflective thinking, we noted Kahneman's reasons why System 2 thinking does not guarantee correctness. One of those reasons he cited was the effect of time pressure on the correctness of reflective thinking. The Mars Climate Orbiter offered an excellent example of this: the team had to multitask to solve several unrelated but time-constrained problems. This contributed to the lack of System 2 thinking (deliberate, reasoned thought). Their recommendation was essentially to include people who have an overall picture firmly in view. These people would act as "conscience keepers" for the project.

The law of unintended consequences (why the USA resists the metric system)

The story of the Mars Climate Orbiter failure got us thinking about why the USA is essentially the last bastion of imperial units. It stands to reason that the Mars Global Surveyor problem would have never happened if the US had gotten onto the metric bandwagon back when the rest of the world did. Taking this idea further, one can argue that the economic cost to America of not adopting the metric system has been far greater than the short term pain of adoption. Notwithstanding blowing the investment in the Mars Climate Orbiter, American organisations that export goods have the overhead of dealing with differing local and global measurement systems. In other words, the USA has a rational and economically sensible reason to make the switch, but has not done so.

This is not for the want of trying as there have been several attempts to adopt the metric system, starting from Jefferson in 1790, right through to the present day. While there may have been good reasons for avoiding metrification in the past, these arguments have been rendered irrelevant or have been debunked. The USA is one of three countries that do not use the metric system (the others being Liberia and Myanmar).

One of the attempts at conversion involved quoting quantities in both systems. This led to chaos and confusion, as is evident from the following quote from Cecil Adams (1995), a writer of a popular question and answer column called "The Straight Dope" in the Chicago Reader newspaper.

> "It was a typical let's-please-everybody muddle. Dual posting of highway signs in miles and kilometers cost money without any compensating advantage and, by calling attention to the fact that one kilometer equals .621 miles, made the metric system seem needlessly complicated. The folly of dual measurements persists to this day. Rather than baffle consumers by pointing out that a gallon of milk equals 3.78 liters, it would be better to simply replace gallons with four-liter containers. The two-liter pop bottle no doubt succeeded because it was just that simple."

It seems to us that the lack of adoption to the metric system is also a case of attribute substitution on a grand scale in that the collective memory of botched attempts resulted in a bias against any new attempts at conversion.

The ubiquity of bias

Even with only our brief introduction to common cognitive biases, you will start to notice that they are rather common, both at work and at home. For example, it is a good bet that Kailash believes he is a better manager than he actually is. As another, his penchant for buying lottery tickets, despite knowing that the odds are stacked against him, can also be explained by bias. On the other hand, it is easy to fall into the trap of attributing all failures of judgment to bias. This, in itself, is a bias—which is kind of ironic. Nevertheless, research indicates that these biases operate even when people are aware of them, so it seems that they are part and parcel of the business of being human.

The ubiquity of cognitive bias and the fact that it is a concept that has gone mainstream (as judged by the number of blog posts and online articles written on the topic) point to a deeper problem: ideas, like the concept of cognitive bias, tend to have a life of their own. They propagate and mutate in ways that the originators of the idea may never have thought of. Furthermore, some "mutations" of the original concept may even be false but gain currency because they are legitimised by continual use or even by authority. In the next chapter, we elaborate on the notion that ideas have a life of their own—regardless of their utility or validity—as this point is central to the main theme of this book.

3

Myths, Memes and Methodologies

"Good teachers produce skeptics who ask their own questions and find their own answers. Management gurus produce only unquestioning disciples" (Russell Ackoff and Herbert Addison)

The thing about standards . . .

In the last couple of decades, projects have become part and parcel of mainstream organisational practice. It seems that every initiative undertaken by organisations ultimately translates to a "project" of some kind. So, it is no surprise that project management is gaining more and more traction in organisations. An all-too-visible manifestation of this trend of "projectisation" is the "Program Management Office" (PMO) that oversees projects and programs within the organisation. Indeed, projects and their management are now seen as strategic imperatives necessary for the growth and development of organisations rather than just a tactical/ operational toolkit of best practice or standard techniques.

There is an old saying that the nice thing about standards is that there are so many to choose from. As such, the plethora of project management methodologies, best practices and standards serve to reinforce the idea that projects have an objective existence. In much the same way, permanent organisations are perceived as being "real" objective entities which have an existence independent of the people and relationships that comprise them.

Implicit in this belief of the objective existence of projects is that there are objectively right ways to manage them, and that it is possible to codify these methods into standards, best practices and methodologies. The advantages afforded by the standardisation of project management are many. To name a few:

- Accepted standards provide a common professional vocabulary and toolset of techniques.
- They are cross-disciplinary—i.e. they provide techniques that can be applied across various unrelated disciplines.
- They are endorsed and disseminated by professional bodies. Two examples of this are: a) the publication of "bodies of knowledge" which outline a professionally accepted standard of knowledge; and b) certification of professionals. A consequence of this is that professionals who wish to be perceived as competent have no choice but to endorse the standard.

While all this is fine and dandy in theory, there are some less obvious downsides of standards and methodologies in practice. Here are a few:

- There's nothing innate in standards that guarantees their validity. However, standards, due to their "market position," tend to shut out the competition. Alternate views of the profession get little or no airtime barring perhaps in academic circles (more on this later).
- Standards are hard to change because of the cost involved and/ or vested interests of the standards bodies and those "certified" as proficient in the use of the standards.
- By definition, standards aim to ensure that organisations do things in the same or similar ways. They aim to eliminate idiosyncrasies in the way organisations do things. However, as we will see in later chapters, this is not always a good thing.

There are security guys and then there are security guys

[Voluntary disclosure: Paul and Kailash hold a good few certs, but read on . . .]

IT security, like many IT sub-disciplines, has certifications that recognise domain skills and knowledge. The pre-eminent security certification is called the Certified Information Systems Security Professional (CISSP) that is administered by the International Information Systems Security Certification Consortium—abbreviated as (ISC)²®. This broad-based certification, which Paul currently holds, is much like the Project Management Professional (PMP®) certification that Kailash holds. The two certifications have similarities in terms of breadth of subject matter covered, professional experience, examinations and periodic re-certification requirements.

However, the CISSP certification is not without its detractors. The IT security profession has a significant number of members with considerable technical prowess (grey or black hat hackers) who consider the CISSP to be a "management" certification that does not accurately reflect hands on skill. Accordingly, a common badge to be found at IT security conferences, like Defcon and RSA, is emblazoned with the words "Not a CISSP."

Figure 3.1 A commonly seen badge at IT security conferences

Our point is not that standards are wrong, incorrect or do not reflect relevant experience, only that practitioners need to look at them with a critical eye rather than accept them as gospel best practices.

To this end, we will outline a couple of common myths and misconceptions regarding project management. We'll begin by looking into the origins of a project management tool that is held in high regard by many practitioners and textbook authors. From there, we'll move on to a discussion of how the (mis)interpretation of a poorly written research paper led to a delivery model that dominated the project management landscape for more than twenty years, and is still pervasive today. Our aim, as stated earlier, is not so much to dump on standards but to encourage a degree of critical thinking in those who use them.

A PERT myth

PERT (Program Evaluation and Review Technique) is a tool to plan, coordinate and manage projects. Among other things, it is a stock standard way to manage project schedule risk. PERT is taught, or at least mentioned, in just about every project management course.

PERT is considered to have originated in the Polaris project, a ballistic missile development effort by the US Navy that took place between 1956 and 1960. Quoting from a project management text (Nicholas and Steyn 2008), the technique was developed for projects where the duration of activities involved a lot of uncertainty:

> "It originated during the US Navy's Polaris Missile System program, the perfect example of a complex research and development program with uncertainty about the kind of research to be done, the stages of development needed and how fast they can be completed . . . The duration of the project is uncertain and there is a great risk that the project will overrun the target completion time.

> To provide a degree of certainty in the duration of the Polaris program, a special operations research team was formed in 1958 with representatives from the Navy's Special Projects Office (SPO), the consulting firm of Booz, Allen and Hamilton, and the prime contractor, Lockheed Missile Systems. The method they devised was called PERT . . ."

The Polaris endeavour is often held up as an exemplar of a project delivered to specification and on time. Accounts, such as the one quoted above, imply that PERT was one of the main reasons for its success. Unfortunately, in this case and others, some aspects of the history have fallen through the cracks of time because the truth with PERT is considerably more nuanced than what many would have us believe.

As it turns out, it was used on the Polaris project more as public relations than project management. It was often applied "after the fact" when generating reports for Congress which held the project purse-strings (It is amazing what people will do when someone else signs the cheques).

An excellent place to start our examination of PERT's history is a RAND Corporation publication entitled "Quantitative Risk Analysis for Project Management—A Critical Review," written by Lionel Galway (2004). The paper was essentially a survey of quantitative risk management and analysis techniques. Galway had this to say about PERT:

> ". . . PERT was a great success from a public relations point of view, although only a relatively small portion of the Polaris program was ever managed using the technique. And this

success led to adaptations of PERT such as PERT/cost that attempted to address cost issues as well. While PERT was widely acclaimed by the business and defence communities in the 1960s, later studies raised doubts about whether PERT contributed much to the management success of the Polaris project. Many contended that its primary contribution was to deflect management interference by the Navy and DoD (Department of Defence) by providing a 'cover' of disciplined, quantitative, management carried out by modern methodologies . . ."

Then, in the conclusion of the paper, he stated:

". . . While the Polaris program touted PERT as a breakthrough in project management, as noted above not even a majority of the tasks in the project were controlled with PERT. [Work done in] the late 1970s, although limited for generalization by the sampling technique, showed less than a majority of organisations using CPM/PERT techniques. And the interviews conducted for this report revealed a similar ambivalence: respondents affirmed the usefulness of the techniques in general, but did not provide much in the way of particular examples . . ."

The authoritative history on PERT is Harvey Sapolsky's (1972) book, "The Polaris System Development: Bureaucratic and Programmatic Success in Government." Among other things, it described how the use of PERT on the project had been grossly overstated. Unfortunately, the book is out of print, but Michael Murphy (2000) has published an excellent review of the book on his web site. Quoting from the review:

". . . SPO (Special Projects Office) Director Vice Admiral William F. Raborn pushed PERT mercilessly. The colorful PERT charts impressed everyone, and coupled with the nature of the project, they exuded management 'sex appeal.' This kept other DoD poachers at bay and politicians off SPO's back. Other government services became so enamored with PERT, they quickly made it a requirement in subsequent contracts. A

> more objective assessment of PERT is that the network analysis is the major benefit. PERT can reduce cost and time overruns, and make its practitioners look like better managers . . ."

Other defence organisations caught onto PERT's effectiveness at keeping annoying managers at bay, too. For example, the Royal Navy was aware of the over inflated success of PERT when it embarked on its own version of the Polaris program.

> "The Royal Navy deliberately adopted PERT, essentially, to keep Whitehall, Parliament and other critics away from their project. It worked just as well for the RN as it did for the USN . . ."

We found the accounts of PERT presented in these sources fascinating because they highlight how project management history can be so much more ambiguous and messier, than textbooks, teachers and trainers would have us believe. Techniques are often taught without any regard to their origins and limitations.

Thus, disassociated from their origins, they take on a life of their own leading to myths where it is difficult to separate fact from fiction. To that end, our next example of this phenomenon is downright scary.

A waterfall or a trickle?

The "waterfall" approach to projects draws inspiration from the industrial revolution inspired, scientific approach to manufacturing and production. The technique, which we'll describe shortly, is possibly the worst way to develop software. Consequently, in modern day software development, the term "waterfall" is a bit of a dirty word.

For the trainspotters among readers, the term is believed to have originated in an influential paper written forty years ago, although tellingly, the author, Winston Royce (1970), never actually used the term in the paper. Nevertheless, the basic idea is likely very familiar to you. Anybody remotely connected to software development or project management will be familiar with the approach of:

Gather data—> Analyze data—> Formulate solution—> Implement solution[1]

For many years, conventional wisdom in project management and software development was to follow an orderly and linear process based—or so it is alleged—on Royce's approach. The term "waterfall model" comes from the image of a project "flowing through" each of the steps. Figure 4.2 shows Royce's diagram in all its glory from page 2 of the paper. The question is: how correct is the commonly accepted interpretation of Royce's methodology?

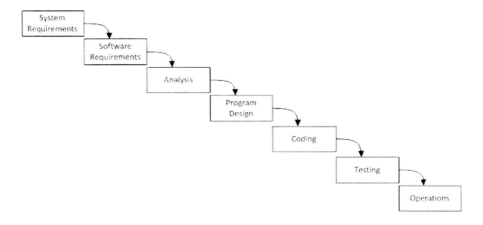

Figure 3.2: The model for software development that came to be known as waterfall

Waterfall: invitation to failure?

Royce, himself, was well aware of potential limitations and criticisms of the model summarised by Figure 3.2. This is evident from the following quote from his paper . . .

> "I believe in this concept, but the implementation described above is *risky and invites failure* . . . The testing phase which

---

[1]   This is an abridged version of the rational-scientific method of solving problems. We'll have more to say about this in Chapter 5

occurs at the end of the development cycle [. . .] Yet if these phenomena fail to satisfy the various external constraints, then invariably a major redesign is required. The required design changes are likely to be so disruptive that the software requirements upon which the design is based and which provides the rationale for everything, are violated. Either the requirements must be modified, or a substantial change in the design is required. In effect the development process has returned to the origin and one can expect up to a 100-percent overrun in schedule and/or costs."

So, Royce, in his original paper, actually *recognised* that the waterfall model is *risky and invited failure!* This fact seems to have been overlooked by those who subscribe to waterfall methodologies. Why hasn't this important fact been mentioned in best practice frameworks that espouse waterfall? We suspect this may be because Royce's work, like many academic papers, is not quite bedtime reading. Furthermore, it is quite confusing in parts. For example, at first glance, Royce appeared to suggest that the method is, in principle, quite sound. Consider this quote:

"I believe the illustrated approach to be *fundamentally sound.* The remainder of this discussion presents five additional features that must be added to this basic approach to eliminate most of the development risks"

Now, if you stopped reading his paper at this point all you would have is Royce's famous diagram and the belief that he endorsed waterfall as "fundamentally sound." However, a further reading of the paper paints a different picture. Indeed, in recent years, it has been recognised that Royce may have been misrepresented.[2] Consider this excerpt from the conclusion of the paper (emphasis ours):

"[There are] five steps that I feel necessary to transform a risky development process into one that will provide the desired

---

[2]   See: http://www.georgeallenmiller.com/2008/10/16/dr-winston-royce-the-plight-of-a-mis-quoted-man/ and http://www.youtube.com/watch?v=X1c2--sP3o0 for example.

product. [...] In my experience, however, *the simpler method has never worked on large software development efforts and the costs to recover far exceeded those required to finance the five-step process listed.*"

While it is true that Royce could have worded his paper better, one would expect that people who quote him would actually have read the paper in its entirety[3], especially if they plan to endorse his approach. Yet, this is precisely what *did not* happen. In a review of iterative and incremental approaches to software development, Basili and Larman (2003) had this to say about Royce's paper:

"Winston Royce shared his opinions on what would become known as the waterfall model, expressed within the constraints of government contracting at that time. Many—incorrectly—view Royce's paper as the paragon of single-pass waterfall. In reality, he recommended an approach somewhat different than what has devolved into today's waterfall concept, with its strict sequence of requirements analysis, design, and development phases. Indeed, Royce's recommendation was to do it twice . . ."

Furthermore, Basili and Larman quoted Royce's son, as having said the following regarding his father:

"He was always a proponent of iterative, incremental, evolutionary development. His paper described the waterfall as the simplest description, but that it would not work for all but the most straightforward projects. The rest of his paper describes [iterative practices] within the context of the 60s/70s government-contracting models (a serious set of constraints)."

This is indeed an irony, especially considering that the US Department of Defence used Royce's paper to justify the adoption of waterfall as a software development standard for many years (Department of Defence

---

[3]   In Chapter 7, we will examine why prose often gets misrepresented and what can be done about it

standard DOD-STD-2167). Why did they adopt Royce's paper? Because it was published by the IEEE[4]—a bastion of peer reviewed excellence.

The final sentence about the context of 60s and 70s contracting models is important too, and we will have much more to say about these in Chapter 11. For now, we'll simply note that it took years to fix the standard: DOD-STD-2167 was finally superseded by an iterative/incremental development approach in 1994 (Larman 2003). However, by then the damage had been done: British, German and French standards, heavily influenced by the DOD-STD-2167, had already been published. The misinterpretation of Royce's paper thus became the de-facto way of running government-related software projects in Europe and the US. Inevitably, it wormed its way into the private sector as well. The myth of waterfall was thus established. The legitimation of waterfall by the US DoD lead to others assuming that it is a "Best practice" and hence worthy of adoption.

As an epilogue to the waterfall affair, Larman described a meeting with the lead author of DOD-STD-2167 as follows:

> "In 1996 I visited the Boston area and had lunch with the principal author of 2167. He expressed regret for the creation of the rigid single-pass waterfall standard. He said he was influenced by common knowledge and practice of the time, plus other standards (e.g, 1521B). He was not familiar with the practice of timeboxed iterative development and evolutionary requirements at the time and in hindsight, said he would have made a strong iterative/incremental development recommendation, rather than what was in 2167 . . ."

What's really interesting is that we were able to find these references with relative ease—the truth about PERT and waterfall is there for all to see. Given this, why do misconceptions regarding these techniques persist to this day? Let's turn to the research literature to see if we can find any explanations for this.

---

[4]   Institute of Electrical and Electronics Engineers

A memetic view of project management

Memetic? What the . . . ? Not more jargon, *please*! We hear you but trust us—this is interesting stuff, especially in light of the two case studies we just examined . . .

Jon Whitty (2005), an academic from the University of Southern Queensland, put forward a somewhat heretical take on the discipline of project management in a paper entitled "A Memetic Paradigm of Project Management." However, because the paper is written in academese—an arcane language, comprehensible only to professional researchers—it remains relatively unknown outside of academia. In the following sections, we take a professional project manager's view of the paper.

Whitty began with the statement that project management has, by and large, failed to live up to the expectations of stakeholders. This statement should be shocking but isn't because it is well documented by studies such as the Standish Report (2009). To quote Whitty, this widespread failure suggests that academics and practising project managers

> ". . . still do not really understand the nature of projects, and that too much research effort has been directed towards clarifying the reasons for project success and failure, while downplaying research on why projects exist and behave as they do . . ."

He believes that the current paradigm of project management cannot help us understand the true nature of projects. Instead, a more critical approach, which considers projects to be a ". . . human construct, about a collection of feelings, expectations and sensations, cleverly conjured up by the human brain . . ." might be a more fruitful way of looking at projects. Here's where the memetic bit comes in.

A memetic interlude

The term meme was coined by another nerd, the evolutionary biologist Richard Dawkins (1976) in his book The Selfish Gene. In this book, he presented the idea that the genes that survive evolution (i.e. those that are passed on from generation to generation) are the ones that contain characteristics serving their own interests. In other words, genes are like those annoying self-centred generation Y co-workers acting "selfishly" to propagate themselves.

More relevant, however, is the parallel he drew between the above view of biological evolution and that of the evolution and propagation of ideas. Ideas, according to Dawkins, propagate themselves through assorted means, ranging from education to mass media. He used the term *meme* to describe

> ". . . an idea (or any unit of information) which gets transmitted (from person to person) through communication or repeated action."

It is important to note that a meme isn't just any random, fleeting thought but an idea that is transmitted with a fair degree of fidelity.

There are many examples of memes, such as folk tales or a really good dirty joke. Consider the power of the "leave Britney alone" meme. Here, a YouTube video of a sobbing teenybopper asking the world to leave Britney Spears alone[5] was viewed by half the world and was even spoofed in a movie[6]. "Memetics" is essentially the study of how memes develop and replicate. As we will see shortly, standards and methodologies are particularly powerful memes.

It's alive and it's coming to get you!

Whitty suggested that the discipline of project management should be viewed as a collection of related memes which propagate as a group. Such groups of memes are collectively called a *memeplex* (darn academics and their jargon).

Taking a cue from Dawkins, this isn't surprising at all. Basically, *any* academic discipline or professional practice can be considered a memeplex. The implications of viewing bodies of knowledge like project management or business analysis to be such "self-serving" memeplexes are rather interesting.

---

[5] http://www.youtube.com/watch?v=kHmvkRoEowc
[6] The movie was Meet The Spartans http://en.wikipedia.org/wiki/Meet_the_Spartans

Firstly, it evokes some interesting mental imagery in the form of one of those 1950s "creature feature" movies with bad special effects. This is where the memeplex body of knowledge is this gooey, pulsating, "ideas blob" which terrorises all and sundry. Anyone who comes into contact with the "memeplex goo" turns into a zombie-like disciple who, when assimilated, makes the memeplex blob even bigger.

Looking deeper into the creature feature metaphor highlights a somewhat counterintuitive implication of the memetic view. As we said earlier, the "ideas blob" creates zombie-like disciples. A memetic view of project management turns the notion of knowledge being created by scholars or practitioners on its head: it is the memeplex that creates the scholars and practitioners, rather than the other way round! Therefore, we can only conclude that scholars and practitioners who were exposed to standard or best practice memeplex goo are now unquestioning disciples (your authors included).

Russell Ackoff's quote about management gurus at the start of this chapter is relevant here. He was a vocal critic of the way management was taught at business schools. In Ackoff's (1986) delightful little book called "Management in Small Doses," he distilled the problem as follows:

> "The major deficiencies in management education are not in what is taught but how it is taught. A major part of management education is devoted to trying to solve problems given to students by teachers. As a result, students unconsciously come to believe that it is natural for problems to be given to them. In the real world however, problems are seldom given; they must be taken. Nevertheless, students are neither taught nor learn how to take problems.
>
> In management, problems usually have to be extracted from complex, unstructured and messy situations. This can only be learned through practice, preferably under the guidance of someone who knows how. In learning, to take problems like learning to drive an automobile, instruction has little value without demonstration and practice."

In one sense, the book you're holding in your hands is simply dripping with memeplex goo (sorry dear reader, but it's too late for you to resist)!

But our intent is not to convert you. If you disagree with some of our arguments, it is likely for one of two reasons.

Firstly, the memeplex goo from your existing body of knowledge is at odds with some of the things we have said. Your current dominant memeplex is trying to preserve itself as all memeplexes do and its immune mechanism is trying to fight off the one from this book.

But there is a second possible reason which we sincerely hope is the one at work. We hope that you are simply reading this book with the same critical intent with which we wrote it. Nothing, but nothing that we do in our professional lives should be exempt from critical examination.

The life and times of a memeplex

Let's look at another example of a memeplex. This time, in homage to the roots of the term, we'll use a biological analogy.

In the beginning . . .

When one person has a radical idea they are usually branded a heretic, like that one person in every office whose stock answer to any question is "Just buy a Mac." But when that mad heretic manages to convince someone else that their idea is good, something magical happens: the heretic becomes the visionary and the ideas behind the heresy become the seed of what will eventually turn into a memeplex.

Adolescence . . .

All of us adults remember the adolescent stage of our lives when we dealt with acne, hair in funny places and making the transition into adulthood. A set of related heretical ideas have to go through a similar process of finding an identity and becoming a full-fledged memeplex.

Organisations are continually subjected to influences from the economic and political environment in which they exist. In terms of the marble board analogy from the Introduction, these forces are the hands that tilt the board in unexpected directions. One of many responses to such influences is to create new organisational roles to deal with the changes. These roles, with the cool titles and position descriptions that accompany them, can be thought of starting the "transition to adulthood" of a memeplex.

Like all new and fresh sounding position titles, there is a period of identity crisis where practitioners try to find their niche in an organisational machine that doesn't quite know where to fit them in. Additionally, within the new discipline, there are various practitioners doing things in different ways depending on their interpretation of their roles.

The effect the new roles have on the organisation and the wider "skills marketplace" may be seen as radical or revolutionary by other well-established disciplines. The latter may at first reject the new discipline because it challenges the "rightness" of theirs. Using our earlier analogy, the new role—which is not yet a full-fledged discipline—can cause the board to tilt in unexpected directions. These changes can threaten the wellbeing of those who are in previously established roles.

An organisation is, quite literally, an organism and organisms respond to changes in ways that tend to maintain the status quo. However, given enough time and a certain critical mass of practitioners, the system begins to accept the changes; the marble board finds a new equilibrium and the memeplex starts to take on an identity of its own. Unfortunately, the new memeplex is still to be established; it needs to do more work for wider acceptance.

The step towards wider acceptance is when professional bodies start to appear. These often begin as informal organisations but are the young memeplex's first steps towards professional respectability. Invariably, after a period, professional bodies begin to develop "bodies of knowledge." From there, it is a short step to certifications that demonstrate a "deep and meaningful" understanding of this codified knowledge. This signals that the memeplex is now approaching adulthood. A few practitioners—the early adopters—now want to be inducted into the "club of the certified" and be considered one of the clique.

More organisations start to notice the new "cool kids" club and decide that their employees should be cool kids too. Therefore, they begin to ask for certifications and professional association membership as a prerequisite for employment. Prospective employees then see this requirement and realise that they also need to be in the club if they want to get a job.

At or around the same time as organisations start to legitimise the new memeplex, educational institutions get in on the act and endorse it further by integrating it into their curriculums. After all, they want to be seen as cool, too.

Maturity . . .

The memeplex has now come of age; it is mature, self-perpetuating and has some cool new job titles to show for it. Disciples of the associated body of knowledge have now been given the "absolute truth" and proceed boldly into the world to preach the good word. The result is that the memes are propagated rapidly. The memes are now a part of conventional wisdom (the status quo) and will "do what they can" to protect and propagate themselves.

With that understanding, we now return to Whitty. In the paper he raised the concern that

> ". . . a large amount of memes in the PM memeplex are today being generated and replicated by University Business Schools. Moreover, as we continue to define organisational success in monetary terms our education systems seem more naturally an extension of corporate training . . ."

The implication being that the memes propagated aren't necessarily good or correct because their propagation is driven by a lopsided notion of what is good. Moreover, the chances of a radically new idea making it through to mainstream are small because new ideas that are even slightly heretical are rejected by the memeplex. This is a consequence of the memeplex "immune mechanism" that we mentioned earlier. The only way that a new idea can survive is:

- By being engulfed and assimilated by the memeplex (the blob of goo visual is particularly apt here); or
- By achieving a "critical mass of acceptance" as mentioned in the previous section. The telltale sign of this is the appearance of a new job description appearing in organisations.

In general, any existing memeplex challenged by a new idea will first attempt to assimilate it and will succumb only if it is unable to deal with the changes wrought by the new competitor.

It is possible that you have not looked at project management, or other disciplines, through a memetic lens up until now. If so, this is an illustration of the power of established memes and the difficulties faced by new ideas in challenging the status quo. Ironically, the fact that Whitty's ideas haven't gained wide acceptance suggests that the memetic view has some validity. Whitty may be a victim of his own metaphor.

The path to the role of "Business Analyst"

Business analysis is a relatively recent discipline that arose out of systems analysis and project management in the early 1990s. While one could make a compelling case that the discipline has been there all along in the form of practices that preceded it, one can make the same argument about many other disciplines and methodologies. Further, the *official* recognition of business analysis as a separate discipline is indeed a relatively recent affair. The International Institute of Business Analysis™ (IIBA®) was founded in October 2003 and the Business Analyst Body of Knowledge (BABOK®) was released in draft form two years later. Interestingly, academic institutions began offering courses on business analysis, oriented around what became the BABOK®, well before the official legitimation of the profession began. Examples include the University of Melbourne "Master of Management (Business Analysis and Systems).[7] Now, armed with the gospel according to BABOK®, budding business analysts go out into the world to spread the good word.

A mature memeplex and the adaptive challenge

Project management is a much older discipline than business analysis and is, therefore, much further along the memeplex lifecycle. In fact, the project management memeplex has itself split into other memeplexes: the business analysis memeplex described in the previous section is one such offshoot.

For a start, project management has given rise to multiple standards, bodies and certifications, representing its continuing legitimisation as a profession. To gain acceptance into the community of project managers,

---

[7] http://www.melbournegsm.unimelb.edu.au/future/business_and_it/mmb.html

a budding aspirant subscribes to one or more of the standards, joins professional bodies and gains certifications, all created by the cycle of the memeplex.

The rapid development of project management as a discipline is a typical mature memeplex characteristic. In the last decade or so, there has been a huge growth of membership in professional project management bodies. Furthermore, in universities and business schools, project management has gained legitimacy as a sub-discipline of management. With this come all the attendant trappings, such as journals, academic conferences, textbooks and degrees.

The larger the project management memeplex gets, the less accommodating it appears to become. This manifests itself in many ways. One example is that, project management practitioners (who have been immersed in the memplex "goo") may feel threatened by any challenge to the "rightness" of their practices and convictions.

But projects continue to fail and, quite naturally, questions get asked about the validity of the gospel according to the memeplex. The traditional project management memeplex is indeed being subject to critical scrutiny by academics, such as Whitty (and those who care to read Winston Royce's paper to the very end!). Professionals too, sense that something is not quite right in the world of the dominant memeplexes like project management and business analysis. Indeed, this book has its roots in such thoughts.

An unexpected tilt of the marble board

Whitty drew attention to the fact that false memes frequently get propagated along with true ones. The point is, once ensconced in mainstream thought, an incorrect idea gets the stamp of legitimacy and thus becomes almost impossible to question or correct. The stories behind the questionable origins of PERT and waterfall highlighted earlier in the chapter clearly illustrate the power of memes taking over mainstream thought.

The point is this: new knowledge is always seen through the *lens of existing knowledge*. To use our marble board metaphor, in challenging a memeplex, you are in effect, tilting the personal marble boards of practitioners in directions that they are unfamiliar with. This, quite naturally, disturbs their sense of wellbeing, so they'll do whatever they can to resist it. Ironically, this is the same sort of resistance that practitioners come up against when implementing *their* projects.

In contrast, taking a memetic viewpoint—wherein it is known that propagated memes aren't necessarily correct—would require that practitioners be critical of ideas and practices handed down by authority. That, in the end, is excellent advice for us all, regardless of whether or not we agree with Whitty's memetic view or Ackoff's contrarian wit.

And finally, a hidden danger

One final point before we close this chapter. It should be clear from the foregoing discussion that well established memes can cause people and organisations to take a blinkered view of the challenges they face. For example, a bureaucratic approach to managing a product development project, wherein "Best practice" processes and procedures are enforced without any regard to their utility, can stifle creativity and innovation—the very qualities one needs when creating novel products. We explore this idea further in the next chapter, where we also meet exemplary innovators from a well-loved children's classic.

4

Managing Innovation:
The Demise of Command and Control

"You tried and you failed. What did we learn? Never try"—(Homer Simpson)

That paperclip

Sometime in 1994 or 1995 we suspect someone excitedly drew a giant paperclip with eyes on a whiteboard in a nondescript office at Microsoft's headquarters in Seattle. Someone else in the room—probably the person who signs cheques—looked at it and said "That's pretty damn cool." Several more meetings would have been held to explore the idea further. Somewhere during this process, a conversation like the following might have occurred:

> "I know—let's call him Clippy."
> "That's a brilliant idea!"
> "I have an even better one. Let's put it in the next version of Microsoft Office as part of the help system."
> "Dude, that's brilliant—you are a genius."

Before long, people decided that this was innovative enough to develop further, and thus a project was born, assigned a budget and nerds got down to coding. And so, from Office 97 to Office 2003, we were blessed with the innovation of the soon to be reviled "Clippy." In fact, such was the dissatisfaction with Clippy that Swartz (2003) even wrote a thesis examining why people hated it so much.

So, was Clippy innovative? Let's chase a definition (in spite of our warnings from Chapter 1), and see what the dictionary says. Merriam-Webster online dictionary defines this term as:

Innovation (n): A new idea, method or device

Okay, so this definition leaves the door wide open, as the meaning of the term can vary from the iPod that creates a whole new market to a new way to organise paperwork so that a book publisher can pay royalties to hardworking authors faster.

Interestingly, this definition also fails to address how an innovation is to be judged. As we discussed above, Microsoft obviously thought that "Clippy" was a tremendous innovation in early versions of their Office product suite. Of course, their users and the world, in general, thought otherwise. That said, Clippy did actually have one unexpected benefit;

it provided an absolute goldmine of material for stand-up comedians worldwide.

Organisations are always interested in doing things better; the present state of affairs is rarely good enough. Even when it is, the world around the organisation does not stand still. To that end, innovation is one of the means to progress to a more desirable future state. When organisations want to innovate, they forget about Clippy and look at examples like Apple's iPod or Nintendo Wii with envious eyes and want the same for themselves. Therefore, they hunt high and low for the magic formula that would enable them to foster and manage this highly desirable thing called *innovation.*

Like all good buzzwords or platitudes, the word "innovation" is sufficiently ambiguous that it can be interpreted to suit one's own ends. This point is underscored by management gurus, consultants and academics who oblige desperate organisations by waxing at length on the best way to inspire and channel innovation. After all, there has to be a process for it, right?

But here's the paradox. Like our hairlines, the more we want it, the further it seems to recede. But does that stop organisations from chasing the mirage?

Managing a mirage?

Both Paul and Kailash have experienced the "call to arms" via the desire of organisations to "innovate." In fact, one of us was witness to an extreme manifestation of the desire to manage innovation: Senior managers in a multinational organisation set up a committee to encourage and manage new creative efforts. The committee was instituted with great fanfare, even greater expectations and chaired by a manager with a suitably pompous title.

The problem with this initiative was that many of the very smart people on the committee had no idea what their brief entailed: What does it mean to "encourage and manage innovation?" Books were read, gurus sought and consultants engaged, but the search for the magic formula led nowhere. The only tangible results were reams of documents filled with well worded platitudes and a couple of (admittedly very nice) presentations on innovation. The committee did not last long; a year or so after being instituted, it was quietly disbanded.

This failed project is a rather typical scenario in organisations that attempt to foster innovation by throwing a kitchen sink of processes and committees at it. It should come as no great surprise that the committee failed to produce tangible results: it failed because people were mistaking innovation as an end, rather than a means to an end. When viewed as an end, innovation suffers from the platitude effect that we described in Chapter 1. To refresh your memory, innovation is one of those platitudinous words that fall into the same category as "quality," "flexibility," "security" and "governance," in that it doesn't really make much sense on its own. Figure 4.1 is a better representation of innovation.

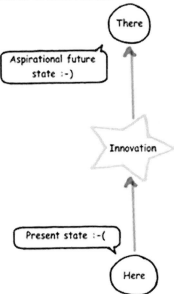

Figure 4.1: Innovation as a means to an end

Innovation is, of course, very easy to see in hindsight because it is perceived through the difference it has made in a particular situation. Nintendo's Wii game system is regarded as innovative, not because it had better or more powerful graphics capability than its Sony and Microsoft competitors, but because it redefined the gaming experience via its unique motion controller.

However, had the Wii been a complete flop in the market, it may not have been considered particularly innovative.

So, how does the star labelled "innovation" enable us to get from our present state to some sort of better future state? Given what we said earlier about the folly of throwing the kitchen sink at "developing and managing innovation," it is only appropriate that we use that humble household fitting to make a point or two. Kitchen sinks hold a special significance for Kailash. Over the next page or two, Paul will take a step back and let Kailash relate a couple of stories from his research days . . .

Tales from the kitchen sink

It was early 1994 and I had started a research degree within the chemical engineering department at the University of Queensland. Given my theoretical leanings, I gravitated towards the mathematically-oriented field of fluid dynamics—the study of fluid flows. I'd spoken to folks working in the area and finally decided to work with "Tony," not only because I found his work interesting, but his quick intelligence and easygoing manner would make for a good work environment. Tony's knowledge in fluid mechanics was wide ranging. That was important, but what really appealed to me was that he was happy to let me follow my own interests rather than his.

I spent a few weeks, or was it months, trying to define a decent research problem, but got nowhere. Tony, sensing that it was time to nudge me towards a decision, suggested a couple of problems to investigate. Realising that I'd already burnt up a few months of a research grant, I agreed to work on a problem he suggested. Very briefly, the problem related to the break-up of fluid jets into drops. This phenomenon is a familiar one, but rather than attempt to explain it, I will follow the advice that a picture is worth several words.

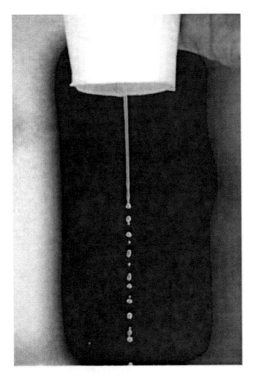

Figure 4.2: Break up of a water jet into drops

The phenomenon has several industrial applications: one example being inkjet printing, which spawned a lot of research in the area in the 1970s and 80s. The specific problem that Tony suggested I work on was a variation of the standard jet break-up problem. I hit the books and research journals, absorbing as much as I could about all the prior work done on it.

I learnt a heck of a lot about the physics of jet break-up, but by the time I'd started my research, the problem had been done to death. At least a hundred variants of the problem had been solved and I realised that my PhD would be at best a minor extension of existing work. I read about and around the problem to try and find an interesting angle until I could procrastinate no more. A yearly review loomed, so I began working on the problem Tony had suggested. Things carried on in this vein for almost a year . . . dull, desultory progress . . . the world was looking very grey indeed . . .

Then came one of those wonderful, but unexpected "Aha" moments when everything changed. One evening in October or November 1994, I was washing up a large pile of dishes when I noticed a curious wave-like structure on the thin jet that emerged from the kitchen sink tap and fell onto a plate an inch or two below. The wave pattern was absolutely stationary and rather striking. Rather than attempt to describe it any further, I will just show you a photograph of the phenomenon.

Figure 4.3: Stationary waves on a water jet

The phenomenon is one that countless folks have noticed, and even though I'd seen it before, I had never paid it much attention. But suddenly among the suds and dishes, I was transfixed by the jet. I saw that this was related to the phenomenon of jet breakup. As crazy as it sounds, this was a transcendent moment for me because I knew intuitively, without working through the maths, that I would be able to explain this pattern.

To me the pattern was, and still is, a thing of beauty. Since I'd been immersed in the theory of fluid jets for so long, I realised the phenomenon was caused by surface tension[1]. Incidentally, Paul tells me I need to get out more. He's probably right . . .

---

[1]   Surface tension is the force that arises from the attraction between liquid molecules. These forces are what make a liquid a liquid—if they weren't present, the liquid would be a gas. The forces are balanced in the interior of a

Wondering if anyone had published any papers on it, I rushed off to the library to find out more. The dishes could wait; better still, they might be done by the time I got back! Google Scholar and decent Internet search engines were still a good few years away so I had to slog through print and library references to dig up relevant papers. I came up with very little and realised that I'd stumbled on to something that could see me through my degree and could even make a worthwhile paper.

The next day, I told Tony about it, and being a fluid dynamics nerd too, he was just as excited about it as I was. He was more than happy for me to switch topics and I worked feverishly on this problem. Within a few months I had a theory that related the wavelength of the waves to jet velocity, fluid viscosity[2] and surface tension. My theory was validated by a fourth year undergraduate student and it was novel enough to get me my degree and a couple of papers.

"Who would have thought . . ."

So, as you can see, the kitchen sink does have value in innovation! Of course, the maths and physics that I learnt over these years have all but dried up and vanished, but what remains with me are a few insights into the creative process, which I list below:

- **Interesting opportunities lurk in unexpected places**: A kitchen sink—who would have thought. Clippy being of more value to stand-up comedians than computer users—who would have thought.
- **. . . But it takes work and training to recognise opportunities for what they are**: If I did not have a background in the physics of fluid dynamics, I wouldn't have seen the waves for what they were.
- **A sense of progress is important, even when things aren't going well**: Tony left me to my own devices initially, but then nudged me

---

liquid because a liquid molecule is on average subject to the same force in all directions. On the surface, however, molecules are subject to a net attractive force (from the interior of the liquid). This unbalanced force manifests itself as surface tension.

2   Essentially a measure of the stickiness of a fluid.

towards a productive direction when he saw I was going nowhere. This had the effect of giving me a sense of progress towards a goal (my degree), which kept my spirits up through a hard time.

- **It is best to work on things that interest you, not those that interest others**: I stuck to my primary interest (mathematical modelling) rather than do something that was not of much interest but may have been a better career choice.

Lab collab

Here's another story from a few years later when I was working as a theorist within a polymer processing laboratory. Most of the other members in the research laboratory were doing practical projects, working in the lab doing stuff with real polymers, whilst I was engaged in modelling imaginary ones using simulations. The folks engaged in the two strands of research did not meet much—incidentally this is quite common in many university departments. Hell, that was fine with me because I was happy working on my own little project.

Then one day, one of "the others" knocked on my door to have a chat. One thing led to another and I was able to contribute to a practical problem that he was working on. The reading and background work I had done up to that point enabled me to solve his problem rather quickly. Progress at last—but not in the way I'd imagined.

Encouraged by this, I started talking to others in the group and soon found that they had modelling problems that I could help with. I published a few papers through such collaborations and kept my academic score ticking along. More importantly though, I got for the first time, a taste of collaborative work and I found that I really enjoyed it. One of the papers that we wrote rated a minor award, which would have helped my academic career had I stayed in the field. However, later that year I decided to switch careers and move to consulting. But that's another story . . .

My stint in the polymer lab, very different from my solo research experience, taught me a few things about the importance of collaboration in creative work. These are:

- **Collaboration between diversely skilled individuals enhances creativity**. It is important to interact with others, particularly professionals from other disciplines. I'm grateful to my colleagues from the lab, Michael, Stewart and Grant, for drawing me out of my "comfort zone" of theoretical work.

- **Being part of a larger effort does not preclude creativity and innovation.** Although I did not do any experiments, I was able to develop models that explained some of the phenomena that my colleagues found.
- **Even modest contributions add value to the end product—great insights and epiphanies aren't necessary:** None of the modelling work that I did was particularly profound or new. It was all fairly routine stuff, done using existing methods and algorithms. Yet, my contributions to the research added a piece that was essential for completeness.

Some reflections on the stories

[Paul rejoins the conversation . . .]

The events mentioned above are based on the experiences of one person in a research environment, but we believe the takeaways have a much wider applicability. Further, although the two stories are quite different and hold different lessons, there are a couple of common themes that run through them. These are:

- When doing creative work, we tend to end up with results that we don't intend or expect to find.
- A shift in perspective may help in generating new ideas. Looking at things from someone else's point of view might be just the spark you need.
- Things often do not go according to plan but it is important to keep your spirits up.
- Background is important; it is critical to learn/read as much as possible about the problem you're attempting to solve.

The above conclusions hold a warning for those who might over-plan and control innovative or creative activities. In both cases, Kailash started out by defining what he intended to solve but ended up solving something else. By the yardstick of a project plan, he had failed. But, by other measures (dare we use the word "innovation"?), he did alright. By definition, the process of discovery is unpredictable and somewhat opportunistic: you have to be willing and able to redefine your goals as you proceed and, at times, even throw everything away and start from scratch. Of course, this is easier said than done.

The legacy of legacy

Kailash's experience of solving a different problem than the one he intended to highlights two lenses by which his performance could be judged. Through the lens of his original project plan he failed, yet through the lens of innovation he did well. The fact that one can judge failure versus success through either of these perspectives tells us that neither gives us the full picture. Furthermore, the stories illustrate another key point: if cognitive bias wasn't enough, those involved in creative activities are often constrained by what *already exists*.

Organisations are conservative when it comes to accepting new ideas. If a new idea is in conflict with an established one, chances are that it will not be accepted easily. This is not necessarily a bad thing. Why go with something new, unproven and costly when there is already something that works. Unfortunately, this line of thinking can also be used as a justification to stick with the old and shun the new. Hence, we have organisations that continue to be beholden to systems and processes that limp on.

Organisations struggle with the question of how aging systems should be replaced. New systems promise much but are complex, expensive to implement and pose many risks. One such risk is that no one quite understands the legacy bequeathed by legacy systems: what they do, how they do it and why they were designed so. Thus, organisations have little choice but to play it safe and as a result, legacy lives on. Despite all the advances in software engineering, software migrations and upgrades remain fraught with problems. This is true even for systems that claim to represent a clean break from the past. *One never has the luxury of a completely blank slate*; there are always constraints placed by legacy systems. As Fred Brooks (1987) stated in his classic article "No Silver Bullet":

> ". . . In many cases, the software must conform because it is the most recent arrival on the scene. In others, it must conform

because it is perceived as the most conformable. But in all cases, much complexity comes from conformation to other interfaces . . ."

While one aspect of legacy is that it serves to constrain whatever attempts to replace it, another, perhaps less well appreciated point is that those creating something new ought to worry about the consequences of their creation. Unfortunately, this is rarely done. We'll illustrate this point through an example. Consider, for example, Figure 4.4. Many of our readers would have seen something like it before because this diagram it is very common in project management books and presentations. It tells us, among other things, that the *quality* of a project output depends on time, cost and scope.

Figure 4.4: The "iron triangle" of project management

Now consider the following example of a project output: the Sydney Opera House. It is a global icon and there are people who come to Sydney just to see it. In term of economic significance to Sydney, it is priceless and irreplaceable. The architect who designed it, Jørn Utzon, was awarded the Pritzker Prize (architecture's highest honour) for it in 2003.

Figure 4.5: The Sydney Opera House

But the million dollar question is . . . "*Was it a successful project?*" If one was to ask one of the two million annual tourists who visit the place, we suspect that the answer would be an emphatic "Yes." Yet, when we judge the project through the lens of the "iron triangle," the view changes significantly. To understand why, consider these fun filled facts about the Sydney Opera House.

- The Opera House was formally completed in *1973*, having cost *$102 million*
- The original cost estimate in 1957 was *$7 million*
- The original completion date set by the government was *1963*
- Thus, the project was completed *ten years late* and *over-budget by more than a factor of fourteen*

If that wasn't bad enough, Utzon, the designer of the opera house, never lived to set foot in it. He left Australia in disgust, swearing never to come back after his abilities had been called into question and payments suspended. When the Opera House was opened in 1973 by Queen Elizabeth II, Utzon was not invited to the ceremony, nor was his name mentioned.

Now, that is harsh. Clearly, when judged through the "quality" lens of time, cost and scope, this project was an unmitigated failure. Yet, the Opera House serves to remind us that, when all is said and done, we judge quality through something deeper than time, cost and scope alone. That something is *legacy*—what it means for future generations.

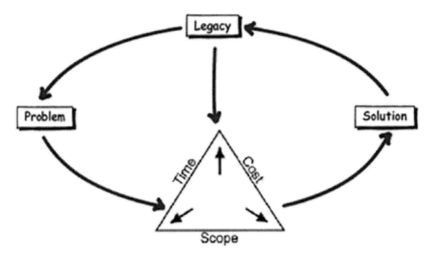

Figure 4.6: Legacy informs the iron triangle

So, we think that the Project Management 101 diagram needs to be redrawn because it misleads, especially for the sorts of complex problems that inspired this book (the characteristics of which, we will examine in detail in the next chapter). Considering time, cost and scope without legacy is delusional and plain dumb. Legacy *informs* time, cost and scope and challenges us to look beyond the visible symptoms of what we perceive as the problem and challenges us to consider the implications of our solutions. Figure 4.6 summarises our view that creative acts are influenced by the legacy of the past and, at the same time, they create a legacy of their own.

With that said, we now turn to the question of managing creativity and innovation in organisational settings.

The greatest CEO and organisation of all time

Over the years there have been many visionary leaders who have had profound influences on the field of innovation, leadership and organisational development. Jack Welch would be a good example, as would be Bill Gates and Richard Branson. Some might say that in terms of pure innovation you would have to hand the gong to the late Steve Jobs of Apple.

But all of these guys pale into insignificance when they are compared to whom we consider to be the most visionary and creative CEO in the history of the modern organisation, especially when judged by the criteria of creativity and innovation. Such has been his influence that we believe his organisation is the archetype by which all self-proclaimed "innovative" organisations should judge themselves.

Academics have coined a term to describe this sort of organisation and, strange as it may seem, that term is not "brewery." Instead, we have this notion of the *post-bureaucratic organisation,* a mythical place where decisions are made collectively through dialogue and consensus, where the hierarchy is flat, employees have a say in issues that affect their work. Table 4.1 compares a post-bureaucratic organisation to a traditional bureaucratic organisation:

Bureaucracy	Post-bureaucracy
Consensus through Acquiescence to Authority	Consensus through Institutionalized Dialogue
Influence based on Formal Position	Influence through Persuasion/Personal Qualities
Internal Trust Immaterial	High Need for Internal Trust
Emphasis on Rules and Regulations	Emphasis on Organisational Mission
Information Monopolised at Top of Hierarchy	Strategic Information shared in Organisation
Focus on Rules for Conduct	Focus on Principles Guiding Action
Fixed (and Clear) Decision Making Processes	Fluid/Flexible Decision Making Processes
Network of Specialized Functional Relationships	Communal Spirit/Friendship Groupings
Hierarchical Appraisal	Open and Visible Peer Review Processes
Definite and Impermeable Boundaries	Open and Permeable Boundaries
Objective Rules to ensure Equity of Treatment	Broad Public Standards of Performance
Expectation of Constancy	Expectation of Change
Dilbert Pointy haired bosses	*Umpa Lumpas*

Table 4.1: Comparison of bureaucratic and post-bureaucratic organisations (from Hodgson 2004)

The post-bureaucratic organisation is epitomised by that fictional chocolate factory, where green haired Umpa Lumpas sing their merry songs and dance their merry dances (Dahl 2007). In such a place, creativity and innovation is found in every nook and cranny, turning out ground breaking products, with loads of "oomph" that the rest of the world marvels at.

That's right. If you want to understand the post-bureaucratic organisation, look no further than Willy Wonka and his chocolate factory. Now, that guy knows how to innovate! Okay, so the iPods and iPhones are cool, but come on . . . the Everlasting Gobstopper was sheer genius!

Other organisations have attempted to emulate Wonka's model with varying degrees of success. Although a number of workgroups within large organisations might function in a post-bureaucratic way, the fact that Wonka-like organisations do not exist suggests that a post-bureaucratic organisation is a utopian and academic ideal, one that is unlikely to survive in the real world.

Why is it just an ideal? Perhaps it is because those who manage organisations, departments or workgroups are generally uncomfortable with employees working autonomously, even if they are four feet tall Umpa Lumpas who are naturally self-organising. This is understandable as it is ultimately the responsibility of managers to ensure that organisational or departmental goals are achieved. How else to do this but through the time-tested *command and control* approach to management? In this approach decision making is top-down, with employees having little say in defining goals and how they will be achieved. It is the antithesis of a post-bureaucratic approach.

Project managing Umpa Lumpas?

We may not all be working for Willy Wonka, but we suspect that many readers would be able to identify characteristics from both columns in their work environments. Many organisations do recognise that a "light hand on the rudder" is needed in order to encourage creativity and innovation. Yet, where does one draw the line between creative freedom and control?

Many organisations see project management as the silver bullet answer to this question. After all, project management, by definition, provides a means to manage collective goal oriented endeavours. Furthermore, many projects, especially those involving a new product, such as software or a revamped Everlasting Gobstopper, have significant creative or innovative elements. It, therefore, seems reasonable that project management is the answer to the problems of managing creative work.

In practice, however, project management emphasises formalized procedures and reporting mechanisms. It tends to be a largely bureaucratic affair. Project management tools and techniques support managerial discipline by providing means to decompose the project into manageable bits by using the much-loved work breakdown structure[3] and then assigning these bits to individuals or small teams. The work assigned can then be tracked and controlled tightly, which—from a managerial perspective—is a good thing. However, implicit in this view is the assumption that project management processes will enable managers to control and direct creative work *without any adverse side-effects.*

This begs the critical question. If you can indeed use project management processes to control or direct creative work, then *why are there no PMBOK® or Prince2® certified Umpa Lumpas?*

While we speculate that Umpa Lumpas might be more philosophically aligned to Agile Methods[4], a more likely answer to this question can be found in a brilliant paper by Damian Hodgson (2004) entitled "Project Work: The Legacy of Bureaucratic Control in the Post-Bureaucratic Organisation." While Umpa Lumpas are not mentioned by name, it explored the tensions and contradictions presented by project management approaches in a Wonka-like post-bureaucratic organisation. Hodgson acknowledged that organisations implicitly recognise the need for a "light hand on the rudder," but he posed the question: If project management is seen as a means to achieve this, how well does it work in practice? In Hodgson's words:

---

3   A project management technique used to decompose the entire work of the project into elements that can be estimated and sequenced accurately.

4   Agile refers to several methodologies that emphasise an iterative and incremental (piecewise) approach to product development. The main difference between these and the traditional waterfall approach (discussed in the previous chapter) is that Agile methods do not attempt to plan the entire project at the start. Another difference is that a working (but incomplete) version of the product is delivered to the customer at frequent intervals

"In response to the challenges of the post-bureaucratic form, project management has been put forward by many as a 'tried-and-tested' package of techniques able to cope with discontinuous work, expert labour and continuous and unpredictable change while delivering the levels of reliability and control of the traditional bureaucracy. . . . I explore some of the contradictions and tensions within a department where such a 'hybrid' mode of control is implemented, embodying both bureaucratic and post-bureaucratic logics. In particular, I focus upon the discursive tactics employed to sell 'rebureaucratization' as 'debureaucratization' and the complex employee responses to this initiative. I argue that the tensions evident here cast significant doubt on the feasibility of a seamless integration of bureaucracy and the post-bureaucratic [organisation]."

The "discursive tactics employed" that Hodgson mentioned are the seemingly reasonable and rational arguments that an organisation uses in its internal marketing campaign to "sell" the idea that the methods and approaches of project management are consistent with the ideals of a post-bureaucratic organisation.

Buzzbank

The arguments Hodgson presented in his paper are based on a case study conducted on a UK bank which he referred to using the pseudonym *Buzzbank*. Buzzbank was a real success story in the banking sector and had expanded rapidly in both market share and turnover via its use of new technology. As Hodgson described it:

"My interest in particular centred on Buzzbank senior management's identification of project management as the prime 'critical success factor' for the organisation; the development of project management expertise throughout the organisation was seen as a key priority to maintain performance into the next decade. To an extent, the project teams researched could scarcely be more 'cutting edge,' representing highly-trained

> 'knowledge workers' developing innovative high technology applications and solutions in a new sector of an enormously profitable industry . . ."

Hodgson conducted interviews and observed operations within the highly successful IT department of Buzzbank over a period of two years. During this period, the organisation was implementing a "strategic plan" aimed at formalizing innovation and creative work using project management processes. The idea, in the words of a couple of senior IT managers, was to *"bring a level of discipline"* and *"bring an idea of professional structuring"* to the work of the department.

The main rationale used to sell project management to the Buzzbank IT team was one that will be familiar to many of our readers: the need to ensure predictability and repeatability of work done whilst ensuring that innovation and creativity would not be impeded. This was portrayed by management as a natural and inevitable consequence of growth. They claimed that the existing "ad-hoc" work culture would no longer be successful because the organisation was approaching its "next stage of evolution."

The immediate benefit of such a metaphor for those members of senior management charged with "rebureaucratizing" the organisation was that it carried a very strong sense of inevitability. As such, it had the effect of framing opposition to such changes as irrational and futile, standing in the way of this natural "evolution." Any employee resistance was dubbed as "natural growing pains," much like those of an adolescent rebelling against the rules imposed by their parents. Cast in this light, dissenting viewpoints were portrayed as natural and unavoidable—and possibly even necessary—but ultimately without any validity.

Another interesting aspect that Hodgson highlighted was the way in which old practices, the successful but "bad" ones, were subsumed in the new (formal) framework. For example, in the old world, employees were given the freedom to experiment and many considered this a strength, not a weakness. In the new world, however, such a practice was seen as a threat. It was considered more important to capture how to do things correctly so that things became repeatable and experimentation would not be necessary. As one manager put it:

"If we capture how we do things right, at least it makes things repeatable, and we can record the improvement required when things don't go right, which doesn't happen in a rapidly-expanding, gung-ho environment."

Hodgson noted that the terms "rapidly-expanding" and "gung-ho," which were used in a negative sense, could just as well be cast in positive terms such as "flexible" or "proactive." The point being that management framed the existing situation in terms that made the implementation of the new procedures seem like a logical and reasonable next step. The processes were touted as a means to achieve change (i.e. be flexible) but in a controlled way. Unsurprisingly, management then went to great lengths to avoid use of terms that would cause their framework to be perceived as being negative. For example, the term "structure" was used instead of "bureaucracy" or "formalization." In this way, management attempted to assimilate the existing values of Buzzbank into the strategic plan.

Spider senses tingling . . .

So, how did the Buzzbank employees take to this new regime? Perhaps unsurprisingly, the managers who instigated this process viewed it positively, however acknowledged that such change gave rise to understandable but irrational resistance. In contrast, when Hodgson spoke to lower level employees, the impression he got was very different indeed (emphasis ours):

"However, in the time spent by myself in the organisation, the tone and target of much of the humour, as well as much stronger reactions, appeared to throw doubt on the extent to which this discourse had permeated among the general employees, particularly within the IT department. Humour was commonplace in the everyday banter both within teams and between teams in the IT division at Buzzbank, and the increasing levels of bureaucratization was the butt of most of the humour, particularly at the lower levels of the hierarchy. *The main experience of project management as reported by many Buzzbank employees was one of intensified bureaucratic surveillance . . .*"

This was exemplified by the reaction of employees to managerial jargon that was used in company circulars and literature intended to promote the strategic plan. The comments provoked by such literature were ironic and cynical, highlighting the gap between managerial intent and employee reality.

Additionally, Hodgson noted that employees often appeared to comply with the new regulations but not in the way intended by management. Employees would "comply" with the formal requirements of the new system in terms of filling in the necessary forms, reporting in at given times, completing the necessary work-logs and so on. But cynicism and subversion were rife.

> ". . . compliance on the part of Buzzbank employees in many cases bore all the hallmarks of instrumental behaviour, accompanied by insubordinate statements and humour ranging from the cynical to the confrontational. At other times, assurances were given to senior management and immediately contravened, fictionalized accounts of project activities were submitted late, or else procedures were observed meticulously to the detriment of deadlines and other constraints. The emergent organisational order was a precarious negotiation between alienated compliance and an autonomous disregard for bureaucratic demands . . ."

Employees clearly did not buy into the strategy or the tactics to "sell" the new regime to staff. References to a "natural process of evolution" and the consequent "growing pains," the framing of terminology to make the changes seem more palatable did not work and such techniques were plainly seen for what they were: methods to "sell the unsellable." In short, there was a clear gap between the perceptions of management and employees as to the success of the newly implemented processes.

Warm and fuzzy

Hodgson saw the case study as exemplifying the problem of control vs. autonomy in emerging post-bureaucratic organisations. Managers viewed project management as a means to address the risks inherent in post-bureaucratic work, whereas employees viewed it as an unnecessary and unjustified imposition. Management was looking for the best of both worlds; a hybrid model that incorporated the best elements of a post bureaucratic model and a traditional command and control approach. The case study casted doubt on whether such a hybrid is possible *solely* through the implementation of standard project management techniques and processes. It exposed some of the tensions and differences in perceptions that can occur when such a model is implemented.

The case study also illuminated a more general problem that pervades organisations: reconciling diverse viewpoints of stakeholders on any contentious issue. In the case of Buzzbank, it was how projects should be managed, but one can see a similar divergence of perspectives in many organisational problems that have no clear-cut, yes/no answers. We'll explore this point further in the next chapter.

Looking over the complaints of the Buzzbank employees, it is clear that most of the problems arose from the loss of autonomy that they had enjoyed prior to the implementation of the new processes. The key message, therefore, is simple and obvious. The more input employees have in making work-related decisions, the more engaged and motivated they will be.

Yes, this does mean letting go of the "reins of control" to an extent but it is clear, as highlighted by Hodgson's work, that holding the reins tightly might cause more problems than it solves. What's called for, above all, is a degree of flexibility. Use project management processes by all means but be open to employee input as to what's working well and what's not.

In concluding this chapter, we can only regret that Willy Wonka did not write a book on leadership or project management.

5

There Are Problems
and There Are "Problems"

"Confidence is what you have before you understand the problem."
—(Woody Allen)

Of pot and thought

Back in the late 1960s hippies would smoke weed, sing kum ba yah and ask each other deep questions like "Why can't we all just get along, man?" and "I'm so hungry . . . where can we get some pizza?" Such was the depth of insight from this era that the cultural and ideological impacts are still felt today—mainly through generation Y's penchant for buying anything that has the word "organic" in it.

Taking a memetic viewpoint of Chapter 3, the hippies spawned a new memeplex on a societal scale. They questioned the status quo and labelled those who held it dear with picturesque terms such as "squares." The resulting ideological and cultural clash of these "hippie vs. square" super-titans raged on for several years. In different guises, this drama is played out time and again, whenever a bunch of heretics set out to change the world and—if they succeed in doing so—spawn a new memeplex.

Around the time that the hippie memeplex was reaching maturity, another group of discontents were starting to question the basis of rational problem solving. They believed the "tried and true" rational methods of analysis that were epitomised in the scientific method were, to put it bluntly, inadequate for many problems. This bunch of pioneers didn't wear tie-dyed shirts and couldn't be identified by shoulder-plus length hair. To understand what they were talking about, one had to read research journals where they published their radical ideas. Back in this era (1960s and 1970s), this silent battle played itself out slowly. Each exchange of fire could take a year or two (that being the lag time between submitting a paper for publication and its appearance in print). The internet and desktop PCs as we know them did not exist and Bill Gates and Steve Jobs were still getting picked on by jocks in high school.

The heretics and their ideas

These academic heretics were from disciplines as diverse as planning, philosophy, design methods, operations research and management/leadership. Despite their varying backgrounds and disciplines—which of course led to them all to use wildly different terminology and metaphors—many of them were actually saying the same thing. In essence, they realised that problems could be classified into two broad categories, each of which had to be tackled using vastly different methods and tools. Table 5.1 below lists some of these category names, along with the heretic who coined them. The key point recognised by all these folks is that the problems on the left-end of the spectrum could be solved using tried and tested traditional techniques of analysis but those on the right were another matter altogether.

Hippie	Left Extreme	Right Extreme
Rittel/Webber	Tame problem	Wicked problem
Simon	Programmed decision	Non Programmed decision
Ackoff	Problem	Mess
Ravetz	Technical Problem	Practical Problem
Heifetz	Technical Problem	Adaptive Problem
Checkland	Hard Systems	Soft Systems
Johnson	Problems to solve	Polarities to manage

Table 5.1: Problem category names, and the people who coined them.

Before proceeding any further, it is worth clarifying what we mean by the term "traditional techniques of analysis." Essentially, this refers to the systematic process of analysis enshrined in the scientific method and page two of Winston Royce's (1970) paper[1]. For our purposes, we can summarise it as involving the following steps:

1. Understand the problem
2. Gather information about the problem
3. Analyse the information
4. Formulate (possibly several alternate) solutions
5. Evaluate alternatives
6. Implement the best solution
7. Test the implemented solution
8. Modify the solution if necessary (cycle through steps 1-8 iteratively)

---

[1] In Chapter 3, we examined the back story of the waterfall method of IT project delivery and how it appears to be rooted in a misinterpretation of a paper by Winston Royce

This technique works brilliantly on many problems—even technically complex ones, such as sending a spacecraft to Saturn. However, it all starts to go awry when it comes to right-extreme problems.

You will note that there are considerable differences in terminology used by these authors. Clearly, these authors would have benefited from a quick chat over coffee or a web search before they published their definitions. But alas, Google did not exist at that time, so such differences were inevitable.

Amongst those listed above, Herbert Simon (1960) was the earliest to make the distinction between the so-called left and right modes of thinking. We first met Mr Simon in Chapter 2 where we learned about the concept of bounded rationality. In his 1960 book "The New Science of Management Decision" he spoke of "programmed" and "non-programmed" decisions. According to Simon, a programmed decision "is repetitive, routine and has a definite procedure worked out for it." In other words, there is a clear, predictable relationship between cause and effect. Moreover, the solution is definitive. It does not call for a novel approach each time a problem comes up; it can literally be "programmed." On the other hand, non-programmed decisions are novel in that they have no pre-set rules and procedures to guide their handling and call for intelligent, adaptive and problem oriented action. He further noted that the techniques for these non-programmed decisions involve judgment, creativity, and intuition. At that time, these were strange, even heretical, words to describe the supposedly rational process of decision making.

Russell Ackoff (1979), who we met briefly in Chapter 1, has the most compelling metaphor for complex (or, in Simon's terms, non-programmable) problems. He called them *messes*. This term is picturesque and conveys a lot—we've heard the phrase "this project is a mess" countless times. That said, the word "mess" means many things to many people so it is true that the term tends to be conflated with its other meanings, thus making the definition of a mess a mess! Nevertheless, the following words from Ackoff summarise the sense in which he uses the term:

"Managers are not confronted with problems that are independent of each other, but with dynamic situations that consist of complex systems of changing problems that interact with each other. I call such situations messes. Problems are abstractions extracted from messes by analysis; they are to messes as atoms are to tables and chairs."

In the fifty-odd years since these intellectual hippies put out their "way out there" ideas, the *wicked* metaphor has turned out to be the most appealing and has gained wide acceptance, especially in the last decade or so. As a result, Horst Rittel, the man who coined the term, is fast achieving the status of a management guru (alas posthumously). Rittel, along with Melvin Webber (1972), drew the distinction between "tame" and "wicked" problems in a seminal paper entitled "Dilemmas in a General Theory of Planning." Unlike their intellectual compatriots who waffled on about the difference between left and right without actually articulating it in a more concrete fashion, Rittel and Webber described ten *defining characteristics* of wicked problems. The criteria can be used to determine whether or not a problem is wicked. They are:

- **There is no definitive formulation of a wicked problem.** In other words, the problem can be framed in many different ways, depending on which aspects of it one wants to emphasise. These different views of the problem can often be contradictory. Take, for example, the problem of traffic congestion. One solution may involve building more roads, whereas another may involve improving public transport. The first accommodates an increase in the number of vehicles on the road, whereas the second attempts to reduce it.

- **Wicked problems have no stopping rule.** The first characteristic states that one's understanding of the problem depends on how one approaches it. Consequently, the problem is never truly solved. Each new insight or solution improves one's understanding of the problem yet one never completely understands it. This often leads to a situation in which people are loath to take action because additional analysis might increase the chances of finding a better solution. Analysis paralysis, anyone?

- **Solutions to wicked problems are not true or false but better or worse.** Solutions to wicked problems are not right or wrong but are subjectively better or worse. Consequently, judgements on the effectiveness of solutions are likely to differ widely based on the personal interests, values, and ideology of the participants.

- **There is no immediate and no ultimate test of a solution to a wicked problem**. Solutions to wicked problems cannot be validated as is the case in tame problems. Any solution, after being implemented, will generate waves of consequences that may yield undesirable repercussions which outweigh the intended advantages. (Offering Britney Spears a recording contract is a classic example).

- **Every solution to a wicked problem is a "one-shot operation" because there is no opportunity to learn by trial-and-error, every attempt counts significantly**. Rittel explained this characteristic succinctly, with the example "One cannot build a freeway to see how it works."

- **Wicked problems do not have an enumerable (or an exhaustively describable) set of potential solutions.** There are no criteria that allow one to test whether or not all possible solutions to a wicked problem have been identified and considered.

- **Every wicked problem is essentially unique.** Using "what worked elsewhere" will generally not work for wicked problems. There are always features that are unique to a particular wicked situation. Accordingly, one can never be certain that the specifics of a problem are consistent with previous problems that one has dealt with. This characteristic directly calls into question the common organisational practice of implementing "best practices" that have worked elsewhere.

- **Every wicked problem can be considered to be a symptom of another problem**. This refers to the fact that a wicked problem can usually be traced back to a deeper underlying problem. For example, a high crime rate might be due to the lack of economic opportunities. In this case the obvious solution of cracking down on crime is unlikely to work because it treats the symptom, not the cause. The point is that it is difficult, if not impossible, to be sure that one has reached the fundamental underlying problem. The level at which a problem "settles" cannot be decided on logical grounds alone.

- **The existence of a discrepancy representing a wicked problem can be explained in numerous ways. The choice of explanation determines the nature of the problem's resolution.** In other words, a wicked problem can be explained in many ways with each "explanation" serving the interests of a particular group of stakeholders.

- **The planner has no right to be wrong (planners are liable for the consequences of the actions they generate).** Those who work with wicked problems (town planners, for example) are paid to design and implement solutions. However, as we have seen, solutions to wicked problems cause other unforeseen issues. Planners and problem solvers are invariably held responsible for the unanticipated consequences of their solutions.

Most of our readers would have had to deal with problems that satisfy one or more of these defining characteristics. While we think that Ackoff's mess of systems is a more comprehensive model than Rittel's because it describes the complex interactions of many problems as opposed to a single problem, it is the clarity afforded by the definition of problem wickedness that makes Rittel's formulation more appealing. The ten characteristics of wickedness are way more concrete than the rather abstract systems viewpoint favoured by Ackoff. This concreteness helps us relate it to our own experiences—an act that sometimes results in one of those rare, insightful "Aha" or "That's so true" moments, when we realise that the problem we are grappling with does not have a solution in the usual sense of the word.

Now, each person in Table 5.1 offered their own methods to tackle "right extreme" problems. The amazing thing is that the methods proposed by these diverse individuals have a fair degree of overlap. In the next chapter we will examine this overlap in some detail, but for now, let's take a look at common first reactions that people have when faced with wicked problems.

Easy listening vs. heavy metal: attribute substitution revisited

The first and most common response to the sort of complexity that comes with problem wickedness is *naive simplicity*. What this means is best understood by referring to commercial talkback radio where one can routinely hear statements along the lines of "Why can't we just . . ."

"Well, can't they just lock them up and throw away the key?"

"Why can't we just send them back to where they came from?"

In fact a fairly good litmus test for whether you are being naively simplistic is the use of the phrase "Surely . . ." or "Why can't they just . . ." at the start of a solution statement. These sorts of solutions, ones that seem so simple and obvious at first glance, usually fail to take into account many important aspects of the problem. Unfortunately, naïve simplicity is something all of us indulge in, often ignoring our better judgement.

A classic example of this bias was when Travis, a friend of Paul's asked him for some advice. Travis is a pretty smart guy, a financial planner by profession and a nerdy one at that. If Paul ever asked him about a particular stock or particular fund to invest in, Travis would immediately launch into a long, detailed discussion about one's personal situation, job security, age, investment mix, risk tolerance, debts and so forth. From that, he would ask a thousand and one questions before he would give an answer consisting of several options. One day, when Travis called Paul for advice on a computer system for his financial planning practice, Paul naturally asked several similar questions to determine what sort of system would suit Travis best. Travis interrupted Paul in the middle of the discussion and asked "Can't you just do it for me?" to which Paul shot back "Can't you just tell me which managed fund to buy?"

This rhetorical question had the immediate effect. When Travis heard his own question reframed in a manner that was relevant to his skills and discipline, he instantly realised his inadvertent double standard and replied "Touché."

This example highlights the *attribution substitution* process that we described in the chapter on cognitive biases (see Chapter 2). A brief recap: When we are asked a question, our mind works like a kind of jukebox which searches for similar situations from memory and then uses these to inform our response to what's being asked. In areas we know a lot about, we have a wider selection of "songs" to choose from. In unfamiliar areas, on the other hand, we build a picture of the world based on the few "songs" that we do know from that genre.

There are several implications of this. Firstly, when we "know" about something, it can take different forms. Theoretical knowledge ("I have studied this") differs from tacit knowledge ("I have lived this"). To understand the difference, consider musical skill: working through a stack of books on how to play a guitar won't make you a virtuoso. Sure, you could argue that you have expert "theoretical" knowledge on playing the guitar: you could identify chords, scales and other aspects of the art of playing the instrument. But despite that, if we handed you a guitar, it would be exceedingly likely that you would completely suck at playing it.

Fresh university graduates often encounter this problem when they enter the workforce with inflated expectations. All that academic knowledge must be worth something in the real world, their reasoning goes. Of course, reality brings them back to earth rather rapidly when they find that some of the most important work skills can only be learnt by experience. This, once again, illustrates how the process of substituting "songs" from your mental jukebox depends on whether you have studied versus whether you can actually play.

Secondly, in an area we do not know much about, we often do not realise that there is much more to a particular musical genre than the few popular songs we hear on the radio. Our Gadget character from Chapter 2 is a classic example. In training, this is referred to as *unconscious incompetence*—when people are not aware of the gaps in their knowledge. (In everyday life this is referred to as blissful ignorance). Training theory states that the person must become conscious of their incompetence before development of the new skill or learning can begin.

But there is another, much more basic implication. Even if we do acknowledge our lack of knowledge in a particular genre, we may *not be interested in learning more about that genre*. This issue is much trickier. While Paul likes heavy metal, Kailash likes something lighter. Despite writing a book together in close collaboration, it is very unlikely that, despite Paul's attempts, Kailash will ever buy a Megadeath album. Conversely, it is exceedingly unlikely that Paul will suddenly start listening to The Shins anytime soon.

This illustrates the conflict that can occur when different stakeholders have their version of what's good and believe (tacitly) that others will feel the same way. To accept alternate points of view requires them to question their own sense of values, beliefs and doubts. While taste in music is a trivial example, the underlying mental process is similar in wicked situations.

Lifting the veil

As illustrated by Paul's exchange with his friend Travis, the veil of naive simplicity can often be lifted by asking the right question or highlighting the *disconnect* between how different situations are handled; the gap between espoused and actual behaviours. Asking the right question at the right time can force people to alter the lens through which they see the world, thus reducing the effect of cognitive bias.

Dr Phil[2] has this down to such a fine art that it is entirely possible that he might be able to get Paul to put aside his disdain for The Shins long enough to understand Kailash's musical point of view. On the other hand, Jerry Springer[3] demonstrates how lifting the veil can be extremely confronting if done the wrong way.

With a difficult problem, conflict is inevitable. After all, conflict is the most visible manifestation of problem wickedness. Without it, the problem would not be wicked. This conflict is amplified as the number of stakeholders increase. We like to think about it this way: each stakeholder occupies their own universe of ideas, values and beliefs. In complex initiatives, the fluidity of the problem definition coupled with nasty constraints almost guarantees that these universes will have little in common. Most of the time people have a natural aversion to conflict. After all, it makes life unpleasant and stressful and tips our finely balanced marble board of wellbeing, a situation nobody enjoys. So, stakeholders pretend to agree with each other, glossing over difficulties with platitudes; those big elephants in the room that nobody sees.

To see the elephant one needs the right "mental eyewear." The two pop-purveyors of mental eyewear take different approaches to the problem. While Dr Phil takes a measured, gradual approach to changing the lens by which someone looks at a problem, Jerry Springer literally tears the veil off, leaving people shocked, naked and in the spotlight unprepared. Given that wicked problems have a social dimension, such radical actions will do more harm than good because they can amplify the conflict and solidify intractable positions.

---

[2]   Dr. Phil, is a television personality, author, psychologist, and the host of the television show "Dr. Phil"

[3]   Jerry Springer is a television presenter, best known as host of the tabloid talk show "The Jerry Springer Show"

From naive simplicity to overwhelming complexity: "It's all too hard"

People deal with conflict in different ways. For those who have had their solutions of naive simplicity flushed down the gurgler, it is almost inevitable that they will feel the problem is overwhelmingly complex. They lose all sense of confidence and start to believe that the problem is unsolvable. Woody Allen characterised this nicely when he said "Confidence is what you have before you understand the problem."

For many, the natural reflex to this situation is to give up and revert to the status quo. This cuts to the heart of the disequilibrium we described in the Introduction. When faced with overwhelming complexity, we invariably experience uncertainty. This in turn affects our marble boards of wellbeing and our natural reaction is to try and resist the tilt and get back to stability. The status quo may not be ideal, but at least it *feels* secure and security tends to win out in unsettled times.

However, when people settle for the status quo, they do so knowing that things could be different. Consequently, they remain unhappy about the way things are as well. In most organisations though, there are bands of brave-hearts who truly believe the problem can be solved. Some of these true believers don their boxing gloves and spar with "The System," whereas others choose the ninja approach which advocates change by stealth from within "The System." The battle is inevitably an unequal one. So, in either case the net result is organisation-wide discontent and unhappiness.

When faced with overwhelming complexity, it is human nature to seek some sort of order. Complexity is chaotic and stressful and there are common visible symptoms of this chaos. Some of these are:

- Lack of coherent purpose: everyone has a different view of the problem and how it should be tackled and thus trying to nail down scope or agree on a problem statement is an exercise in futility
- Lack of trust between individuals who comprise the team
- Resistance (overt and covert) to change
- Positioning for defence and blame avoidance
- Paralysis; lack of action

The problem with symptoms is that they are just visible manifestations of the problem. Often the root cause is not where the pain point is. In medicine, treatments for some ailments often take place far from where the pain is experienced. An example used by Ackoff is that you would not use brain surgery to cure a headache, despite the pain being felt in your head. Instead you would take a pill, even though there appears to be no direct relationship between the pill and to the pain being experienced.

Unfortunately though, organisations often use brain surgery for their headaches because visible symptoms are often mistaken for the root cause of problems. This leads to incorrect solutions being applied. Moreover, there are plenty of snake-oil purveyors who claim to have silver bullet cures for organisational headaches. These solutions are often referred to as *best practices*: techniques or processes that are generally considered to be better than all others at delivering particular outcomes.

Figure 5.1: A snake oil cure for organisational ills?

The false promise of best practices

Many of the problems organisations face have wicked characteristics. Some examples include: reacting to changing markets, dealing with new regulations, market competition, strategic investments and so on . . . the list is endless. In all these, the key question for decision-makers is "What should we do about X," where X is the problem. The point to note is that although the problems may look generic, they usually have key elements that are organisation-specific (the "uniqueness" characteristic of wickedness). Further, stakeholders, be they board members, middle management or front-line employees, hold diverse opinions on what exactly the problem is and how it should be tackled (the "diverse viewpoints" characteristic of problem wickedness).

A common response to such problems is to seek advice from consultants, preferably from one of the Big Quartet. Now, Big Q consultants, like all consultants worth their sodium chloride, generally claim their advice to be based on some form of best practices: techniques or methods that are "proven" to be better than all others at achieving desired outcomes.

The "better than all others" claim is problematic in itself, but there's a bigger issue that lurks within the concept of best practices. The fundamental premise behind this concept is that it is possible to reproduce the successes of those who excel by imitating them. At first sight, this assumption seems obvious and uncontroversial. However, most people who have lived through an implementation of a best practice know that following such prescriptions does not guarantee success. Actually, research suggests the contrary: that many attempts at implementing best practices fail (Wareham and Cerrits 1999). Furthermore, as we discovered in Chapter 3 with PERT and waterfall, just because someone is doing it, doesn't mean that it is right or good. Memeplexes are notorious for legitimising questionable or downright poor practices.

This paradox remains unnoticed by many managers and executives who continue to commit their organisations to implementing best practices that are, at best, of dubious value. Yet, at the same time, these same managers know that if they wanted to become guitar virtuosos, they would need to invest a considerable amount of time and hard work to achieve the necessary proficiency.

The question arises as to why the best practice approach to solving organisational problems fails. In our opinion, there are two key reasons why this happens. We'll look at these in brief next, deferring a detailed discussion and potential solutions to the remainder of this book.

Lack of understanding

Best practice methodologies tend to presume that the group, be it an organisation or a part thereof, has a shared understanding of the problem being addressed as the starting point. This presumption is often wrong, particularly for wicked problems. Much of the visible project symptoms that we outlined from the Chaos Report in Chapter 1, such as vague, incomplete and changing requirements, are a result of this underlying issue.

The only real means to achieve shared understanding is through dialogue. Unfortunately, in this day and age where hours are equated to cash and naïve simplicity reigns, time spent on understanding problems is viewed as time wasted. Management demands action, not talk, and collaborative analysis—particularly the kind that involves debate and discussion—is seen as "just talk." This is understandable considering the average person's disdain for meetings that go over the same ground and never seem to progress. Hence, as described in the introduction, there is a pressure to short-circuit the process of understanding and analysis and jump to solutions.

The problem thus remains poorly understood by the group and, more often than not, results in analysis based on simplistic or flawed perceptions driven by cognitive bias as well as memeplex goo. Such solutions are often couched in platitudinous terminology that hides the fact that they aren't well considered. Witness the witless organisational restructure aimed at "achieving efficiency" and "better customer service." Although the problems with such half-baked solutions may be obvious to those working at the coalface of the problem, their voices are not always heard. This is because of the *filters* that alter a message as it traverses the organisational hierarchy. As we saw in the Introduction, due to people filtering the message based on their instinctual needs, what begins as excrement at one level is transformed into fertilizer and powerful growth by the time it gets to the top.

Given the above points, it is easy to see why best practices have prospered. They offer decision makers ready-made "solutions" that have been "proven." Moreover, these solutions have gained considerable mindshare; indeed they are well-established memeplexes that are well ensconced in organisational theory and practice.

From the perspective of decision-makers, the pressure and temptation to follow the best practices route to problem-solving is, therefore, considerable. For one, such solutions are, or claim to be, "best" so these present a safe choice for decision-makers whose credibility may be on the line. Secondly, if the solution fails, the failure of best practice can be attributed to a flawed implementation rather than a problem with the practice itself. This brings us to the second point.

The tacitness of best practices

It is not well appreciated that much of the knowledge pertaining to best practices is *tacit*—it cannot be codified in writing or speech.[4] In the resource-based view of organisations, the knowledge held by an organisation is a strategic resource. However, not all kinds of knowledge are strategic.

The term *explicit knowledge* refers to knowledge that can be written down or otherwise recorded. It is therefore a tradeable commodity that can be bought and sold. This reduces its strategic value simply because other firms can copy the pioneers. On the other hand, tacit knowledge requires extended contact between expert and novice and is therefore harder to acquire (Maskell and Malmberg 1998). Consequently, it is tacit knowledge that distinguishes firms from each other and sets the "best" (however one might choose to define that) apart from the rest. Tacit knowledge thus confers a strategic advantage to firms. It is precisely this knowledge that best practices purport to capture but can't.

Tacit knowledge is always context and history dependent. Among other things, it depends on a practitioner's experience *within a particular tradition.* Winograd and Flores (1987) use the term *pre-understanding* to describe this "taken for granted" background knowledge that practitioners have but do not (or cannot) articulate. Clearly it is hard—maybe impossible—to extract, codify and transfer such knowledge in a way that makes sense outside its original setting. The only way to gain it is via an iterative and incremental process of learning by practice. Such learning

---

4   The difference between explicit and tacit knowledge is nicely summed up in Michael Polanyi's aphorism "we know more than we can tell." The former refers to what we can "tell" (write down, or capture in some symbolic form) whereas the latter are the things we know but cannot explain to others via writing or speech alone (Polanyi 1966).

requires close interaction between the teacher and the taught. In light of this, it is easy to understand why adapting and adopting best practices is hard. Best practices are incomplete because they omit important elements—all the tacit bits that can't be written down, which means organisations have to (re)discover these in their own way. The explicit and rediscovered tacit elements then need to be integrated into new workplace practices that are invariably different from standardised best practices. The resulting practices are unique to the implementing organisation.

Another point worth noting is that most practices that get embedded in organisations are customised to a point where they are quite distinct from the generic practices that they are derived from. This can invite criticism from methodology-obsessed purists who'll complain that the practices have been bastardised beyond recognition. This tussle between methodology purists and pragmatists is worthy of a good-vs.-evil epic of its own. Indeed, such an epic is currently being played out in the field of agile software development.[5]

The inherent wickedness of organisational problem-solving

We've traversed a fair bit of territory in this chapter so it is worth a recap. We began by pointing out that the problems faced by people and organisations fall into two broad categories: tame and wicked (although there are several other terms used to describe these). The former term applies to problems that can be solved using traditional methods of analysis whereas the latter applies to problems that are essentially hard to define, let alone solve.

A typical first response to wicked problems is naïve simplicity, summarised by the "Why can't we just . . ." attitude. Once it is realised that this will not work, the reaction is either to give up altogether or look for tried and tested "silver bullet" solutions that have worked for others. This is where best practices come in. Yet, as we have discussed, best practices are incomplete. They cannot incorporate the tacit knowledge required to make these practices work effectively. Implementing organisations have to rediscover this knowledge in their own way.

---

5   http://steve-yegge.blogspot.com/2006/09/good-agile-bad-agile_27.html

This brings us to the key question as to how tacit knowledge and assumptions can be surfaced and explored. The best way to do this is the most obvious one; through open dialogue and debate involving all those who care about the outcome. However, therein lies the problem. Notwithstanding that most people dislike long, laborious meetings, most organisations find it difficult to have truly open and honest discussion about contentious issues in the first place.

In the next few chapters we look at what open dialogue means and how organisations can create an environment that fosters it. This gets to the heart of the main theme of this book—establishing collaborative means to tackle wicked problems.

6

In Praise of Dialogue: From Bounded to Communicative Rationality

"The real cause of this dispute is something I like to call Nerd Law. Nerd Law is some policy that can only be enforced by a piece of code, a public standard, or terms of service. The only way to adjudicate Nerd Law is to write about a transgression on your blog and hope that it gets to the front page of Digg. Nerd Law is the result of the pathological introversion software engineers carry around with them, being too afraid of confrontation after that one time in high school when you stood up to a jock and ended up getting your ass kicked. If you actually talk to people, network, and make agreements, you'll find that most are reasonable." (Ted Dziuba) http://www.theregister.co.uk/2009/05/11/dziuba_firefox_extensions/

The secret to Borg success . . .

You would think that after our gushing praise of Willy Wonka in Chapter 4, we would claim Umpa Lumpas (who work at the chocolate factory—the poster child for the post-bureaucratic organisation), to be the epitome of self-motivated and adaptable workers. While we have respect for the talents of Umpa Lumpas, we believe the gong for shared understanding and adaptability to change should go to the Borg from Star Trek.

The secret to Borg success is the collective "hive mind." Each Borg individual is linked to the collective mind by a sophisticated network that ensures each member is under constant supervision and continual guidance. The collective consciousness not only gives the Borg the ability to share the same thoughts but also to adapt instantaneously to tactics used against them. Star trek crew members had to recalibrate their phasers constantly if they wanted to take out a Borg drone because the Borg would quickly adapt to the phaser and thus be immune to subsequent shots.

Of course, dialogue with the Borg was tricky because they had a tendency to assimilate you into the collective mind which, if the movies are anything to go by, looks kind of painful. But when you think about it, this is highly efficient because once it happens, all your thoughts are integrated into the collective and you reap the benefits of a very deep and tacit understanding of all Borg knowledge.

Imagine how handy this would be in complex project delivery. Let's say that a Borg drone becomes aware of a constraint that will affect project timelines. In an instant, the problem is automatically known to every other drone in the collective. Further still, you now have the entire collective wisdom of the Borg to determine a corrective course of action. A Borg drone could study PMBOK® or assimilate a PMP® certified project manager (we like the images this evokes, despite one of us being a PMP®) and all other Borg drones become, in effect, PMP® certified. This is not only an efficient means to transfer knowledge of questionable utility but also saves a lot of money in certification costs. This is why Borg projects are *always* completed on time and on budget—and if the customer doesn't like the result, the Borg simply assimilates them too.

The reason we are invoking the Borg is that we are going to talk about some heavy stuff that the Borgs know implicitly: the concept of *communicative rationality* and its implications. This is a philosophical notion which, by the time we are done explaining, may make you feel that the Borg are the only group that could possibly practice it!

Dialogue, rationality and action

A fundamental human desire is the need to be taken seriously. Thus, when we participate in discussions we want our views to be given due consideration by other participants. Consequently, we present our views through statements that we hope others will see as being rational—i.e. based on sound premises and logical thought. However, as we have seen in Chapter 2, we humans are at best boundedly rational. Any analysis or argument we make is limited by the information we have, the time that is available to us, our cognitive limits (we aren't all Einsteins) and our biases (and don't we have a stack of those?) We are also guided by our sense of wellbeing, which manifests itself in our value judgements: our sense of ethics, morality and even our political affiliations. In short, just because we think we are being rational doesn't mean that we are. As such, those who we are communicating with may think that our statements are "pots of manure that stinketh"[6]. This is to be expected when each of us has our own world views. It is presumably the reason why the Borg evolved the way they did: one collective mind implies one world-view—no arguments, no problem.

When someone makes a claim about something, such as a possible root cause for a problem or why a particular course of action should be taken, others have to judge that claim based on the *validity of the statements* made. Thus, although Paul knows that Opeth is the best band ever, when he states this "fact," he needs to justify why he thinks so.

The philosophy underlying such a process of dialogue is described in the theory of *communicative rationality* proposed by the German philosopher Jurgen Habermas (see Ulrich 2001a and 2001b or Finalyson 2005 for very readable expositions of the theory). We'll now describe the bare essentials of the theory in brief.

The basic premise of communicative rationality is that rationality (or reason) *is tied to social interactions and dialogue.* In simple terms, communicative rationality implies that:

---

[6] See "The Plan" at the start of the Introduction.

- You are willing to sincerely state what you think or feel in some sort of forum;
- You are prepared to offer reasons why you think or feel that way;
- You are willing to change your mind when presented with evidence contrary to your statements.

If you aren't willing to do the above then you are not being rational in the sense of communicative rationality. Essentially, you are full of your own opinions and not much else. According to Habermas, rationality doesn't exist in our heads, neither does it in the statements we make. Rationality resides in the *dialogue that we have with people* when our statements are being tested for their *validity*. In this view, rationality lies in the ongoing dialogue in which statements are presented, argued and then accepted or rejected.

Of course, we should not forget that the practical aspect of organisational dialogues is that they lead to some sort of action based on what transpires. Habermas referred to actions based on rational dialogue, in the sense described above, as *communicative action*. Such action is based on commitments made as a result of the deliberations. Indeed, Winograd and Flores (1987) referred to organisations as *networks of commitments* between individuals who comprise organisations. These commitments could be formal or informal agreements to perform actions ranging from recurring, operational tasks to resolving one-off issues—essentially the things that make an organisation tick.

That said, we now take a closer look at what communicative rationality entails.

Validity claims

According to Habermas, statements made in discussions have implicit or explicit *validity claims*—they express a speaker's belief that something is true or valid, at least in the context of the dialogue. In the theory of communicative rationality, every statement makes the following three validity claims[7]:

---

[7] There is a fourth claim: validity. This refers to the implicit claim that the utterance is expressed in a way (language, terminology etc,) that the listener can understand. We take this point as a given. Further, when a statement isn't

- It makes a claim about objective (or external) reality. Habermas referred to this as the *truth* claim.
- It says something about social reality. That is, it expresses something about the relationship between the speaker and listener(s). Habermas referred to this as the *rightness* claim.
- It expresses something about subjective reality. That is, the speaker's personal viewpoint. Habermas referred to this as the *truthfulness* claim.

It is easier to understand these three claims from the point of view of the challenger to a claim than a claim itself. A claim can be disputed because it is factually inaccurate (the *truth* claim). However, truth goes beyond facts. For example, Darwinists will likely dispute the statement that "Intelligent Design should be taught in schools" not because of any factual issue, but because they do not accept the *rightness* of intelligent design in the first place. As far as the creationist making the statement is concerned, they are speaking the sincere truth. This is the essence of rightness claim: it talks about the social or ethical reality in the discourse. Finally, a claim might be disputed because the person making it is simply a tosser and they are not genuine in what they are saying. In other words, they are being political and twisting things to serve their ends. They make a statement that is both factually and ethically true to participants, but they are not being completely sincere (the *truthfulness* claim).

The unholy trinity of truth, rightness and truthfulness—heavy stuff, eh? Now you know why we started this chapter with the Borg. We can think of no one else who could actually pull this off. It seems that, to truly be rational, you need a hive mind so that truth, truthfulness and rightness are visible and unambiguous to all.

Requirements for ideal discourse

In real life, where contentious matters are discussed, politics, hidden agendas and emotions trump the rational validity claims of truth, rightness and truthfulness. So, readers may be wondering if any real-life dialogue

---

comprehensible, the listener can always ask for clarification. See Goldkuhl (2001) for more on this point.

could ever be considered rational. We agree: in this philosophy, the only way to be rational is for all participants to converge around one single, shared truth.

For this to happen we either take the Borg approach and simply assimilate everything into a hive mind, or we all have to be willing to listen and be prepared to change our own world views (Kailash might have to give heavy metal a go and Paul might have to accept that Opeth may not be the best band after all). Therefore, we consider the philosophy of communicative rationality hopelessly idealistic, as do many other academics and practitioners (see Flyvbjerg and Richardson 2002, for example).

Yet, even if it is idealistic, there are some ideals that are worth striving for, particularly if they can guide us towards a better understanding of some of the intractable problems we face at work and in life. To put in terms we have used earlier, if we agree that a Borg-like hive mind is out of the question (and therefore the convenient fallback of simply assimilating dissenters), then what can we, as small cogs in big organisations, do to encourage open, rational debate that might approximate this ideal?

To answer the question, we first need to know the (possibly ideal) requirements for open dialogue to occur. Habermas himself noted the following requirements (Flyvbjerg 1998):

- **Inclusion**: all affected parties should be included in the dialogue
- **Autonomy**: all participants should be able to present and criticise validity claims independently
- **Empathy**: participants must be willing to listen to and understand claims made by others
- **Power neutrality**: power differences (levels of authority) between participants should not affect the discussion
- **Transparency**: participants must not indulge in strategic actions (i.e. lying!)

While we agree with the intent of this list, it is just as hopelessly idealistic in the real-world as the theory of communicative rationality itself. While it is possible, via structure, rules and process to deal with inclusion, autonomy and power neutrality, the requirements of transparency and empathy are another matter altogether. The latter two are *internal* to participants and cannot be mandated unless we head down the Borg path.

So, we have to be a bit more realistic and accept that the best we can do is *approximate* these requirements. This *might* get us to a point where validity claims are challenged robustly enough that opinions and mindsets of participants converge to a shared understanding of the problem. We'll take a look at what we need to make this happen a little later. First, let's look at how the concepts formulated by Habermas fit in with some of the ideas we have presented in earlier chapters.

Second generation systems analysis

Now that we have examined the notion of communicative rationality and the five requirements for open dialogue, it is worth turning our attention back to Horst "Mr Wicked Problem" Rittel. Rittel (1972) referred to the scientific approach to problem solving as "first generation systems analysis" and used the phrase "second generation systems analysis" to refer to techniques that could be used to tackle wicked problems. The first generation, according to Rittel, is the world of logic and reductionism: breaking a problem into its components and applying the waterfall-type approach to problem solving (see Chapter 3). Rittel then outlined some characteristics of second generation methods and their implications. As we examine them below, keep in the back of your mind the five requirements for open dialogue as prescribed by communicative rationality.

Rittel stated that when solving problems, nobody wants to be "planned at." Additionally, the knowledge required to solve a wicked problem never resides with a single person. Instead, there is a *symmetry of ignorance* "where both expertise and ignorance is distributed over all participants and no-one 'knows better' by virtue of degrees or status."

Rittel suggested that a second generation problem solving process must involve those who are directly affected by the problem. These are the key stakeholders "living" the problem, rather than experts who "know" the problem theoretically. The aforementioned experts should *guide* the process of dealing with a wicked problem but not impose solutions. In Rittel's words, the planner is the "midwife of problems rather than the offerer of therapies." It is *the group* that must come up with the answers.

Rittel realised that in order for generally accepted solutions to evolve, "everybody must be able to exercise his or her judgement about a plan." In other words, *empathy* and *power neutrality* are required because "there is no way of saying that A's judgement about a plan is superior to B's judgement." This necessitates a problem solving model which he called a *conspiracy model*. In a conspiracy model, participants are seen as *accomplices*, willing to embark on the problem and as a result, *share the risks along with the rewards*. Furthermore, any solution cannot be based on scientific-rational considerations alone; it must incorporate issues pertaining to politics, morality and ethics. In other words, Rittel was talking about communicative rationality and the three validity claims: truth, truthfulness and rightness.

So, how do we achieve all of this? Rittel's answer was "by making the basis of one's judgement explicit" and communicating it to others through a process of *objectification*. He described objectification as "successfully exchanging information about the foundations of our judgement." In this context, objectification is essentially communicative rationality at work.

In short, Rittel recommended using an argumentative process; one where questions, positions, arguments and their evidence *are made explicit*. In his words

> "If you only look at the outcomes, you can't reconstruct which statements have entered into the argument leading to a solution."

Basically, one needs to capture the decisions along with the *rationale behind them*. Every step of the planning process has to be understandable, communicable and transparent. In doing so, Rittel hoped that people would:

- **Forget less:** by explicitly capturing different world views help to better understand the nuances of the situation
- **Stimulate doubt:** because only doubt is a test of validity
- **Raise the issues that needed to be raised:** the questions that are worthwhile—those that demand to be addressed because they have the greatest impact or are the most contentious.

It isn't hard to see that Rittel was describing the environment needed to achieve, or at least approximate, the five requirements for communicative rationality.

Heifetz and the qualities of the adaptive organisation

Ron Heifetz (1994) is one of the academic hippies we cited in the previous chapter who recognised the nature of adaptive (wicked) versus technical (tame) problems. He is well known for his work on the theory and practice of adaptive leadership: how to mobilise people through what he termed *adaptive change*—"Change that requires people to transform their expectations, values and ways of working."

One of the key strategies of adaptive leadership is to *give the work back.* Heifetz warned that when a leader undertakes to solve a problem, the leader becomes the problem in the eyes of many stakeholders. By placing work where it belongs—with those responsible for doing it—Heifetz argued that issues will be internalized and owned by the parties best placed to deal with them. The best solutions, he maintained, are when the people with the problem become the people with the solution.

Heifetz, along with Grashow and Linsky (2009), also examined the qualities of what they termed an adaptive organisation. We note these below, linking them to the conditions for rational discourse:

- Elephants in the room are named (*transparency* by another name). In other words, thoughts can move from "inside people's heads, to the coffee machine, to the meeting room." *There are support structures, incentives and support for speaking the unspeakable.*
- Responsibility for the organisation's future is shared (*inclusion*). This is reckoned by the extent to which people act for the entire organisation versus their individual silos.
- Independent judgement is expected (*autonomy* and *power neutrality*). Value is placed on individual judgments and tolerance of errors.
- Leadership capacity is developed (*inclusion*). "To what extent do people know where they stand in the organisation and their potential for growth and advancement? Do they have an agreed upon plan for how they are going to reach their potential? And to what extent are senior managers expected to identify and mentor their successors?" This is more than leadership in the conventional sense. It is a collective notion which includes individual aspirations as well as those of the organisation. To this extent, it is an inclusive concept.

- Reflection and continuous learning are institutionalised (*empathy*). These are support structures for "individual and collective reflection and learning from experience." Reflection necessarily requires that we consider other viewpoints, hence the connection to empathy.

A pattern is already emerging between the visions of the Wonka, Habermas, Rittel, Heifetz (and even some elements of Borg philosophy). Rittel spoke of what is needed to solve wicked problems and both Heifetz and Wonka offered a glimpse of what those principles look like when embodied into organisational life via the adaptive or post-bureaucratic organisation. Both Rittel and Heifetz talked of governance in the form of "models" and "supporting structures" that enable Habermas' themes of inclusion, autonomy, empathy, power neutrality and transparency.

When you distil these messages, it all comes back to *rich dialogue* and the supporting structures that should be in place to facilitate it. But does that do enough to approximate communicative rationality as Habermas envisioned?

A Habermas machine?

We are counting on the fact that some of you picked up a book called "The Heretics Guide to Best Practices," not just because of the catchy title, but because it might offer some insights into reasons why your experiences with best practices may not have been entirely satisfactory.

Yet at this point, after a heavy dose of Habermas, Rittel and Heifetz, this book might seem like it belongs in the new-age section of your local bookstore rather than a serious management text. Another page or two and we will be advising you to sit in a circle, hold hands and sing kum-by-yah. Fear not, we aren't about to do that.

We know that the actions of individuals are driven largely by self-interest, aimed at satisfying whatever they deem to be their sense of wellbeing. For example, if you get a thrill by feeling powerful and superior, you will act to preserve that state on your marble board. (We have just described every politician right there!).

The problem is that Habermas' notion that statements can be contested on the grounds of rightness is all well and good, but it isn't going to cause the person making the claim to suddenly think "Hey, I'm not being rational, so I should change my mind." People usually stick to their views, especially when they feel their wellbeing is threatened. Try reasoning with someone who is going to lose their office because space is needed for open plan cubicles . . . for the greater good of course, and they'll give you a thousand perfectly valid reasons why they shouldn't lose their office. Any talk of the greater good will not help them see the light.

What we need is a "Habermas Machine," a device that all participants can climb into and converse with complete communicative rationality. The question is would people have the courage to climb in?

Imagine if all sides of the Climate change is true/Climate change is hooey issue got into such a machine[8] and through some magical process, all dialogue was rational in accordance with Habermas' three validity claims and five requirements for open dialogue. We doubt that people would ever get into such a device because of what it might lay bare (a manifestation of loss aversion[9]). The truth is not only stranger than fiction, it is also harder to live with because it is . . . well, *true*.

Although we, the authors, have spent considerable time researching, debating and then writing about these topics, it does not mean for a second that we have any more collaborative maturity than the next person. In fact, Paul had a recent experience demonstrating the hard truth that the truth is hard to take.

"No, not the squash court"

Paul bumped into the mayor of his local area one day. The mayor, familiar with Paul's work in the area of sense-making, mentioned that Paul could have been very handy at a recent planning meeting. The conversation then ranged over various topics, and eventually arrived at the concepts of shared understanding and collaborative project delivery. Ever the professional, Paul was articulate and spoke with authority on these matters using clever anecdotes and a few metaphors stolen from Ackoff. However, when the mayor made a casual comment that he thought that the local squash courts

---

[8]   In fact there is a precedent for this: the closest thing we have to a Habermas machine at present is the wikileaks site. And most people whose rationale has been exposed via it are not too pleased about that contraption!

[9]   Loss aversion is a cognitive bias that we covered in Chapter 3

would be better as a community centre, Paul instantly had a mental snap and blurted out "No, not the squash court!" before he had even thought about it.

As it happens, Paul is a squash player and uses the court from time to time. His immediate reaction to the idea that his beloved court might be taken away triggered a negative reaction. That in itself was not unusual, and reminded Paul why Rittel is absolutely correct when he said that solutions to wicked problems must involve those affected. However, at the same time, Paul felt guilty and hypocritical.

From a validity claim point of view, the Mayor was absolutely right. The squash court only served one purpose and squash is a sport that had its peak in the seventies and is on the decline. In his heart of hearts, Paul could not dispute the validity claims that the mayor made. The squash court is a candidate for being made into a community centre (truth), the squash court ought to be made a community centre (rightness) and the mayor truly believed this was the right thing to do (truthfulness). Yet, Paul was *still* not prepared to let go of his squash court. Whilst this form of wellbeing might be irrational to some, Paul loved playing squash on Friday nights with friends to the point of exhaustion and then drinking beer afterwards. Squash was for him a lifestyle activity that kept his waistline in check and it gave him a lot of pleasure (not to mention the odd hangover). There was no way he wanted to give it up.

The attachment to a squash court is, of course, a trivial example compared to say, a fishing community whose entire livelihood and heritage is threatened by cuts in the quotas of how much they can catch. If the plan to get rid of the squash court went ahead, Paul, by his own admission, would side with the "pro squash court" crowd and channel his energies into saving it. He would make all sorts of logical arguments as to why it should stay, all the while knowing that those arguments would not survive the Habermas test of rationality.

If there was a Habermas Machine that ensured communicative rationality and if Paul were to climb into it, he would likely lose his squash court—at least in its current form. Next door to the squash court is a tennis court, a basketball court and an oval. Seen from a purely rational point of view, Paul had various other exercise options, none of which got in the way of drinking beer. But Paul doesn't play tennis. He plays squash and has done so since he was a kid.

An imaginary conversation ensues . . .

"Besides," Paul says, "the courts are just a two minute walk from my house."
"There are courts available a five minute drive away. Did a 5 minute drive make that much of a difference?" asks the planner.

Regardless of the reasonable answers given to him and the rationality of the opposing argument, Paul wanted the squash court to stay!

How powerful is self-interest?

Paul's behaviour around the squash court issue actually reflects the standard model of human behaviour assumed in classical economics. It is called "rational choice" or "game theory"[10] and it assumes that individuals' actions are driven by rational self-interest—the well-known "What's in it for me?" factor. So, in a situation where an individual has access to a resource that is also available to others, classical economics predicts that the individual will aim to maximize his or her benefit without necessarily regarding the common good. In short, a squash court vs. community centre smackdown.

While rational choice is the clear pattern in highly competitive situations such as the stock market where personal gain is the whole aim of the game, it totally sucks in situations that demand *collective* action. However, there might be hope for the mayors of this world after all: Elinor Ostrom (1998), one of the 2009 Nobel Prize winners for Economics, has demonstrated empirically that, given the right conditions, groups can work towards the common good even if it means forgoing personal gains.

Ostrom referred to two ways in which individuals in a group work towards outcomes that are superior to those predicted by rational choice theory.

Communication: In the rational choice view, communication makes no difference to the outcome. Individuals can talk all they want, making promises and commitments to each other

---

[10]   Okay, for the 1% of academics reading this, "non co-operative game theory to be precise

(through communication), but they will invariably break these for the sake of personal gain . . . or so the theory goes. In real life, however, it has been found that opportunities for communication *significantly raise the cooperation rate* in collective efforts. Moreover, research shows that face-to-face is *far superior* to any other form of communication (Frey and Bohnet 1997, Lengel and Daft 1989) and that the main benefit achieved through communication is exchanging mutual commitment ("I promise to do this if you'll promise to do that") and increasing trust between individuals. Did you catch that? It is important so we'll say it again: *the main role of communication is to enhance the relationship between individuals rather than to transfer information.*

Innovative Governance: Communication by itself may not be enough; there must be consequences for those who break promises and commitments. If Paul faced a public flogging as a result of negotiating in poor faith, then he might decide that the squash court wasn't that important after all and the 5 minutes of car travel to the alternative courts not such an imposition. Ostrom stated that working for a common good can be encouraged by implementing mutually accepted rules for individual conduct and imposing sanctions on those who violate them.

In case you have not made the connection yet, both Rittel (1972) and Heifetz et al. (2009) made similar points. Rittel spoke about governance with his notion of a "conspiracy model" of problem solving where there was a *sharing of risks* along with the rewards. Heifetz spoke of support structures, incentives and support for open communication, such as naming elephants in the room, nurturing shared responsibility and ownership of problems, encouraging independent judgement and institutionalising reflection and continuous learning.

Ostrom (1998) made one additional point that is very important however. Designing a governance structure to support the collective work of problem solving must be *done by the group itself.* Rules imposed upon the group by an external authority are unlikely to work.

Collaborative behaviour and effective governance

Command and control approaches to managing innovative projects were examined in Chapter 4, where we saw Buzzbank as an illustration of how inappropriate governance can have negative consequences on the organisation. So, how does one create a governance scheme that fosters co-operation and has a mechanism to punish non-cooperation but in a way that avoids adversarial and uncooperative behaviour?

Fortunately, our genetic predisposition to punishing people if they don't do the right thing by us runs deep. We can leverage our innate capacity for *strong reciprocity*. Strong reciprocity is characterized by the saying "Do unto others as you would have them do unto you . . ." with the addendum ". . . but if others don't do unto you, then nail their asses, even at personal cost to yourself."

A great example of this is a game that Paul played when attending a team building day some years ago (coincidentally the same team building day that we mentioned in the BOHICA section of Chapter 1). Participants were divided into two teams and played a game called RedBlue. The rules were simple. Each group chose a colour red or blue.

- If both teams chose red, they would get $10000 each
- If one team chose blue and the other chose red, the team choosing blue would get $20000
- If both teams chose blue, both teams lose $10000

The teams had to play two rounds without contact before they could have a "negotiation." Paul was nominated as the representative for his team. Ever the optimist, Paul convinced his team that they should go red—a win/win scenario. His logic was that going blue was a zero-sum game because if the other team did choose blue, his team could then choose blue and they all would lose. Therefore, they wouldn't choose blue as it would not be in their interest.

As it happened, the other team *did* choose blue, so Paul's team was $0 and the other team's ledger was $20000. Paul's team members argued that they should choose blue this time, and Paul fought hard to insist that red was the only way to go. Once again the other team chose blue, increasing their winnings $40000 while Paul's team was still at zero and baying for blood.

Now it was time for negotiation. During the negotiation process, Paul argued to his counterpart that if Paul's team chose blue from here on in, team B would lose all of their winnings. He made it clear that if this meant his team also lost money, so be it. Paul's team would rather see the opposition lose money even if it meant that his team also lost.

Faced with that threat, team B made an undertaking to choose red from then on, but Paul made one additional proviso. As a show of good faith and to account for the first two rounds where his team had suffered, on the next round team B would choose red, while Paul's team would choose blue. After that, Paul promised that his team would choose red.

Negotiation over, the game was on. Collective tension was high and both teams held their breath. True to their word, team B chose red and Paul's team chose blue. Although there was still a price differential between them, Paul's team felt that this was enough and chose red for subsequent rounds. Team B also chose red, and by the end of the game (with the last round being an all or nothing choice), both teams came out with lots of metaphorical cash.

The twist to this team building game was that there was another pair of teams in the room that started with a red/blue combination and never recovered. The desire to punish created a loss of trust and both teams voted blue/blue for the remainder of the game, ending with both teams losing all possible money.

Paul's behaviour of being prepared to vote blue for the remainder of the game, for the purpose of denying Team B the opportunity that they were seeking, is an example of strong reciprocity. In punishing Team B for acting in self-interest, he and his team were prepared to wear the same pain. The opposing team realized that if Paul's team opted to choose blue, they would lose all that they had gained. In short, each team had the power to deny the other.

Returning to Ostrom (1998), she identified reciprocity as one of three core, interacting relationships that promote cooperation. The other two variables are reputation and trust.

Reputation: This refers to the general view of others towards a person. As such, reputation is a part of how others perceive a person, so it forms a part of the identity of the person in question.

In situations demanding collective action, people might make judgments on a person's reliability and trustworthiness based on his or her reputation.

Trust: Trust refers to expectations regarding others' responses in situations where one has to act before others. Clearly, trust is an important factor in situations in which people have to depend on others doing the right thing.

According to Ostrom, face-to-face communication and innovative governance can change the structure of dysfunctional collective situations by providing those involved with opportunities to enhance these core relationships. On the flip side, heavy-handed interventions and increased competition between individuals will reduce them. The Buzzbank case study described in Chapter 4 is a good example of how imposed governance frameworks can destroy trust and thus reduce collective creativity.

Emergent themes

If we take stock at this point and distil the messages of Wonka, Habermas, Rittel, Heifetz and Ostrom, some key themes emerge. Habermas gave us the notion of communicative rationality, validity claims and noted that it needed the conditions of *inclusion, autonomy, empathy, power neutrality* and *transparency.*

Independently, Rittel (1972) echoed the notion of validity claims via the need to have inclusive dialogues with those affected by issues and that this dialogue must incorporate issues pertaining to politics, morality and ethics. He emphasised the idea that the planner is the "midwife of problems rather than the offerer of therapies"—someone who helps the group come up with the answers that are within the members of the group. Furthermore, he spoke of the need for a problem solving model he called "A conspiracy model of planning," based on the idea of *shared ownership/ shared risk/shared reward.* Rittel spoke about the conditions of inclusion, autonomy and power neutrality that are required for open dialogue in the sense of Habermas.

Rittel also was more explicit about how the process of objectification could take place. He suggested that this could be done via an argumentative process in which questions, positions, arguments and their evidence are made explicit. In other words, by utilising tools and practices that make dialogue and arguments transparent.

Heifetz et al. (2009) also spoke about Rittel's midwife in the sense that a leader had to "give the work back" by placing it where it belonged; to those who were impacted by the problem. He also spoke of the structures required for an adaptive organisation.

We also noted that while inclusion, autonomy and power neutrality can be created with process and rules of engagement, empathy and transparency cannot be. Typically, the latter two conditions are *internal* to each person in a group and you have no way of forcing them on a group as a whole. Ostrom (1998) showed that, even so, they can be fostered through communication and innovative governance, underpinned by the three core relationships of reciprocity, reputation and trust.

But how do we foster these feel-good themes like inclusion, autonomy, empathy, power neutrality reciprocity, reputation, trust and transparency (not to mention objectivity via argumentation) into a governance model? How can we create the sort of *environment* or *space* that would allow these desirable qualities to take root and flourish? One thing is certain: if it were easy, we would all be doing it by now because there would be a best practice for doing so and legions of consultants to show us how.

The fact that we don't means that there isn't a best practice. There is no yellow brick road to open dialogue . . . but there is a road.

Towards a holding environment

Many of the behaviours we display in our interactions with others are based on the *norms* of the group that we are working in. Norms refer to commonly accepted or approved behaviours or values within a group. Typically these specify conduct, beliefs and attitudes expected of group members. They are essentially values that are learnt through experience with the group, rather than formal education. They are entrenched in the sense that we often follow them without conscious thought. This is why it is hard to change behaviours, why we hear the "That's just how it is around here" cliché.

This is relevant to our discussion because the ideal of communicative rationality can only be arrived at through changing group norms, and as a consequence, the behaviour of individuals as well. The focus of the group and the individual has to shift from self or factional interest to that of the greater good. This involves a great deal of learning and adjustment, which can be facilitated and fostered via an appropriate environment.

People have different terms for this environment or "space" that facilitates such a process of learning and adjustment. Terms include "Ba" (Nonaka and Konno 1998) "Art of hosting" (Art of Hosting 2011), "Presencing" (Scharmer 2009) and "The learning organisation" (Senge 1994). But we like the term *holding environment*, in the context that Ron Heifetz (1994) used it. But we are getting ahead of ourselves. Let's begin at the beginning and let the story unfold.

The term holding environment was first used by the psychoanalyst Donald Winnicott (1960) to describe the earliest stages of the relationship between mother and infant. Winnicott described the main function of such an environment as being "the reduction to a minimum of impingements to which the infant must react . . ." The point being that infants do not have the ability to deal with external stimuli in a sensible way; all they can do is react to them. The function of the holding environment is to give an infant the space it needs to develop the ability to cope with events that it cannot control.

The term these days generally applies to any psychologically supportive environment. A holding environment gives the parties involved a protected space in which they can develop the behaviours necessary to *adapt* to the specific situation and environment they are in. The process of adaptation is difficult because there is a great deal of uncertainty and people are therefore unsure of how to act and react to specific situations.

Generalising this concept, one can say that a holding environment is a safe space in which the individuals involved can discover or invent their own solutions to their problems. Rittel (1972) described the midwife role, which is apt, given the mother/child analogy from which the term originates. Heifetz (1994) called this process of discovery *adaptive work.*

"Adaptive work can mean clarifying a conflict in values, or bridging the gap between the values that we stand for and the current conditions under which we operate. When you have a problem or a challenge for which there is no technical remedy, a problem for which it won't help to look to an authority for answers—the answers aren't there—that problem calls for adaptive work."

It is clear that the issues that are of concern to us in the book (i.e. wicked problems) involve adaptive work in the way Heifetz described it. Indeed the process of managing a wicked issue or problem is essentially adaptive. It involves exploration, trial-and-error and iteration to align participants' shared sense of truth, rightness and truthfulness. Once we see this, it is clear that adaptive work in organisations requires a holding environment too.

According to Heifetz, a holding environment enables adaptive work by containing and regulating the stresses that such work generates. The idea is not to eliminate stress but to control it: one needs to maintain a level of stress that mobilizes people without overstressing them.

Figure 6.1 shows what Heifetz called a technical problem and what Rittel called a tame problem. It also illustrates, on the Y axis, the tolerance users have for change (called the productive range of distress). While the level of distress is not high, we have the business-as-usual situation or status quo (the area below the productive range of distress).

With a tame or technical problem, everyone sees what the problem is and the acute distress felt prompts action. Once the problem is solved we return to business-as-usual. The arrow below illustrates the path of distress when solving a tame problem.

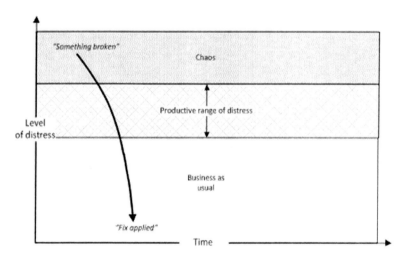

Figure 6.1: A tame problem (adapted from Heifetz 1998)

With a wicked or adaptive problem, however, such as in Figure 6.2, the problem is not universally understood by participants. In fact, some stakeholders may not believe there is a problem at all. Consequently, they may not understand the need or justification for a solution.

In this case, the solution is often beyond the tolerance for distress of users and, like all humans when faced with stress, we seek a *return* to business-as-usual, not because it is optimal but because it is *safe* and we won't lose our marbles.

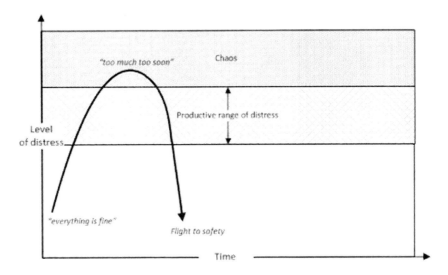

Figure 6.2: An adaptive or wicked problem (adapted from Heifetz 1998)

According to Heifetz, the key to governing adaptive or wicked problems is to "regulate the temperature" so to speak. Without any distress users will not leave their comfort zone. Apply too much heat and people will pull back to what is safe. Figure 6.3 shows the effect of raising the temperature within tolerable levels. Fairly soon, the new practices become business-as-usual and we can again raise the temperature. This is known as building adaptive capacity.

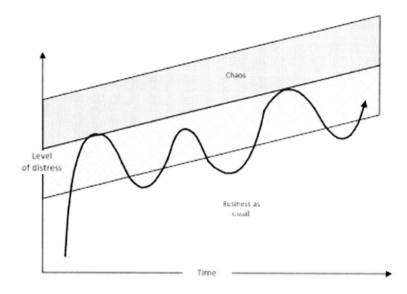

Figure 6.3: Building adaptive capacity (adapted from Heifetz 1998)

In the context of this book, a holding environment can take many forms and operate in different ways. But what they have in common is *participation safety* and *decision influence*. Free-flowing discussion is possible, one in which people feel free to speak up with the knowledge that their contributions will be taken seriously, with people who are willing to listen and revise their opinions when presented with demonstrably superior arguments. In short, that dialogue and decisions are made on a more communicatively rational basis.

Implication for organisations

The importance of communication in organisations cannot be overstated. Many organisational failures (failed projects being an example) can be attributed to a breakdown of communication, leading to a lack of shared understanding of the problem. Ostrom's (1998) work reiterated the importance of communication, specifically emphasizing the need for face-to-face interactions. From experience we can vouch for the efficacy of face-to-face communication in defusing crises and clearing up misunderstandings.

In most organisational environments, governance is imposed by management. Most organisations have followed methodologies which have excruciatingly detailed prescriptions on how projects should be controlled and managed. Ostrom's work suggested that a "lighter touch" may work better. Such a view is supported by research in organisational theory (consider, again, the example of Buzzbank from Chapter 4).

If a particular organisational control doesn't work well or is too intrusive, change it. Better yet, seek the team's input on what changes should be made. In fact, most methodologies give practitioners the latitude to customize processes to suit their environments. Unfortunately, many organisations fail to take advantage of this flexibility and consequently many managers come to believe that control-oriented governance is the be all and end all of their job descriptions. Is it any wonder that organisational work groups often complain about unnecessary bureaucracy getting in the way of work?

Finally, it isn't hard to argue that the core relationships of reciprocity, reputation and trust would serve organisations just as well as they do other collectives. Teams where individuals help each other (reciprocity) are aware of each other's strengths (reputation) and know that they can rely on others if they need to (trust), not only have a better chance of success but also make for a less stressful work environment. Unfortunately, these relationships have long been dismissed by project rationalists as "warm and fuzzy" fluff, but perhaps the recognition of these in mainstream economic thought will change that.

If we were to summarise this chapter in a few lines it would be that *rationality lies in dialogue and action based on mutual agreement, not in individual statements or unilateral actions. The holding environment that nurtures such rationality is the key to collaborative problem solving in organisations.*

Interlude:

From problems to solutions

"It isn't that they can't see the solution. It's that they can't see the problem."
(G. K. Chesterton)

Remember our infomercial inspired introduction to this book? We asked you some loaded questions around the sort of dysfunctional patterns people observe in organisations. Now that we are done with Part 1, it is a good time to revisit them and in doing so, reflect on the journey thus far and the one that lies ahead.

If you stretch your mind back to the introduction, you will recall that the very first question that we asked was whether readers have ever had the feeling that something is not quite right in organisations but could not articulate why. We hope that via our journey through platitudes, biases, management myths and wicked problems, you can now put some names to what you have instinctively felt. Although the areas that we covered might have seemed unrelated at first, we hope you will agree that they all serve to highlight the gap between what we are often asked to do at work and our own sense of wellbeing.

Another point we made in the introduction was that the organisations we work for are bigger than any individual. They consist of many people, each with their own sense of wellbeing. The problem of disconnection between work and internal motivations is thus multiplied many-fold. Addressing the issue requires that these different viewpoints and motivations be *aired and reconciled*. It follows from the above that when it comes to the failings of best practices, different people will have different perspectives on what the issue is, or indeed if there is any issue at all! Indeed, this is why our approach in Part 1 highlights what, in our opinion, are the issues with pretty much anything labelled "best practice," especially when it comes to dealing with wicked problems.

Since different people have different views on what is wrong, any solution must take into account the diversity of viewpoints before attempting any fixes. This insight informs the approach we take in Part 2, where we expand on the notion of rational dialogue and what is needed to foster it by examining some approaches to *creating, developing and nurturing a holding environment*.

To that end, we will focus on techniques that help in getting a diverse group of stakeholders to reach a shared understanding of the issues being debated and a shared commitment to a course of action. It is a fact of organisational life that most meetings in which controversial topics are discussed tend to be fractious affairs that generate more ill-will than understanding. The techniques we discuss are *squarely aimed at addressing this issue.*

Our discussion will cover several areas. Firstly, in Chapters 7 and 8 we look at the power of visual representations of problems and how they can structure problems and capture the essentials of conversations in *real-time*. This enables participants to surface tacit or incorrect assumptions and better understand the various world views of others. We compare a few argument visualisation techniques before focussing specifically on the one that underpins our case studies in Part 3.

However, capturing dialogue is only a part of the story. One also needs to ensure that the *right questions are being asked*. To this end, in Chapter 9, we focus on how to find the right questions using techniques that come under the banner of "Problem Structuring Methods." We will take you on a whirlwind tour of several methods, before focusing on their commonalities and distilling the core ingredients of a good problem structuring method.

We round out Part 2 by taking a detailed look at what it takes to create an environment in which the right questions can be asked and answered in a truly open and cooperative manner. We do this by examining the trials and tribulations of an industry sector where you might least expect to find the answer.

As you journey through Part 2 of this book, you will notice that our proposed solutions are not prescriptive; they will not tell you the "one truth," but will help you discover *your* truth that works for you in your situation and organisation. To paraphrase a famous bard, the solutions to our problems lie within us, not in our stars or any other (heavenly or terrestrial) authority.

PART 2

What to do about it . . .

7

Visualising Reasoning

"Man always has two reasons for the things he does; the logical one and the real one." (unknown)

How to become the alpha programmer

The story we're about to relate is from a time when Paul was working for an IT company with a large team of computer programmers. To set the context for those who aren't familiar with the inner workings of an IT department, we'll first spend some time presenting a potted sociology of programmers.

Like any primate, computer programmers often spend their time in large social groups or, as we like to call them, "development packs." These groups are strictly trait based, meaning that they are usually tied to a particular technology. Programmers from a pack rarely migrate outside of their home range and usually avoid each other. They are generally aggressive towards those who work in broader IT disciplines such as Business Analysts, System Administrators and Project Managers. Consequently, social interactions between members of different packs are fairly uncommon.

Like all primate groups, development packs have a strict hierarchy. The group is led by an alpha programmer who achieves this status by displaying real—or more often imagined—programming prowess. Alpha programmers often get to where they are by bluffing and calling the bluffs of other members of the development pack. There are showdowns when an individual in the alpha position is challenged—and this happens often because programmers tend to overrate their abilities and hold strong opinions (cognitive bias again). Consequently, alphas often have to "fight" individuals in their group in order to hang on to their position.

As part of a grander cycle, junior programmers have to go through the process of "developer adolescence/puberty." If these juniors see something wrong and dare to say anything about it, they risk being "shot down" by the alpha senior. This happens regardless of whether the junior is right or wrong; the norms of the social hierarchy require that alphas assert themselves so as to maintain their top dog status. As time goes on, the "developer adolescent" becomes an adult and in the process, learns that attaining alpha status in the development pack is achieved by trampling on others' opinions and abilities. The way to the top is paved with deflated programmer egos, so to speak. Achieving alpha status means that one has "arrived." Among other things, alpha programmers' opinions and ideas are rarely questioned: they get their way most of the time.

When an alpha is challenged, the forum is almost always email, with the rest of the pack being cc'd in on the battle. Paul was witness to such a challenge when he was working in a group in which a newly hired senior programmer—who had reached adulthood in a different development pack—questioned the implementation approach of the current alpha programmer. The incumbent alpha had written a detailed technical specification outlining his preferred solution and why it was the right thing to do. Paul questioned the approach because he saw that it would have a negative impact on the area that Paul was responsible for. However, try as he did, Paul could not get the alpha programmer to see the point. There were two reasons for this. Firstly, the argument was conducted via email: Paul opted to counter the alpha's wordy email with more prose. As anyone who has attempted to argue via email will know, countering prose with more prose rarely works. Secondly, since Paul was *not* a programmer, and was an outsider as far as the development pack was concerned, trying to go up against the alpha was futile.

Paul's saviour was the alpha challenger, who was able to usurp the incumbent with an email that contained no text whatsoever—just the two images shown in Figure 7.1.

Figure 7.1: The image that defeated the alpha programmer

The point made here was so obvious that it needed no elaboration. There was no reply from the incumbent alpha; he slunk off to the back of the pack, his status forever relegated to that of a junior pack member. Needless to say, his solution went the way he did.

Why the manual sucks (and people never read it)

Most people dislike writing reports or essays. Firstly, the effort it would take to codify a deep, hour-long conversation between two people into a written form is substantially greater than effort involved in the conversation itself. Secondly, it is much harder to explain complex ideas in prose than in a face-to-face conversation. In the latter, one has the advantage of being able to see the other person's reaction and adjust the explanation to match their understanding.

Yet, most of us have been saddled with the riveting task of writing business documents such as project proposals, business cases, technology evaluations, functional specifications and so on. The typical organisation generates and prints reams of these documents daily, so there's no escape for the average corporate minion.

Typically, business documents are aimed at conveying positions or ideas to a specific audience. For example, a business case might detail the rationale behind, and hence the justification for, a project to executive management. The hardest part of composing these is the *flow*—how ideas are introduced, explained and transitioned one after the other. The organisation of a document has to be carefully thought through because of the difficulty in conveying complex, interconnected ideas in writing.

That's not all, there is a deeper problem: prose makes it hard to systematically evaluate ideas because the relationships between those ideas are not immediately evident. Since we all have differing world views, readers have to decode the relationships and connections between ideas in prose. In writing this book, Paul and Kailash have often read the same paper and come away with differing interpretations of the ideas discussed.

This is the reason why Ikea[1] manuals contain no prose at all. As shown in Figure 7.2, the power of images in conveying ideas cannot be overstated.

---

[1]   In the minute chance that readers are not aware of Ikea, they are a multinational company that designs and sells ready-to-assemble furniture

After all, it took only two cleverly juxtaposed images to vanquish a certain alpha programmer.

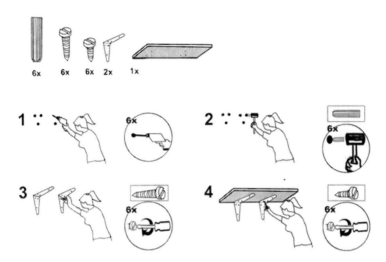

Figure 7.2: An example pictorial instruction manual

From walnuts to mice and men

Edward C. Tolman (1948) was one of those professors who liked to put hungry rats in a maze to observe how they learned to find food hidden in it. After performing a series of experiments, Tolman argued that, over time, rats built "cognitive maps" which provided them a mental representation of the maze. This enabled them, over time, to navigate the maze and find the food faster.

Similarly, someone who cannot remember what happened on a night of alcoholic over-indulgence may yet manage to find their way back home, despite not being able to explain how they did so. Like the rat that has memorised where the food is, the fact that someone completely plastered can still wake up in their own bed, despite having a hazy recollection of the night before, suggests that we all possess cognitive maps of concepts and relationships that we have learnt and experienced. The commuter

---

such as beds and desks, appliances and home accessories. The company is the world's largest furniture retailer.

who drives home on "auto-pilot" is another good illustration of this. One can be thinking about other things but still find one's way home.

Our grey matter seems to have many of these cognitive maps laid down and refined over time. They enable us to see and interpret a given situation in different ways, depending on context, need and even mood. Sometimes we experience one of those serendipitous moments where we can suddenly "see" information in a different light or make a connection between our cognitive maps that we previously were not aware of. This is essentially the process of learning: making sense of the world through building connections between what we know and what we have just become aware of. It isn't a stretch to say that many great discoveries arose from well posed, incisive questions which enabled people to change their frame of reference and experience an "Aha" moment. The power of a well framed question, which enables us to see something in a completely different light, cannot be underestimated. Clearly, asking the right question can lead to insight and breakthrough.

If we accept that cognitive maps are internal, mental maps of concepts and relationships—or more picturesquely, signposts for thought—then, it is quite plausible that *external* representations of concepts and their relationships to each other could also augment our thinking and learning processes. In simple terms, pictures can help us learn, and in doing so, help us better understand

However, vanquishing alpha programmers and assembling cheap furniture is one thing, solving issues such as climate change or peak oil quite another. As discussed in Chapter 5, the latter problems are *wicked*. They are so complex and intractable that there is no agreement as to what the problem actually is, let alone the solution. If wicked problems were solvable simply by displaying questions and rationale in the form of clever cartoons or pictures, then surely, we would have solved them all by now. As it stands, many of us can't even put together an Ikea bookshelf without swearing at the manual.

Nevertheless, visual representations can be helpful in disentangling complex, intertwined issues that make up wicked problems. To this end, we are going to spend some time examining how pictures, symbols and text can be used to understand and communicate complex problems. In particular, we'll focus on figuring out the key elements for effective visual communication of complex ideas.

Visualising complexity

Anytime you draw a shape like a circle and write some text in it, you are creating a symbol that represents something—an object, idea or a concept. Draw a similar symbol, put an arrow between the two and you have now created—or at least implied—a relationship between them.

Even if the meaning of the symbols and lines are not specified, in the absence of any other cues our minds tend to assume that there is some sort of relationship. Further, if there is an arrow, like the one shown in Figure 7.3, we tend to assume that the relationship is a *directional* or a *causal* one. What this means is that one node is contingent on, or a consequence of, the other. The point is that our minds know at once that "This" has some sort of effect on "That."

Figure 7.3: An example of a causal relationship represented visually

Visually representing the causal relationship between concepts is a useful way of making knowledge of the relationship *explicit*. Imagine a group of stakeholders trying to come to a common understanding of a complex issue. Many times the chain of causality is not apparent to all participants. This fundamental truth is aptly demonstrated every Christmas day when desperate parents literally tear the house down, looking for batteries to turn their child's fancy new paperweight into the toy it allegedly is. We suspect that more batteries are bought on Christmas and the day after than any other day of the year, due to parents overlooking the fact that toys with an "on" switch need power and that batteries are *not* included. We also suspect that every one of these toys comes with an instruction manual that clearly states that fact, but as we mentioned earlier—the manual sucks. To top it all, there's the human tendency not to read the manual until *after* something has gone wrong. (In light of Chapter 2, we call that the "Instruction Manual Superfluity" bias).

Many projects also suffer the same "forgetting the batteries" issue in the form of a critical fact or assumption that was not given due attention.

By the time the issue is noticed, it is too late and the cost of going back to deal with the oversight is usually painful, expensive and frustrating. Therefore, mapping the cause and effect relationship between elements of a problem, system or situation, enables a group of stakeholders to explore each other's understanding of that issue *without the overhead of writing and comprehending an essay.*

The example "this and that" of Figure 7.3 is known as a *causal map* and it is likely that readers have drawn this type of map at one time or another. Yoda from Star Wars could have drawn a causal map to help him think through his chain of logic when providing advice to a young Anakin Skywalker at the Jedi Council (see Figure 7.4).

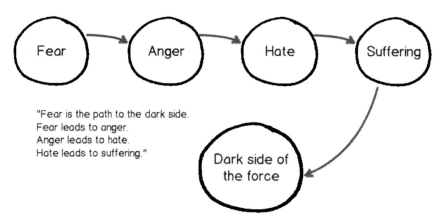

Figure 7.4: Sample causal map—Yoda's advice to Anakin Skywalker

A causal map of a complex problem will consist of several interconnected nodes, reflecting the tangled relationship between concepts or components of a system. Such diagrams have been around for a while, so we doubt that readers would find the foregoing statements particularly earth-shattering. What is interesting, however, is the manner in which this basic relationship can be augmented. There are a wide variety of incarnations of causal maps, each with their own elaborations of this simple relationship.

One popular form of causal map that is all the rage among process improvement nerds is the "fishbone" or "cause-and-effect" diagram invented by Kaoru Ishikawa in the 1960s (Figure 7.5 shows a Middle

Earth[2] inspired example). In these diagrams, the relationship between nodes is a two or three level hierarchy which resembles a fish skeleton. Each of the major "bones" represents a category of causal factors that affect an outcome or problem which is represented by the "head" of the fish on the right. Each category of causes also contains sub causes.

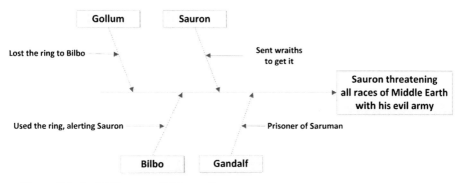

Figure 7.5: An Ishikawa or fishbone diagram

Comparing the fishbone diagram with our simple example, it should be clear that there is considerable flexibility as to what constitutes a causal map. Another example of a causal map is described by John Thorp (1999). Thorp's version of a causal map, which he called a "Result Chain," used a single hierarchy of nodes but offered flexibility via different *types* of nodes. As can be seen in Figure 7.6, a Result Chain diagram uses different geometric shapes to signify node types, which are classified as *outcomes* (circles), *initiatives* (rectangles) and *assumptions* (hexagons). The arrow, or relationship, between these nodes is called a *contribution*. When you think about it, Thorp's scheme is simply another way to describe a cause/effect relationship.

---

2   Middle-earth is the fictional setting of the majority of author J. R. R. Tolkien's fantasy writings. The Hobbit and The Lord of the Rings

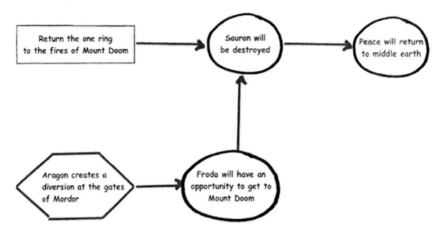

Figure 7.6: A Result Chain

A result chain diagram provides a roadmap to support the shared understanding of the benefits expected from a project or initiative. Figure 7.6 illustrates a Middle Earth strategy meeting where the initiative of returning the one ring to the fires of Mount Doom was discussed. The immediate desired outcome of this initiative is the destruction of Sauron. However, there is a major assumption here: we need Aragon to create a diversion at the gates of Mordor, so as to enable Frodo to get to Mount Doom. If this happens, then the ultimate outcome will be achieved and peace will return to Middle Earth.

The result chain diagram neatly summarises what was perhaps the most important Middle Earth strategy meeting. It is important to note that there are no minutes necessary . . . and definitely no tedious essays.

Serendipity on the back of a napkin

Our next example of a causal map was described to Paul by Mike Kapitola, a senior Project Manager who works for a government agency that is responsible for the road network in Western Australia. This conversation, as you will see in the case studies, turned out to be one of those serendipitous moments.

Paul and Mike were at a cafe, discussing project governance and the difficulty of achieving and maintaining shared understanding among the project team. Mike is the master of visual metaphor, and during the course of the conversation, used a bar napkin to draw a type of diagram that he would typically use to better align a group to the goals of a project. "Imagine this is your project," he said. "This is the *What*."

Figure 7.7: A graphical representation of a project or outcome to be achieved

He then proceeded to explain that a project cannot exist all on its own. One thing that a project must have is a desired outcome—a goal. "Therefore," he continued, "we ask ourselves, *why* are we undertaking this? The answer to this question can be drawn as another node which is placed to the *left* of the initial node."

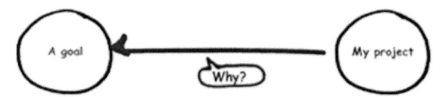

Figure 7.8: A graphical representation of the justification for a project

"Often there are several *Whys*, supporting the *What*," he explained, as he continued scribbling on the napkin.

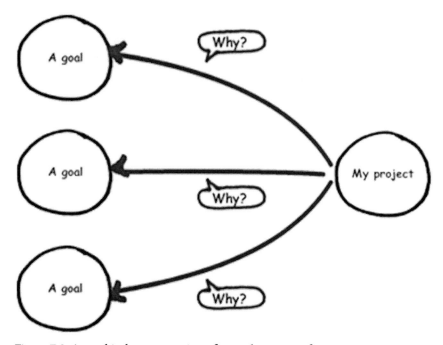

Figure 7.9: A graphical representation of several outcomes for a given project

"That's fine as it goes but projects need to be *done*. So, the next thing we have to ask ourselves is *how* will we achieve the goals of this project? This time we draw nodes to the right of the original *What*. The result is a kind of butterfly shaped diagram summarising the goals and outcomes."

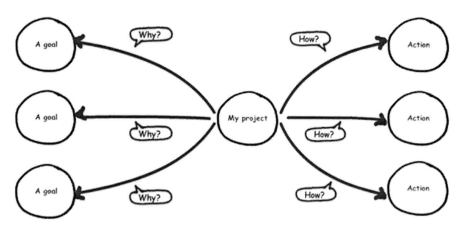

Figure 7.10: A graphical representation of linking project outcomes to actions

Reflecting on this conversation, Paul was struck by the simplicity of the diagram and the fact that it summarised so much so clearly using no more than the real estate on the back of a napkin.

There are two interesting aspects to this map that makes it different to the others. The first is that this process can be repeated for *any* node in the map. Thus, we can look at any of the circles in this diagram and ask the same question "Why" or "How." The really important point here is that *whatever node you are looking at becomes the "What"*—a goal to be achieved.

Any answers regarding why this goal should be achieved, Mike would draw to the *left* of the current node and any answer to "how" the goal should be achieved would be placed to the *right* of the current node.

This highlights the other aspect to this map. Remember that whatever node you are focusing on at any given moment is the "What." Anything to the left of the "What" is a *goal* and anything to the right of the map is an *initiative*. The nodes in this diagram change their meaning based on *which node you choose to focus on*. The diagram can be read in two directions and each direction tells a different story.

Start on any circle and consider it a "What." Then by asking "Why," you read the map in a right-to-left direction to see the *underlying purposes* for that particular "What." Start on any node and by asking "How," you read the map from a traditional left-to-right direction to see the legwork needed to achieve the "What." As an example, consider the Star Wars inspired pathway in Figure 7.11. It pretty much lays out the whole "dark-side of the force" strategic plan (if only the Jedi had found it in time, eh?).

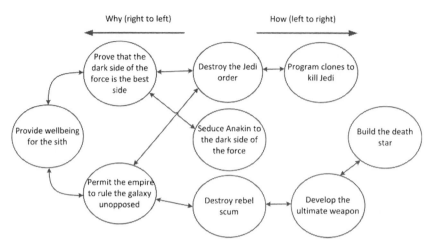

Figure 7.11: A sample causal why/how map from the perspective of the Sith

Figure 7.11 is still a causal map because each node is contingent upon any nodes to its left, and each node requires those to its right to happen to achieve it. The important logic to Mike's causal map—Paul refers to this as the "Kapitola Pathway"[3]—is that as you add more and more nodes to the right, you should be seeing things are more tangible and hence more measurable. This is because as we ask "How" over and over again, we eventually get to a point where someone actually has to *do something*; there is some *measurable action*. Conversely, as you move to the left, you will be unpacking the *underlying purpose* of the project or program, and the strategic ends that it serves.

We will revisit the Kapitola Pathway via the case studies in Chapter 12. Unlike the result chain map, the pathway map does not signify different types of nodes via different shapes or symbols. Instead, it often labels the *arrows between nodes* to make the causal relationship clear.

This is important as it illustrates another way in which we can increase the visual richness of maps and what they convey. Rather than proliferate different shapes or types of nodes, we can label the *connections between them* with text.

---

[3]   Kapitola adapted this map from an earlier diagraming method he had come across called Link Thinking Hierarchy (LTH), developed by David Stevens (http://www.profstevens.com/). Stevens in turn developed LTH as a refinement of Functional Analysis Systems Technique (F.A.S.T) diagrams, developed Charles W. Bytheway in 1965.

Labelling relationship arrows between nodes also allows us to expand the notion of what a relationship actually is. After all, relationships between concepts or subjects are not always about cause and effect. However, once the relationship between nodes is no longer based on cause and effect, by definition, it is no longer a causal map. Instead it becomes its close cousin—the concept map.

Concept maps

The key difference between a concept map and its causal cousin is that the relationships between the nodes aren't necessarily those of cause-effect; they can represent pretty much *any* relationship. Since it is cumbersome, if not impossible to develop visual representations for all types of relationships and associations, the links are generally labelled with text describing the relationship. The Kapitola Pathway is, in this sense, a concept map. As an example, Figure 7.12 is a simple concept map that represents the entire expert knowledge that Paul and Kailash have of country music.

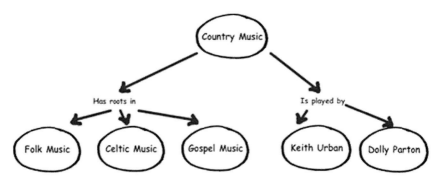

Figure 7.12: A simple example of a concept map

The main difference between this map and the examples preceding it is that the arrows display relationships that are no longer causal. For example, the fact that country music has its roots in folk music means that it is *related* to folk music, not a result of folk music.

The most important point with concept maps is that the relationships between the circles are specific to a particular map. Another concept map on say, spaghetti bolognaise, is unlikely to have a relationship with a label of "is played by." Thus, the relationship arrows are the key to understanding what the nodes represent and what the map attempts to convey.

The term "concept map" is an umbrella term that refers to a broad category of diagrams that have many subtypes. Some concept maps, like our county music example, are free-form in the sense that they do not place any restrictions on nodes and the relationships that can be defined. This means that a map is pretty much unrestricted in terms of how nodes are related to each other.

Much as in the case of causal maps, concept maps can use variations in the shape, colour or size of nodes to convey meaning. Typically, concept maps have a limited palette of objects and relationships available. This forces mappers to think about how their specific situations and problems can be expressed using a limited number of elements and relationships between them.

Powerful and expressive notations have been invented by combining a limited set of relationships with a well-defined set of node types. A good example of this is the Argument Mapping notation of Figure 7.13, invented by Tim van Gelder (2003).

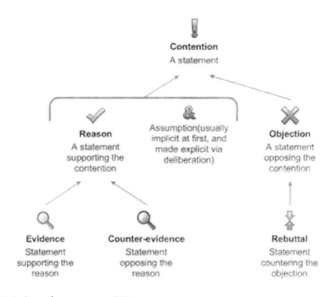

Figure 7.13: Sample Argument Map

In this map the top level node is a *contention*, which is a statement or conclusion that is supported or opposed by the rest of the map. Each block below the contention is called an *argument*. Arguments support or oppose the contention, as well as other sub-arguments. Although the figure is in greyscale, argument maps utilize colour in addition to icons to provide visual cues to the reader. The supporting text provides further detail on the argument.

Within argument nodes, one can have *reasons* which support the contention along with implicit *assumptions* and/or explicit *co-premise* nodes (co-premises are not shown in Figure 7.13, since they are similar to assumptions). One can also have *objections* to contentions, and statements rebutting objections.

Argument maps have one feature in common with the fishbone diagram. Both are multidimensional in the sense that one node can contain sub nodes. In the case of argument mapping, each argument node contains a *premise* and one or more *assumptions* or *co-premises*. In Figure 7.13, the supporting argument has a premise with an assumption.

Schemes such as argument mapping provide a common vocabulary for those using the maps. This generally leads to a more succinct expression of the problem or situation than would have been possible otherwise which, in turn, helps develop shared understanding.

Symbolism and abstraction

Now that we have examined a few types of maps, it is worth stepping back and looking at some general considerations that apply to all of them.

Firstly, in the argument and the result chain maps, colours and shapes are used to enhance the visual impact of a node. These visual differences are leveraged to convey different meanings for nodes *without the use of text*.

But there is a problem with the use of shapes: when looking at a result chain diagram or argument map (and a fishbone diagram to a lesser extent), the meaning of a shape isn't obvious. One needs a legend or key to explain what each shape represents or else, training in use of the notation.

Consider the Result Chain as an example. A hexagon does not automatically make the reader think "assumption." With the argument map, the icons do not intuitively imply "premise," "co-premise" or "assumption." This is because there is little or no obvious relation between the symbol used and the meaning intended to be conveyed. In other words, the symbolism is *abstract*.

What do we mean by "abstract symbolism?" Consider the sledge-hammer and walnut example in Figure 7.1 used at the start of this chapter. In this case we don't have a map but a photograph of two very real, easily identifiable objects. Yet, the intent behind the combination of photos is to convey something very different to the objects in the photo. The visual icons have nothing to do with the concept being conveyed. If you have never cracked open a walnut before, the significance of the metaphor may be lost on you and the juxtaposition of the two symbols would make no sense. You would take the information literally and see two real world objects with no obvious relation.

There is an important implication of the use of abstract symbols in maps. The more abstract a symbol, the *greater the need for shared experience* between the author and the reader in order for the reader to make sense of it. If the notation is being used to map a wicked problem involving stakeholders from diverse backgrounds (in skills, interests, values or culture), then it is highly likely that there will be varying interpretations of symbols within the group. Therefore, anything that can reduce the cognitive overhead of figuring out what symbols mean is a good thing.

The use of symbols and colour for argument maps is a great example of making the meaning of the symbol more intuitively clear[4]. People would generally associate arguments for and against a contention, in line with the general association of green with OK (or go-ahead) and red with not OK (or stop). Compare this, for instance, to the use of a hexagon to denote an "assumption" in the result chain diagram. Looking at a hexagon, would you automatically think that it is an assumption?

At this point you might be wondering why we have taken this relatively deep exploration into various types of maps and the issues around the use of symbolism, colour and text. The reason we have done so is that it sets the scene for examining our final type of concept map, which we will dwell on at length from here on. This type of map incorporates elements of all the maps we have discussed so far. Further, it addresses some of the issues of abstraction and cognitive overhead that we just alluded to. Like the other maps, it is designed to visualise complex reasoning, but it attacks the problem from a very different perspective.

---

[4] While our diagrams in the book are black and white, rest assured that the actual diagrams themselves are colour

Issue mapping and IBIS

Issue mapping is based on a notation called Issue-Based Information System (IBIS) invented by Horst Rittel and Werner Kunz (1970). We will discuss the origins and background of IBIS in the next chapter in detail. Here we'll simply introduce the notation and compare it to the others we have discussed earlier in this chapter. Consequently, our approach here is deliberately light on theory. After a quick introduction we move straight on to an example. As you'll see, the notation is so intuitive that you can start applying it almost right away. If you keep in mind the discussion on abstraction in the previous section, you will notice that IBIS addresses that issue rather elegantly.

IBIS consists of three main elements:

- **Issues** (or questions): These are issues that need to be addressed.
- **Positions** (or ideas): These are responses to questions. Typically the set of ideas that respond to an issue represents the spectrum of perspectives on the issue.
- **Arguments**: These can be Pros or Cons arguing for or against an idea respectively.

When IBIS was developed back in the 1970s, computers were far from mainstream, so the original notation was designed for pen and paper. The notation took on its modern form in the 1980s, using vastly more intuitive elements. It can be argued that the change in notation accelerated mainstream acceptance of IBIS. This is a point we'll discuss in depth in the next chapter but for now, we'll get on with our quick-start introduction.

These days, IBIS maps are most commonly created using a free software tool called Compendium, which can be downloaded at the Compendium web site maintained by the Open University UK[5]. In Compendium, the IBIS elements are represented as nodes as shown in Figure 7.14. *Issues* (questions) are represented by blue question nodes; *Positions* (ideas) by yellow light bulbs; *Pros* by green "plus" signs and *Cons* by red "minus"

---

[5]   http://compendium.open.ac.uk/

signs. Compendium supports a few other node types, but these are not part of the core IBIS notation.

The IBIS node types *imply* the relationships between nodes—the arrows take on different meanings depending on the nodes that are connected. Ideas or positions *respond to* questions, arguments are *for* or *against* an idea and questions of course, *question* any other node.

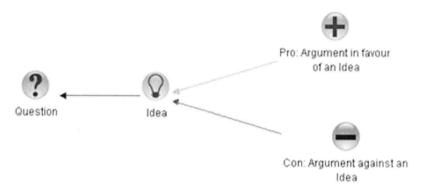

Figure 7.14: The IBIS elements and how they relate to each-other

Additionally, IBIS specifies rules in which the above nodes can be connected to each-other. The rules are as follows:

- Issues can be raised anew or can arise from other issues, positions or arguments. In other words, *any IBIS element can be questioned.* In terms of the notation: a question node can connect to any other IBIS node.
- *Ideas can only respond to questions.* The "light bulb" nodes can only link to question nodes. The arrow pointing from the idea to the question depicts the "responds to" relationship.
- *Arguments can only be associated with ideas.* The + and - nodes can only link to "light bulb" nodes (with arrows pointing to the latter)

The legal links[6] are summarized in Figure 7.15.

---

6   Compendium does not force these rules on users of the tool. Indeed, the form of IBIS we describe here is "pure IBIS" in the sense of how Rittel and subsequently, Jeff Conklin (2005), envisioned it to be.

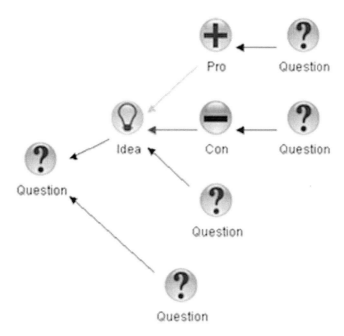

Figure 7.15: Legal IBIS links

Now, all this may look very abstract and theoretical, so let's look at an example of the application of IBIS in visualising arguments using a real life story of Paul's 5 year old boy.

"I want a cat for Christmas"

What follows is a completely true account of how IBIS can help stakeholders see the implications of decisions and show the full context of an argument. Paul was teaching his eleven year old daughter how to perform issue mapping and learn the IBIS grammar. Each night, the family would pick a relevant topic, discuss all of the issues around the topic and Paul's daughter would map the discourse using the Compendium software.

One evening, the question of the day was whether Paul's five year old, Liam, should get a cat for Christmas. The family already has a cat named Jessica, who happens to be owned by Liam's sister. Jessica also happens to be very well behaved, having been trained as a kitten to leave the goldfish alone.

A detailed conversation ensued where Liam outlined his reasons to the family. By the time the conversation was done, Liam changed his mind and decided that he'd rather ask Santa for Lego.

The root question of "Why should Liam get a cat?" was put into the map with some relevant background information. Liam cited two reasons for a new cat: (1) Jessica could have a friend, and (2) Liam would be able to play with the new cat.

Figure 7.16: "I want a cat" base map

Round 1: Liam's parents challenged the initial idea by pointing out that Jessica and the new cat might fight. A con code stating this fact was added to the "Jessie can have a friend" idea. Liam then asked why this would be the case and is informed that cats often do not like other cats. Unfortunately for mum and dad, Liam had the perfect comeback that they found hard to argue with . . . Santa will take care of it!

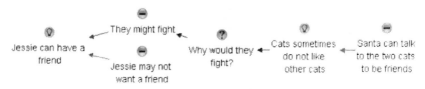

Figure 7.17: Round one of Liam's cat justification in IBIS rationale

Round 2: Liam offered a new reason why he should get a cat. It will help him with spilt milk in the event that he might drop some. When challenged on the grounds of the new cat eating fish as well as milk, and the possibility of the cat not liking milk, Liam offered to "hiss at the cat" to protect the fish.

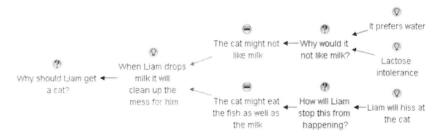

Figure 7.18: Round two of Liam's cat justification in IBIS rationale

Round 3: Unable to get buy-in for the milk idea, Liam switched tack and came up with quite a clever idea that has some merit. The incumbent cat has a particular talent for catching mice and then leaving what is left of them at the back door for family approval. Liam suggested that the family could grow vegetables in the garden because of the fact that two cats are now hunting mice, thereby reducing the mice population (not bad logic for a 5 year old). Unfortunately for Liam, he is reminded that the current cat also has a habit of chewing plants in the herb garden now and the other one might do the same thing.

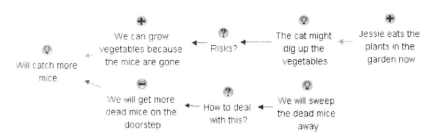

Figure 7.19: Round three of Liam's cat justification in IBIS rationale

Final round: Liam's mother suggested that Liam should *not* get a cat because there will be more cat poop to clean. When asked who would clean said poop, Liam was adamant that it would not be him. When pressed for suggestions, he firstly said he would cover the mess with Kleenex and as another alternative, suggested that we can get a "cleaner man" to pick up the cat poo. When Liam was further challenged as to who the cleaner man was and how to find him, he suggested the police would help. He also then hit upon the idea of teaching the cat not to poo as well!

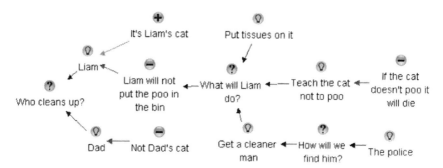

Figure 7.20: Round four of Liam's cat justification in IBIS rationale

At this point, the visual mapping of discourse had its intended effect and a wicked problem was averted. Faced with the prospect that he would have to clean up after the cat, Liam conceded defeat and asked for Star Wars Lego instead. The summary of the discussion is shown in context in Figure 7.21.

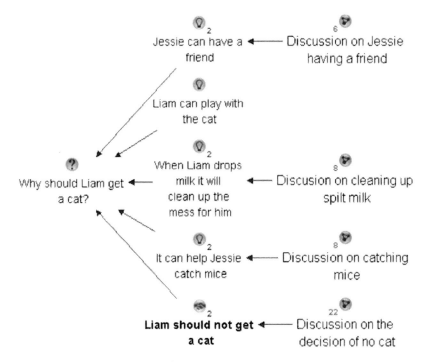

Figure 7.21: The summary map of the "I want a cat" discussion

Abstraction revisited

IBIS is a type of concept map with four basic node types and a strict syntax expressing relationships between those nodes. It shares much with argument mapping in terms of the use of colour and the type of relationships between nodes (supporting and opposing arguments). Moreover, like Result Chain maps, it also uses symbols to distinguish between different types of nodes.

An IBIS node incorporates a picture, prose and a colour, combining all the previous map elements covered so far. But the big difference between IBIS and all of the other maps examined so far is the level of abstraction, or more correctly, the lack of it.

For a start, the symbolism in the nodes is iconic. By clever design, modern IBIS happens to use icon types that have well known symbols. A question node uses a question mark, an idea node uses a light bulb and an argument node uses a + and - symbol to denote pros and cons. All of these symbols have an intuitively obvious relationship to their intended meaning and most readers would immediately understand what the symbols mean. Unlike a result chain where a hexagon means "assumption" only after you have learnt the notation, or an argument map where a white box in an argument is a premise or co-premise, the symbols used in an IBIS map are immediate cues to what the node stands for. No one who looks at a question node will think it is anything other than a question. Furthermore, it is pretty clear that anything connected to a question node is likely to be a response to that question. This is further reinforced through the use of a light bulb symbol. The idea that a light bulb is an "idea" is way more obvious than say, a hexagon being an "assumption."

There is another more subtle but critically important aspect to abstraction that we have not yet talked about. Since the nodes themselves are based on conversational elements (question, idea, etc.), an IBIS map is quite literally mapping the conversation itself. If a question is asked, a question is captured. If someone offers an answer, then the answer is captured.

This is a fundamental difference between IBIS and most other mapping techniques: the other methods cannot map the actual discourse. What they do is create a more abstract, high level representation of the problem. This is not to say that creating a high level visual representation of a problem is a bad thing. On the contrary, it is critically important. But looking at a causal map, you would not get a sense of the depth of discussion behind the map. With IBIS, you will.

In the next chapter we will delve more deeply into this idea of abstraction and compare different techniques in a semi real-world scenario.

Augmenting prose

So far in this chapter we have looked at a few different ways of representing reasoning using visual notations, and how they can enhance and augment deliberations. We'll close this chapter by looking at reasons why visual representations of argumentation enable people to comprehend complex arguments better than prose alone. Our discussion is based on Tim "Mr Argument Mapping" van Gelder's (2003) analysis supplemented by our own observations.

Prose has to be interpreted: As prose is not expressly designed to represent reasoning, readers have to decode relationships and connections between ideas. The choices they make in the process of decoding will depend on individual interpretations of the meaning of words used and the grammatical structure of the piece.

Prose is sequential, arguments aren't: Reasoning presented in written form flows linearly, i.e. concepts and ideas appear in sequence. A point that's made on one page may be related to something that comes up five pages later, but the connections will not be immediately apparent unless the author specifically draws attention to it. One only has to look at flame-wars on blogs or discussion forums to see the limitations of linear conversational structures when the issues that come up in a conversation are typically related in a non-linear way.

Prose neglects representational resources: Prose in most languages is a stream of words and, aside from the odd smilie :-) and **boldface**, does not use other visual elements such as colour, shape, position or graphical structures (trees, nodes, connectors). The brain processes and comprehends visual elements and connectors much faster than it can interpret prose. Hence, the use of these can lead to quicker comprehension with much less effort. Further, as Van Gelder mentioned:

". . . Helpful authors (of prose) will assist readers in the difficult process of interpretation by providing verbal cues (for example, logical indicators such as "therefore"), although it is quite astonishing how frugal most authors are in providing such cues . . . ."

This is true, and we would add that writers—particularly those who write analytical pieces—tend to be frugal because they are taught to be so.

Metaphors cannot be visually displayed in prose: According to Lakoff and Johnson (2003), metaphors are central to human understanding. They also argued that metaphors are grounded in our physical experience because our brains take input from the rest of our bodies. For this reason, most of the metaphors we use to express reasoning relate to physical experience and sensation: *strength* or *weakness* of an argument, support for a position, *weight* of an idea, external *pressure* etc. Van Gelder claimed that visual representations can depict these metaphors in a more natural way. For instance, in IBIS and argument maps, cons are coloured red (Stop) whilst pros are green (Go).

The above points are taken from van Gelder's paper, but we can think of a few more:

Visual representations can present reasoning "at a glance": A complex argument which takes up several pages of prose can often be captured in a single page using visual notations. Such visual representations, if properly constructed through the use of appropriate levels of abstraction, are also more intuitive than the corresponding prose representation. Our next chapter on argumentation will show some more examples.

Less abstract visual representations have less ambiguity: IBIS and argument mapping excel at displaying relationships between ideas. As a consequence of the limited syntax and grammar of visual representations, a given relationship can be expressed in only a small number of ways. Hence, there is little or no ambiguity in depicting or interpreting relationships in a visual representation. This is not the case with prose, where much depends on the skill and vocabulary of the writer and reader.

Visual representations can augment organisational memory: A well-structured archive of issue maps is so much more comprehensible than reams of documentation. This is because maps, unlike written documents, can capture the essence of a discussion minus all the conversational chaff. Much like geographical maps, these can help knowledge workers navigate their way through vast tracts of organisational knowledge (Conklin 2001).

Visual representations can catalyse knowledge creation: Visual representations, when used collaboratively, can catalyse the creation of knowledge. This is the basis of the technique of Dialogue Mapping which we will describe in Chapter 9. A visual representation serves as a focal point that captures a group's collective reasoning and understanding of an issue as it evolves.

To summarise, visual representations serve to augment reasoning because they are better at capturing the nonlinear structure of arguments; easier to interpret, leverage visual metaphors, depict relationships effectively and present arguments in a succinct yet intuitively appealing way. Above all, visual representations can facilitate collaborative creativity, something that is much harder to do with prose alone.

8

Argumentation-based Rationale

"Ladies and gentlemen of the supposed jury, I have one final thing I want you to consider: This is Chewbacca. Chewbacca is a Wookiee from the planet Kashyyyk, but Chewbacca *lives* on the planet Endor. Now, think about that. That does not make sense! Why would a Wookiee—an eight foot tall Wookiee—want to live on Endor with a bunch of two foot tall Ewoks? That does not make sense!

But more importantly, you have to ask yourself: what does that have to do with this case? Nothing. Ladies and gentlemen, it has nothing to do with this case! It does not make sense!

Look at me, I'm a lawyer defending a major record company, and I'm talkin' about Chewbacca. Does that make sense? Ladies and gentlemen, I am not making any sense. None of this makes sense.

And so you have to remember, when you're in that jury room deliberating and conjugating the Emancipation Proclamation . . . does it make sense? No! Ladies and gentlemen of this supposed jury, it does not make sense.

If Chewbacca lives on Endor, you must acquit! The defense rests"

(The Chewbacca Defense. South Park episode.27).

Decision rationale

The previous chapter was all about the power of visual representations and how they can be more effective than prose alone (this book excepted, of course!) in helping a group achieve shared understanding of a problem. We ended the chapter with an introduction to the IBIS notation and showed how it could be used to map a family debate in real-time. Not only did IBIS assist the Culmsee family in reaching a collective decision on the cat question, it also captured the discussion for posterity in an easy to understand format. That map serves as an at-a-glance summary of how the debate unfolded and the rationale behind the decisions made.

Most readers would have had no trouble following the discussion and the resulting map. Given that the only introduction provided to IBIS is a couple of figures and a paragraph or two of supporting text, it is a great illustration of the simplicity and power of the notation.

While parents might think that convincing their small boy that his desire for another cat is indeed a wicked problem, tantrums aside, it really isn't. So, the example of the previous section does not illustrate the real power of IBIS. As we have mentioned in the last chapter, the notation was conceived by Horst Rittel and Werner Kunz (1970) as a means to document diverse viewpoints on wicked problems. If you recall our journey into communicative rationality in Chapter 6, Rittel (1972) suggested that one of the strategies for addressing wicked problems was to make "the basis of one's judgement explicit and communicating it to others." IBIS was invented expressly for this purpose.

Although Rittel described IBIS as a "second generation design method," IBIS was the first of a family of tools and techniques that came to known as Design Rationale. According to John Horner and Michael Atwood (2006) of Drexel University, Philadelphia, "design rationale is the reasoning and argumentation that underlies the activities that take place during the process of designing something—be it an artefact or a system of some kind."

While design rationale encompasses the notion of making the basis of one's judgement explicit, we don't like the name overly much and prefer to use the term "decision rationale." Not everything is about design. For example, deciding whether Santa was to bring a cat or Star Wars Lego was certainly not a design activity. For this reason we'll use the term *decision rationale* or simply *rationale*[1], rather than design rationale.

Now, truth be told, Rittel and Kunz's vision of IBIS design rationale circa 1970 is pretty different to what it looks like today, but we will get to that later. Right now, we are going to delve deeper into the applicability of IBIS in real world problem solving. We'll present a "realistic" story of how IBIS helped a team achieve a common understanding of a problem and reach a commonly agreed decision in an *organisational setting*. Our intent is to provide an illustration of the use of IBIS in a relatively simple, yet real-world situation before moving on to the more complex and wicked problems that are the subject of the case studies in Chapter 11 and 12.

The Approach: an IBIS story

Jack could see that the discussion was going nowhere: the group had been arguing over competing approaches for over half an hour, but they kept going around in circles. As he mulled over this, Jack got an idea. He'd been playing around with a visual notation called IBIS for a while and was looking for an opportunity to use it to map out a discussion in real time. "Why not give it a try," he thought. "I can't do any worse than this lot."

Decision made, he waited for a break in the conversation and dived in when he got one . . .

"I have a suggestion," he said. "There's this conversation mapping tool that I've been exploring for a while. I believe it might help us reach a common understanding of the approaches we've been discussing. It may even help facilitate a decision. Do you mind if I try it?"

"Pfft . . . I'm all for it if it helps us get to a decision," said Max. He'd clearly had enough too.

Jack looked around the table. Mary looked puzzled but nodded her assent. Rick seemed unenthusiastic but didn't voice any objections. Andrew—the boss—had a here-he-goes-again look on his face (Jack had a track record of "ideas") but to Jack's surprise, said, "OK. Why not? Go for it."

Jack hooked his computer to the data projector and within a couple of minutes had a blank IBIS map displayed on-screen. This done, he glanced

---

[1]   Yeah, yeah, we know. We just defined a term something and know that it has a limited shelf life, based on our discussion of "definitionisation" in Chapter 2.

up at the others: they were looking at screen with expressions ranging from Mary's curiosity to Max's scepticism.

"Just a few words about what I'm going to do," he said. "I'll be using a notation called IBIS, or issue based information system, to capture our discussion. IBIS has three elements: issues, ideas and arguments. I'll explain these as we go along. OK, let's get started with figuring out what we want out of the discussion. What's our aim?" he asked.

His starting spiel done, Jack glanced at his colleagues. Max seemed a tad more sceptical than before, Rick ever more bored while Andrew and Mary stared at the screen. No one said anything.

Just as he was about to prompt them by asking another question, Mary said, "I'd say it's to explore options for implementing the new system and find the most suitable one. Phrased as a question: How do we implement system X?"

Jack glanced at the others. They all seemed to agree, or at least didn't disagree with Mary. "Excellent," he said. "I think that's a very good summary of what we're trying to do." He drew a *question node* on the map and continued. "Most discussions of this kind are aimed at resolving issues or questions. Our root question is: What are our options for implementing system X, or as Mary put it, How do we implement System X."

How do we implement
system X?

Figure 8.1: A root question

"So, what's next?" asked Max. He still looked sceptical, but Jack could see that he was intrigued. Not bad, he thought to himself.

"Well, the next step is to explore ideas that address or resolve the issue. So, ideas should be responses to the question: how should we implement system X? Any suggestions?"

"We'd have to engage consultants," said Max. "We don't have in-house skills to implement it ourselves."

Jack created an idea node on the map and began typing as he spoke. "OK—so we hire consultants," he said. He looked up at the others and continued, "In IBIS, ideas are depicted by light bulbs. Since ideas respond to questions, I draw an arrow from the idea to the root question, like so."

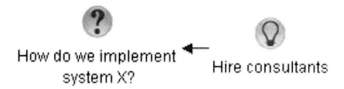

Figure 8.2: A potential answer to the root question

Gesturing to the map, he continued, "Max has also offered a reason why we should hire consultants. We add this in as supporting argument—a pro." He added a "pro" node and Max's reason to it.

Figure 8.3: A supporting argument for a potential answer to the root question

"I think doing it ourselves is an option," said Mary. "We will need training and it might take us longer because we'd be learning on the job, but it is a viable option."

"Good," said Jack. "You've given us another option and some ways in which we might go about implementing the option. Ideally, each node should represent a single point. So, I'll capture what you've said like so." He typed as fast he could, drawing nodes and filling in detail.

As he typed he said, "Mary said we could do it ourselves—that's clearly a new idea—an implementation option. Max already said that lack of in-house skills is the reason he suggests the consulting option. I capture this as an argument against the idea; a con, depicted as red minus in the map."

Figure 8.4: Another potential answer (with argument against it) to the root question

"Mary, you said something about training didn't you?"

"Yes, I think that with the right training we could do it ourselves. We'd also be learning on the job."

"But it will take longer," reminded Max.

"Okay," said Jack. "I've added in 'How?' as a question and the two points that describe how we'd do it as ideas responding to the question." He paused and looked around to check that everyone was with him, then continued. "But as Max tells us, there is a shortcoming of doing it ourselves, it will take longer."

He paused briefly to look at his handiwork on-screen, then asked, "Any questions?"

Figure 8.5: A follow-up question with answers to the "Do it ourselves" idea

"So, does anyone have any other options?" asked Jack.

"Umm . . . not sure how it would work, but what about co-development?" suggested Rick.

"Do you mean collaborative development with external resources?" asked Jack as he began typing.

"Yes," confirmed Rick.

"What about costs? We have a limited budget for this," said Mary.

"Good point," said Jack as he started typing. "This is a constraint that must be satisfied by *all* potential approaches." He stopped typing and looked up at the others. "This is important . . . criteria apply to *all* potential approaches, so we should add any criteria or constraints to the root question," he said. "Does this make sense to everyone?"

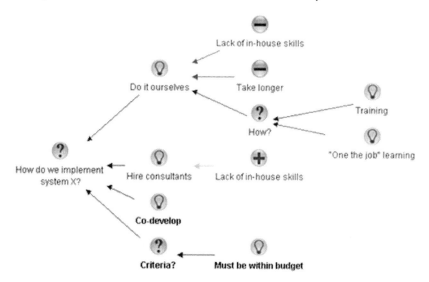

Figure 8.6: An additional potential answer to the root question and criteria surfaced

"I'm not sure I understand," said Andrew. "Why are the criteria separate from the approaches?"

"They aren't separate," Jack replied. "They're a level higher than any specific approach because they apply to all solutions. Put another way, they relate to the root issue—How do we implement system X—rather than a specific solution."

"Ah, that makes sense," said Andrew. "This notation seems pretty powerful."

"It is, and I'll be happy to show you some more features later, but let's continue the discussion for now. Are there any other criteria?"

"Well, we must have all the priority 1 features described in the scoping document implemented by the end of the year," said Andrew. (One can always count on the manager to emphasise constraints).

"OK, that's two criteria actually: must implement priority 1 features and must implement by year end," said Jack, as he added in the new nodes. "No surprises here," he continued. "We have the three classic project constraints—budget, scope and time."

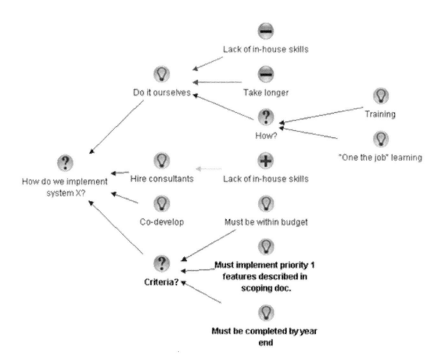

Figure 8.7: Additional criteria captured

The others were now engaged with the map, looking at it and making notes. Jack wanted to avoid driving the discussion, so instead of suggesting how to move things forward, he asked, "What should we consider next?"

"I can't think of any other approaches," said Mary. "Does anyone have suggestions, or should we look at the pros and cons of the listed approaches?"

"I've said it before and I'll say it again: I think doing it ourselves is a dum . . . Sorry, not a good idea. It is fraught with too much risk . . ." started Max.

"No, it isn't," countered Mary. "On the contrary, hiring externals is more risky because costs can blowout by much more than if we did it ourselves."

"Good points," said Jack, as he noted Mary's point against the "hire consultants" idea. "Max, do you have any specific risks in mind?"

"Time—it can take much longer," said Max.

Jack gestured to the map. "We've already captured that as a con of the do-it-ourselves approach," he said.

"Hmm . . ." Max pondered. "That's true, but I would reword it to state that we have a hard deadline. Perhaps we could say 'may not finish in allotted time,' or something similar."

"That's a very good point," said Jack, as he changed the node to read "Higher risk of not meeting deadline." The map was coming along nicely now, and had the full attention of folks in the room.

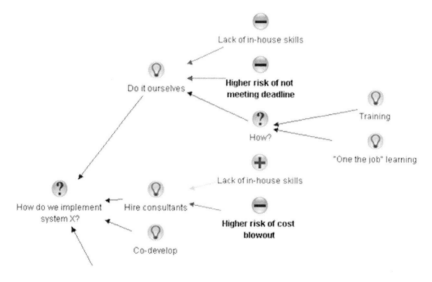

Figure 8.8: Additional arguments against
two of the potential answers to the root question

"Alright," Jack continued. "So are there any other cons? If not, what about pros—arguments in support of approaches?"

"That's easy," said Mary. "Doing it ourselves will improve our knowledge of the technology; we'll be able to support and maintain the system ourselves."

"Doing it through consultants will enable us to complete the project quicker," countered Max.

Jack added in the three pros and paused, giving the group some time to reflect on the map.

**Figure 8.9: Additional arguments
in favour of two of the potential answers to the root question**

Rick and Mary, who were sitting next to each other, had a whispered side-conversation going; Andrew and Max were writing something down. Jack waited.

"Mary and I have an idea," said Rick. "We could take an approach that combines the best of both worlds—external consultants and internal resources. Actually, we've already got it down as a separate approach—co-development, but we haven't discussed it yet." He had the group's attention now. "Co-development allows us to use outside expertise where we really need it and develop our own skills too. Yes, we'd need to put some thought into how it would work, but I think we could do it."

"I can't see how co-development will reduce the time risk—it will take longer than doing it through consultants," said Max.

"True," said Mary, "but it is better than doing it ourselves and, more important, it enables us to develop in-house skills that are needed to support and maintain the application. In the long run, this can add up to a huge saving. Just last week I read that maintenance can be anywhere between 60 to 80 percent of total system costs."

"So, you're saying that it reduces implementation time and results in a smaller exposure to cost blowout?" asked Jack.

"Yes," said Mary.

Jack added in the pros and waited.

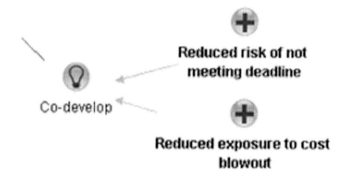

Figure 8.10: New arguments supporting a potential answer to the root question

"I still don't see how it reduces time," said Max.

"It does, when compared to the option of doing it ourselves," retorted Mary.

"Wait a second guys," said Jack. "What if I reword the pros to read 'Reduced implementation time compared to in-house option' and 'reduced cost compared to external option'?"

He looked at Mary and Max. Both seemed to OK with this, so he typed in the changes.

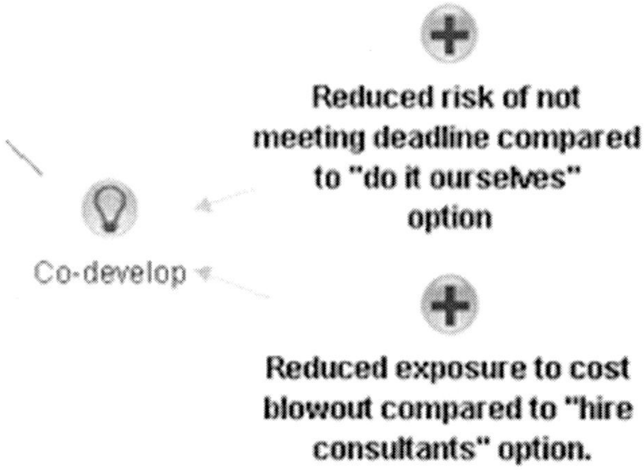

**Reduced risk of not
meeting deadline compared
to "do it ourselves"
option**

**Reduced exposure to cost
blowout compared to "hire
consultants" option.**

Figure 8.11: Clarified arguments supporting a potential answer to the root question

Jack asked, "So, are there any other issues, ideas or arguments that anyone would like to add?"

"From what's on the map, it seems that co-development is the best option," said Andrew. He looked around to see what the others thought: Rick and Mary were nodding but Max still looked doubtful.

Max asked, "How are we going to figure out who does what? It isn't easy to partition work cleanly when teams have different levels of expertise."

Jack realised that although Max asked a question, it was the contextual argument about the difficulty to partition work that was the key point. Accordingly, Jack left the question off and typed in "Hard to work between teams that have different levels of expertise" as a con to the "Co-develop" idea.

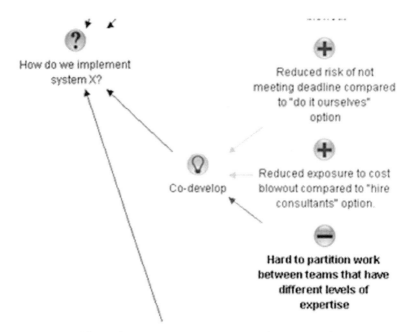

How do we implement
system X?

Reduced risk of not
meeting deadline compared
to "do it ourselves"
option

Co-develop

Reduced exposure to cost
blowout compared to "hire
consultants" option.

Hard to partition work
between teams that have
different levels of
expertise

Figure 8.12: Additional argument against a potential answer to the root question

"Good point," said Andrew. "There may be ways to address this concern. Do you think it would help if we brought some consultants in on a day-long engagement to workshop a co-development approach with the team?"

Max nodded. "Yeah, that might work," he said. "It's worth a try anyway. I have my reservations, but co-development seems the best of the three approaches if we can resolve the partitioning issue."

"Great," said Andrew. "I'll get some consultants in next week to help us workshop an approach."

Jack typed in this exchange, as the others started to gather their things. "Anything else to add?" he asked.

Everyone looked up at the map. "No, that's it, I think," said Mary.

Jack marked the "Co-develop" option as a decision to distinguish it from the other nodes.

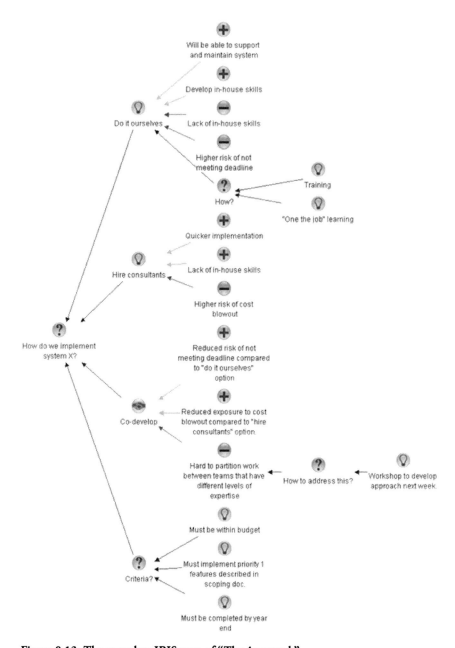

Figure 8.13: The complete IBIS map of "The Approach"

Jack looked around the group. Helped along by IBIS, a shared display and his facilitation, they'd overcome their differences and reached a collective decision. He had thought it wouldn't work, but it had.

Some remarks

As seen from the story that we just related, the structure of IBIS makes it an excellent tool to capture and communicate decision rationale in an organisational context. Figure 8.13 is a fairly complete summary of the essential points of the discussion, stripped of conversational fluff. Each element of the map represents a rhetorical step in the discussion. As the discussion progressed, questions were raised and responses sought and debated. The best way forward became apparent to all through dialogue. It is important to note that the discussion did not require or assume any predefined "selection criteria" for decision making. These criteria *emerged* through the discussion. This is a key point which we'll return to later in this chapter.

Before we move on, it is worth illustrating just how much of a difference the right sort of visual representation of can make to arguments. When Kunz and Rittel first described IBIS back in 1970, issue maps were part of a much larger (and much scarier) system. Their paper is easy to find online and quite amusing when you read it nowadays as it is positively antiquated[2]. Of course, we are talking about a time before PCs and most people in 1970 were freaking out about the news that the Beatles had just split up.

To give you a glimpse of the origins of IBIS, Figure 8.14 illustrates what our "Approach" IBIS map might have looked like in this earlier era. Notice how it loses a lot of its inherent intuitiveness because of its reliance on shapes and textual labels alone.

---

[2]   At the time of writing the paper is online and available at: http://www.cc.gatech.edu/~ellendo/rittel/rittel-issues.pdf

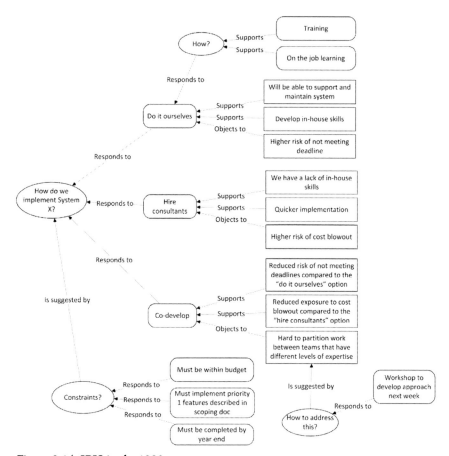

Figure 8.14: IBIS in the 1980s

IBIS is by no means the only type of map that can be used for capturing decision rationale. We've mentioned Argument Mapping in the previous chapter, but there are many others. It is worthwhile taking a look at a couple of these and evaluating how they stack up against IBIS, particularly since some of the other approaches were designed to augment, or address perceived shortcomings of IBIS maps. To do so, we will redraw the previous discussion with Jack and his colleagues using these alternate notations.

Questions, options and criteria

Questions, options and criteria (QOC) is an argumentation-based design rationale representation tool proposed by McLean and co-workers (1991). QOC consists of the following elements:

- **Questions** are akin to question nodes in IBIS. They represent design issues to be resolved or clarified, or problems to be solved.
- **Options** are much like idea nodes in IBIS. They are responses to questions, and represent alternatives that are explored.
- **Criteria** are standards or rules that are used to evaluate the options that are proposed.
- **Arguments** are akin to IBIS pros and cons: they are positions used to support or oppose questions, options or criteria. Dashed lines between options and criteria denote negative influence whereas solid lines indicate positive influence. i.e. arguing against or for an option.

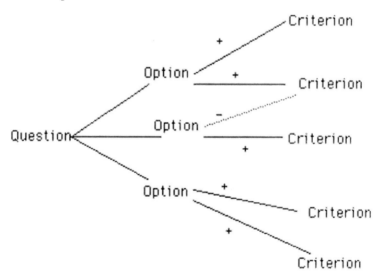

Figure 8.15: The Questions, Options and Criteria ontology

QOC is similar to IBIS in that it has questions, options (ideas) and arguments for or against the options. However, there are several important differences too.

- Evaluation of an idea is performed by assessing how well the alternatives satisfy *criteria*. In IBIS this is done by stating pros and cons against the ideas

- Arguments for or against the identified criteria are denoted *via lines*, and not nodes. A supporting or opposing argument is based on whether *a line is dashed or solid*.

- IBIS focuses on capturing the flow of deliberations, whereas QOC questions are generally more constrained and focused. QOC questions are intended to provide a structure for exploring and explaining the options. IBIS questions, on the other hand, can be about any topic under discussion.

- Finally, and perhaps most importantly, criteria in QOC can only be developed *after reflection*, whereas IBIS arguments can capture potential criteria on the fly.

It is interesting that IBIS was mentioned in the original QOC paper. The authors claimed that QOC is *specific to design rationale* while IBIS isn't (If you recall the start of this chapter, we mentioned that IBIS is considered to be one of the earliest *decision* rationale notations invented). So, we agree with the authors of QOC on this point. Thus, to be fair with our comparison, the example of Jack and his colleagues may not be suited to QOC as their discussion is not really about design.

Nevertheless, Figure 8.16 is the IBIS discussion between Jack and his colleagues in QOC format. Keep in mind that solid lines represent positive influences and dashed lines negative ones.

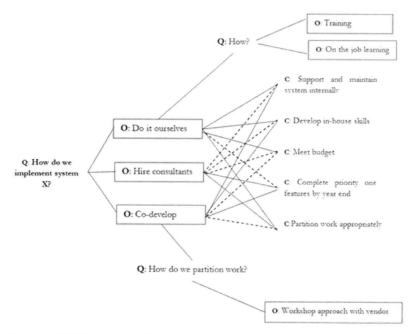

Figure 8.16 "The Approach" discussion using the QOC format

In Figure 8.16 we have marked out the "root question" in bold, although this is not mandated by the notation. Advocates of QOC view it as a notation that can summarise IBIS by distilling the key points of the argument and using the *criteria as a focal point*. The creators of QOC call this "criteria by reflection."

Using our story, a key difference between the QOC map and its IBIS counterpart is that the QOC map has *five* criteria as opposed to three in the IBIS version. However, there is no contradiction here: if you look at the IBIS argumentation it will become clear that some of the pro arguments, such as in-house support and maintenance, are in fact *emergent* criteria. Accordingly, these criteria should be "lifted" out of the arguments and listed explicitly. This is exactly the process of "criteria by reflection" that the originators of QOC refer to.

Despite making the criteria more explicit, the QOC diagram simply isn't as navigable or inherently readable as IBIS. To be fair, the IBIS diagram circa 1980 in Figure 8.14 has the same problem when compared to its modern incarnation. So, to even up the comparison, Figure 8.17 is an attempt to draw the QOC diagram utilising Compendium, leveraging its capability for iconic nodes.

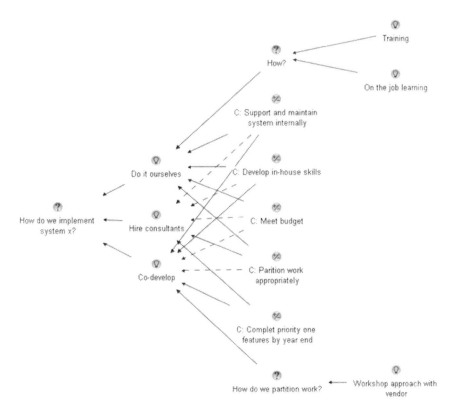

Figure 8.17 "The Approach" discussion in QOC map format utilising Compendium

We think that Figure 8.17 is a little better than the shape oriented map in Figure 8.16. Despite that, the many-to-many relationships between options and criteria make this map far too difficult to read. This problem would be compounded for each additional set of criteria added, and the five listed above are already enough to make one cross-eyed. Additionally, for the criteria nodes, there is no visually appealing symbol that people would intuitively associate with the word "criterion."

Nevertheless, if you think that diagram is scary, you haven't seen anything yet!

Decision representation language

Decision representation language (DRL) is another alternative to IBIS and QOC. In the words of Jintae Lee (1989), the creator of the notation:

"DRL (Decision Representation Language) is a language for representing decision processes. The goal of DRL is foremost to provide a vocabulary for representing the qualitative aspects of decision making—such as the issues raised, pro and con arguments advanced, and dependency relations among alternatives and constraints, that typically appear in a decision making process."

The basic objects in DRL are:

- **Goals**, which specify the properties of an ideal decision option.
- **Alternatives**, which are the available (or considered) options.
- **Claims**, which are arguments for or against alternatives. Claims can be *supported, denied* or *qualified*, and can depend on other claims.

These objects can be hierarchically arranged: goals can have sub-goals, alternatives, sub-alternatives etc. The notion of goals in DRL was something that Lee specifically mentioned that was a shortcoming in IBIS[3].

> "Notably lacking in IBIS, however, is again the notion of goals. Of course, goals cannot be absent in decision making. In IBIS, they appear implicitly in Arguments. The explicit representation of goals allows modular representation of arguments, forces people to articulate the goals and their subgoals, lets people argue about them, provides a basis for precedent management as well as multiple viewpoints."

As an example of Lee's point, the IBIS map from "The approach" discussion has a "do it ourselves" idea. It was argued that it's a good choice because "we will be able to support and maintain the system." There is an implicit goal here to "support the system via internal resources" which would have to go into a DRL map as an *explicit goal*. This makes a DRL map like QOC. In QOC you need to perform additional reflection or synthesis to develop criteria. DRL requires a similar reflective process to extract *goals* from the rationale and make them explicit.

---

[3]   Lee also listed several other shortcomings of IBIS which can be found in http://dspace.mit.edu/bitstream/handle/1721.1/47039/comparativeanaly00leej.pdf?sequence=1

By the way, we aren't done describing DRL yet. It has several other supporting objects including:

- **Questions**, which represents an uncertain state that needs more information for its resolution. For example, how can we achieve goal X.
- **Procedures**, which are step-by-step descriptions for carrying out processes. Procedures could be responses to questions (for example, *this* is how we achieve X) or detailed specifications of alternatives.
- **Groups** represent a set of related objects.
- **Viewpoints** are groups of objects that have the same set of underlying scenarios or assumptions.

The DRL ontology (ontology being a fancy term for the relationships between DRL objects) is depicted in Figure 8.18

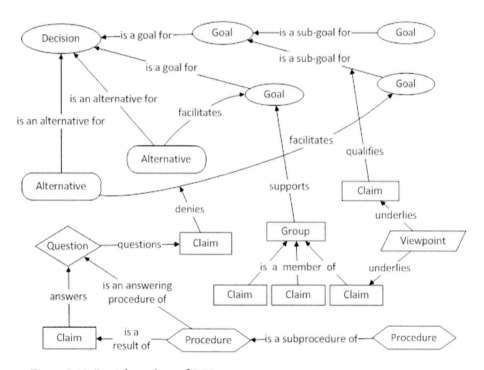

Figure 8.18: Partial ontology of DRL

Now if you think that looks a little confusing, consider that the diagram *does not show all possible DRL relationships.* For example, viewpoints can be associated with any object, not just claims. Further, in its original form DRL used the same shape for all objects. We found this seriously confusing, so we have used distinct shapes for each type of object in our "The Approach" example in Figure 8.19. Note that the decision to be made is depicted at the top left of the diagram as an oval. There are three goals that match the three criteria discussed and the alternatives and how they relate to those goals are listed.

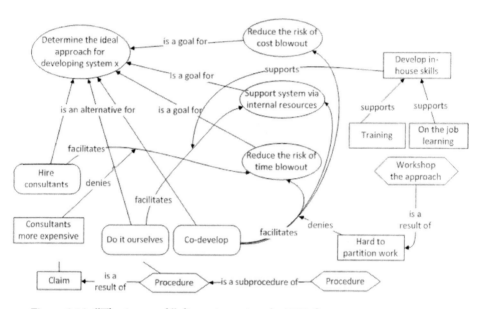

Figure 8.19: "The Approach" discussion using the DRL format

Needless to say, the plethora of objects and relationships make DRL very confusing for the novice user. Fans of the technique may argue that DRL is more about the language than the visual notation and the richness of the language enables designers to capture and mine rationale much more accurately than is possible with IBIS or QOC. This may be true, but as far as the exploratory phase of problem solving is concerned, we believe that the simplicity of IBIS trumps DRL any day.

Argument mapping

The final notation we will look at is Argument Mapping, developed by Tim Van Gelder (2003). Argument mapping is designed to make the reasoning—called a *contention* in Argument Mapping terminology—behind a particular conclusion explicit. In argument maps, contentions are supported by one or more *reasons* and opposed by one or more *objections*. Reasons and objections are based on *assumptions*, which may be hidden at first, and emerge only after analysis. Assumptions may be supported by *co-premises* (claims that serve to establish the relevance or validity of reasons). Objections can be argued against or *rebutted*. Typically reasons and objections are supported by *evidence* or opposed by *counter-evidence*. Evidence or counter-evidence must be based on facts, typically references to the literature or other authoritative, or convincing, sources.

Figure 8.20 is one possible argument map of the discussion between Jack and his colleagues. We emphasise that this is one possibility—there are other ways to cast the discussion in argument mapping terms.

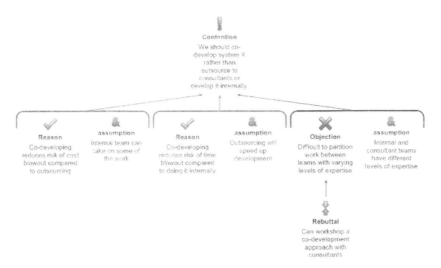

Figure 8.20: The Argument Mapping ontology

The first thing to note is that, like DRL, we start with the decision and build in reasons why we arrived at that decision. Along the way we record objections and attempt to surface all assumptions, some of which may be hidden. A weakness of the sample argument mapped in Figure 8.20 is that it does not include any evidence or counter-evidence. However, recall that our IBIS map is based on a live discussion and though protagonists may quote evidence in the course of a discussion, such claims can typically be confirmed only after the discussion is over. Another important point is that evidence can be captured within IBIS nodes too—as ideas or arguments—with appropriate references to authoritative sources.

The showdown

The obvious question that follows from the discussion so far is how QOC, DRL and Argument Mapping stack up against IBIS in mapping the issue that Jack and his colleagues were grappling with.

Both QOC and DRL were designed, among other things, to address shortcomings with IBIS. Argument mapping is specifically designed to make the reasoning behind a conclusion explicit, not for an open discussion of contentious issues. An important point to note is that all non-IBIS notations offer more node types than IBIS. This may make a more complete ontology, but it makes these notations much harder to use.

The conversation for the conversation

IBIS is easier to use in real time by virtue of the fact that you have only four basic nodes (questions, ideas, pros and cons). This enables mappers to map the dialogue as it occurs without having to spend too much time consciously thinking about how something should be captured. This is more difficult to do with QOC and we would fear to so much as even think of trying to using DRL. This is not surprising, given that their creators go so far as to state that they shouldn't be used in real time anyway. For example, the originators of QOC stated that criteria in QOC can only be developed *after reflection.*

But to reflect on something, we need the "raw materials" provided by dialogue. Since IBIS captures the essence of a conversation as it progresses, it enables participants to "see" and "explore" new themes as they emerge. IBIS does not prescribe or frame the conversation; it counts on the participants moving things forward through discussion. Decision-making is, or should be, a dialectical process, so IBIS is eminently suited to it. We think Socrates would have loved it.

Nevertheless, the IBIS map produced in our story was *not* a mere transcription. Jack did in fact, *synthesise on the fly*. He had to listen to what was said and in his mind, *unpack* statements into their ideas and arguments for and against, all the while doing it quickly so as to *not constrain the conversation*. Notably, he realised that a criterion that was discussed in relation to one option actually applied to all options. Consider this exchange:

> Rick: "Umm . . . not sure how it would work, but what about co-development?"
> Mary: "What about costs? We have a limited budget for this."
> Jack: "Good point. This is a constraint that must be satisfied by *all* potential approaches."

First, Jack realised that co-development was actually an idea, although it was worded as a question. Further, Jack could have inferred that co-development was costly based on Mary's response, which he then could have captured "Costly" as a con against "Co-Development." But he didn't. Instead, he created a question called "Constraints?" and added "Must be within budget" as an idea. The conversation then moved on.

Conversely, the other methods actually *direct* the conversation because they focus much more on using map elements to guide the conversation. In other words, they *prescribe* that conversations ought to occur in such a way as to eke out goals, criteria or premises for a problem *up front*. But we are talking about wicked problems here! Half the time, participants cannot agree what the problem is, let alone goals or criteria. Starting with a question such as "What are the goals?" or "What are the criteria?" with an unaligned group is a recipe for long, pointless and heated arguments.

In our example, the criteria *emerged* from conversation and were captured as they were suggested by stakeholders. The important point is that participants were not pushed into "discovering" criteria. The creators of QOC actually suggested that you could use an IBIS map as the basis for the reflection and synthesis required to create a QOC map. Surely, this suggests that you ought to have another conversation—a free flowing one—prior to the more structured one that uses QOC, DRL or Argument Mapping.

Yet, the emergent, non-prescriptive nature of IBIS is also the reason for the criticisms against it. Indeed, this is one of the reasons why these other notations were invented. Goals, criteria, assumptions and context can be *spread far and wide* across an IBIS map, depending on how the conversation goes. In our example, a QOC map listed five criteria, not the three that were captured in IBIS. So, we actually *strongly agree* with the criticisms of IBIS put forth by the creators of these alternative notations. We do need to make goals, criteria, and core arguments explicit.

However, we do not think this is best done through a *more complicated notation*. We'll explore this point further in the next chapter but for now, let's get back to a comparison of the notations because, in our opinion, the other notations have another not-so-obvious shortcoming in comparison to IBIS.

Cognitive overhead

It seems that for a number of years, designers of rationale representations chose to complicate matters by adding new node types rather than changing the representation of the nodes themselves. Compare, for example, the "old IBIS" map (Figure 8.14) of the discussion with that of QOC (Figure 8.16). The problem with old IBIS is not the node types but *how nodes are represented*.

We suspect that if the late, great Steve Jobs had ever decided to create a graphical representation of rationale, he would have spent more time on the visual representation than the preciseness of the notation—and with good reason too. Any mental effort directed towards figuring out a notation is overhead which should be avoided as far as possible. We believe this *cognitive overhead* is the key difference between the notations: it makes some easier to use than others.

Specifically, the diagrams produced by the non-IBIS representations are harder to understand compared to the IBIS map for two reasons

- Shapes do not have an immediate and obvious meaning. One has to know that a rounded rectangle in a DRL map represents an alternative. In contrast, it is pretty obvious that a green + icon in IBIS represents an argument supporting a particular position. The accessibility of IBIS comes from the visual intuitiveness of the symbols used and the simple grammar. This point applies to much more than just notations for decision rationale. As Steve Krug (2005) mentioned in his book on web site usability, "People don't read pages, they scan them." Any visual artefact, be it a Web page or a notation, must therefore be designed with this in mind.

- The additional flexibility of an expanded notation is offset by the cognitive load of using and processing the notation. It is sometimes hard to decide what a particular element should be represented as. Consequently, there is scope for confusion in creating and interpreting the map. For example, in the QOC map of the discussion, we represented "develop in-house skills" as an argument for the option "do it ourselves." We could have just as well labelled it a criterion. To be fair this is also true of IBIS, but we believe there is less scope for confusion in the latter.

Tim Van Gelder (2003) addressed these issues by using colours and icons liberally in his Argument Mapping notation. We think that as a result of this, argument maps are the closest to IBIS in terms of readability. However, there is *more to it than icons and colour alone*. What also matters is the degree of intuitiveness of an icon.

Early incarnations of IBIS referred to a question as an issue (hence the "I" in IBIS). But it is difficult to come up with an intuitive symbol that represents an "issue." However, since an issue can almost always be cast in terms of a question, the question mark was used in later versions of IBIS. This change, in our opinion, was a stroke of genius. It moved IBIS from being of purely academic interest to something that anyone could use.

By clever design, modern IBIS uses terms that have well known, concrete symbols. IBIS symbols have a near iconic relationship to their intended meaning and most readers would immediately understand what the symbols mean. Argument Mapping attempts to do this, but trying to find symbols that make you think "main contention," "premise," "co-premise," "objections," "rebuttals" and "lemmas" is considerably harder.

A paper by Neil Cohn (2005) entitled "A Cognitive Approach to Visual Signs and Writing" offered some deeper insights into understanding why it is easier to "get" some notations more than others. Cohn introduced what he termed the Cognitive Map of Graphic Signs (CMGS). The CMGS is basically a means of categorising writing systems in terms of how they are perceived by the human mind. Cohn contended that all writing systems can be classified as lying somewhere within a continuum defined by the following types:

- **Sound Based**: refers to symbols that represent sounds. The obvious example of this is the English alphabet.
- **Iconic**: refers to signs or symbols that are immediately "understood" because they stand for something "universal." An example is the much overused ☺.
- **Abstract**: Cohn uses this as a "catch-all" bucket for symbols that are neither sound-based nor iconic. An example of this is the use of diamond shaped figures to denote decision points in flow diagrams.

Cohn depicted the CMGS as show in Figure 8.21, with the space enclosed in the triangle being the continuum mentioned above.

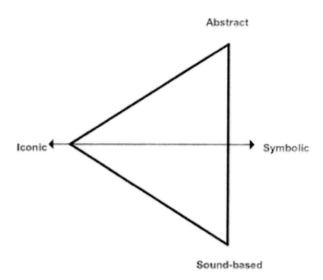

Figure 8.21: Cohn's Cognitive Map of Signs

As far as visual notations are concerned, what is important is the distinction between iconic and abstract symbols. The gradation from one to the other is represented by the line that runs from the iconic apex on the left, to the midpoint of the abstract/sound-based edge.

According to Cohn, the iconic end is characterised by a *fast speed of acquisition* (or understanding) whereas the symbolic end by considerably slower understanding. Further, the iconic end is more accessible to direct perception whereas the symbolic end requires more cognitive effort to comprehend.

With this background it is now obvious why some notations are worth a thousand words while others aren't. Those that rely on iconic representations such as the "?" "+" or "-" of IBIS, short-cut the comprehension process whereas others like DRL, QOC or even Argument Mapping, have an added cognitive overhead. In IBIS it is possible for a novice to tell, at a glance, whether an icon represents an issue, an idea or an argument. In contrast, in DRL it isn't immediately obvious from what each icon represents.

Cognitive overhead and degree of abstraction are well and good, but the real test lies in what novices find easy to learn and practitioners easy to use. So, we'll leave it here, asking you to judge how each visual representation fared in the showdown.

Looking ahead

Recall from Chapter 7 that the key to solving organisational problems—particularly those involving diverse stakeholder groups—lies in rational debate or dialogue. Hence, our preoccupation with finding a tool that can help capture the essence of such discussions in real-time. In this chapter we have attempted to compare some popular notations for visualising reasoning from the point of view of their utility in capturing dialogue. We have argued that IBIS fits the bill best.

Nevertheless, a tool to map dialogue does not by itself guarantee that a discussion will actually cover issues that are important. To that extent we agree with the intent behind Argument Mapping, QOC and DRL. In IBIS, participants could spend hours debating irrelevancies and minutiae. The key to productive debate lies in asking the right questions, and IBIS is silent on how this can be achieved. This point leads us on to the next chapter: the art of surfacing questions that matter.

9

Problem Structuring Methods

"Ah, beer. The cause of and the solution to all of life's problems" (Homer Simpson)

The quest for principled simplicity . . .

In Chapter 5, we noted that there are three stages of coping with wicked problems. The most common initial response to such problems is *naive simplicity*. This is where people think that the solutions are so bleeding obvious that they are amazed that nobody has rolled up their sleeves and simply "gotten it done already." Often people will persist with this line of thinking, no matter what contrary evidence is presented to them. This is a classic case of confirmation bias, where people seek information that supports their preconceptions, regardless of whether or not the information is true.

Nevertheless, let's say that you have managed to get a group of stakeholders to see through the veil of naïve simplicity. Unfortunately your problems have just begun; naïve simplicity is usually replaced by the stage of "overwhelming complexity"—the trough of despair where people start to wonder whether the mess can be solved at all. This stage is characterised by adversarial behaviours in the form of open conflict between stakeholders who, while attacking the ideas of others, do all they can to avoid taking on any responsibility themselves. This phase is also characterised by lack of rational communication or dialogue. No wonder then, that these situations are fertile ground for best practices. A panacea sounds good when the disease appears incurable.

What we are really looking for in these situations is *principled simplicity*. This is where all stakeholders have achieved a common understanding of the problem to the point where, based on what they know and the information they have, are able to commit to a solution or action that they know will lead to an improvement on the present state. It seems that you have to pass through the stages of naive simplicity and overwhelming complexity before you can reach this level of enlightenment. This is a difficult path to realisation and is hence elusive. Certainly for many if not most wicked problems, it is never found.

It should be emphasised that a solution of principled simplicity is rarely one through which the problem is "solved" in the usual sense of the word. This should be no surprise, given that one of the characteristics of wicked problems is that they are never solved definitively. It may well be that only certain aspects of the problem are addressed—perhaps only those that are important to the stakeholders *as a group*. It could also be that shared understanding results in some problems becoming non-problems, as paradoxical as this may sound.

In the last two chapters, we examined the power of visual reasoning and the use of notations to display rationale to better understand problems. Now, in some cases it might well be that this is enough to create a holding environment in which shared understanding can occur (recall that two juxtaposed images worked a treat when putting a certain alpha programmer in his place). If an IBIS map, or any of the visual methods we examined, enables stakeholders to achieve a shared understanding of the problem and as a result, a solution of principled simplicity emerges, then you have yourself the beginnings of a holding environment. Nurture it!

While the benefits of visualising rationale are significant (and we believe that our case studies will demonstrate this further), we know that for many organisations and problems, mapping dialogue or arguments *won't be enough.* Visualising reasoning is one facet of creating a holding environment to deal with wicked problems. It helps the *transparency* aspect of communicative rationality because all viewpoints and arguments are accepted and treated on the same footing in the map. But if drawing visual representation of argumentation were the be all and end all of managing wickedness, then there would be no contentious issues left to tackle, there would be a best practice for managing wicked problems and Ikea wouldn't need call centres!

No . . . there's more to it than just visual notations. Consequently, we need to cast our net wider.

Framing problems

Our examination of QOC, DRL and Argument Mapping revealed that these maps have more node types than IBIS. QOC for example uses a notation in which *criteria* are explicitly represented, DRL on the other hand uses a notation based on *goals* (and a host of other things) and Argument Mapping uses constructs like *assumptions* and *co-premises.*

When you think about it, these additional constructs have an effect of *framing the problem in a particular way.* This framing preselects the sort of questions that are asked, and sharpens the focus of discussions—at least in theory. Asking the right questions is, of course, a good thing. But we believe that there is a better way to frame problems and questions than to use a complex mapping notation and the cognitive overhead that it entails.

Our next stop involves revisiting our group of academic heretics from Chapter 5, people like Ackoff, Rittel and Simon, all of whom, in their own way, distinguished between tame and wicked problems. Just as there are a wide variety in metaphors and acronyms for naming "wickedness," the solutions they offered to deal with wickedness also vary in concepts, tools and methods. This is unsurprising given the variety of disciplines our gang of intellectual hippies came from. Additionally, the solutions they offered have been adapted and extended by subsequent generations of revolutionaries. Many of these upstarts are from relatively new disciplines like IT and business analysis and yes, even project management.

Nevertheless, despite differences, all the solutions are in essence *Problem Structuring Methods* (PSMs). This term was coined by Jonathan Rosenhead and John Mingers (2001). To quote Rosenhead and Mingers from their book "Rational Analysis for a Problematic World revisited":

> ". . . problem structuring methods . . . accept as a fact that the most demanding and troubling task in formative decision situations is *to decide what the problem is*. There are too many factors; many of the relationships between them are unclear or in dispute; the most important do not reduce naturally to quantified form; different stakeholders have different priorities. Problem structuring methods often use models (often in the plural, and with little or no quantification) to help (mostly) group decision making—since it rare for such issues to provide enough structure that those who take responsibility for the consequences of the choices which are made, do so in a coherent basis and with sufficient confidence to make the necessary commitments."

The aim of a PSM is to help a group *frame* a problem in a way that allows a solution of principled simplicity to emerge. By definition, this means that the method chosen needs to encompass varying perspectives so as to engage all stakeholders. To achieve this, a PSM must enable stakeholders to *contribute directly* to the process of problem solving and more importantly, enable them to *own the process*. This echoes the messages of Habermas (Ulrich 2001a and 2001b), Rittel (1972), Heifetz (1994) and Ostrom (1998) that we looked at in Chapter 6.

Analysis vs. facilitation

In 2009, Paul attended and spoke at a conference for Business Analysts (BAs). When talking to some conference participants he noticed that they seemed to think that their main role was to serve as "translators" between IT and "the business." After all, nerds and the rest of humanity can't communicate, right? Enter the Business Analyst, whose job is to get the two sides talking to each other. In this paradigm BAs act as listeners and interpreters, but they are relaying messages *second-hand.* "No you can't talk to the users—talk to the BA" is a common organisational refrain in IT projects.

PSM's repudiate this altogether. According to Rosenhead and Mingers, the very notion of an "analyst" is a relic of the traditional problem solving methods because "analysts can develop a model in the back room." In contrast, with a PSM, "working in the group is *the* distinct activity." Accordingly, most PSM's require a *facilitator* rather than an analyst or translator. The facilitator is responsible for helping a group use a PSM to develop *mental models* that enable them to make sense of the problem space. This is a critical point that cannot be over-emphasised.

In contrast to the analyst worldview, the facilitator paradigm aims to resolve problems using *dialogue between stakeholders.* This is dialogue aimed at achieving a shared perception or understanding of the problem situation. Unlike the analyst paradigm, there are no back-room deals or approaches. Part of the role of a facilitator is to leverage the wisdom of the crowd by creating an environment in which participants can articulate their thoughts, desires and fears—whether they are irrational or rational. This is the essence of a holding environment.

The *mental models* that Rosenhead and Mingers referred to are means of "representing the structure of a problem" in a way that would make it understandable to the participants. Given that we spent two chapters examining maps of various kinds and the visual representation of rationale, you might expect that PSMs use similar maps—and you would be completely right. However, as we will soon see, PSMs use other types of diagrams, in various combinations to boot.

So, we have the following combination of elements that interact together to create a PSM: a *shared space* where all stakeholders can build a model, a *common language or notation* that everyone in the group understands and, last but not least, a *facilitator* who can keep the discussion moving in the right direction.

The PSM smorgasbord

There are a large number of PSMs out there. At first glance you might think that this is somewhat surprising, especially since most people who work in business or professional environments have not heard of these at all. But once you start to look at a lot of them a little more closely, you'll see why this is the case (and why this was a hard chapter to write!).

Many of these methods, although not all, have come from academia. Moreover, their roots lie in the physical and social sciences from which they borrow concepts and terminology. As a result they can be a bit daunting for non-academics. This is part of the problem with them. Techniques that deal with complexity are often complex themselves and therefore struggle to gain traction in the real world.

Yet, at the heart of each PSM are nuggets of simplicity and brilliance. In examining, using and reflecting on them, recurring patterns begin to emerge. Understanding these patterns is critical because it paves the way to a better understanding of how we can frame complex problems. To this end, we will take a whirlwind tour of a number of PSMs. Our treatment attempts to avoid systems terminology and jargon, focusing instead on the rationale behind the methods.

For the record, some of the PSMs we have researched or used include:

- **Soft Systems Methodology**: Peter Checkland (1999)
- **Breakthrough Thinking**: Gerald Nadler and Shozo Hibino (1998)
- **Polarity Management:** Barry Johnson (1992)
- **Dialogue Mapping:** Jeff Conklin (2007)
- **Back of a Napkin:** Dan Roam (2008)
- **Quest**: Nilofar Merchant (2009)
- **Journey Making**: Colin Eden and Fran Ackermann (1998)
- **Strategic Choice Approach**: John Friend and Allen Hickling (Friend 2001)
- **Robustness Analysis**: Jonathan Rosenhead and Shiv Gupta (Rosenhead 2001)
- **Drama Theory**: Jim Bryant, Peter Bennett, Morris Bradley and Nigel Howard (Bennett, Bryant and Howard 2001)

We will examine the first four of these briefly before drawing out the common elements between them. Note that we are deliberately taking a "just enough" point of view. Also, our synthesis is the first attempt ever, as far as we know to explain them all from a simple and conversational point of view. So, grab a strong coffee and let's go traipsing through the world of problem structuring methods. Take your time with this chapter . . . we have a bit to get through.

Soft Systems Methodology

Soft Systems Methodology (SSM) could be described as the granddaddy of PSMs. It has been in continual development and refinement since it was first proposed by Peter Checkland (1999) in the late 1960s. Because of its vintage and development over time, SSM is often the one PSM that people might have heard of.

Yet, having heard of it is one thing, understanding it quite another. Among other things, SSM is rooted in systems theory and systems theory for the uninitiated is like trying to understand the Matrix[1] movies without the car chases and kung-fu. All one is left with is seemingly incomprehensible dialogue. Thus, when attempting to understand SSM in all its gory detail, it is advisable to begin with a double-shot coffee or something stronger if your preferences run that way.

To get an overview on the systems perspective, it is useful to start with Rittel. To begin with, the term wicked problem is in some ways misleading because it implies that there is *a single problem* that has wicked characteristics. However, by Rittel and Webber's (1970) definition, a wicked problem actually consists of *many interrelated issues and perspectives*, each of which is a problem in its own right—wicked or otherwise. Therefore, we are actually talking about many problems, entangled in a complex mess of ever-changing interdependencies. To top it all off, affected individuals have different perspectives on those fluid interdependencies.

This is why Ackoff (1979) used the term "mess." In his words, "Every problem interacts with other problems and is therefore part of a set of interrelated problems, a system of problems." SSM takes this idea even

---

[1]   The Matrix is a 1999 science fiction-action film written and directed by Larry and Andy Wachowski, starring Keanu Reeves, Laurence Fishburne, Carrie-Anne Moss, Joe Pantoliano, and Hugo Weaving.

further. Checkland (2001) described a mess as a state of "flux," which is the continual unpredictable interaction of ideas and events over time. According to him, "The world immerses all of us in such a flux." Checkland made the point that a manager performing the task of management is actually evaluating the flux and taking appropriate actions based on what he or she perceives at that time. These actions in turn became part of the flux, "leading to new perceptions and further actions." (We told you it's like the Matrix movies).

To cut a long, acronym-laden story short, this implies that organisational situations are unique because among other things, people see similar situations differently[2]. This is entirely consistent with our discussions in Chapter 2 on bounded rationality and cognitive bias. SSM, with its penchant for long words from European languages, refers to this as *Weltanschauung*—a German word that translates to "World view." For a given problem, SSM attempts to make each identified Weltanschauung explicit via *conceptual modelling*—the visual bit which we will see in a moment.

The construction of conceptual models begins with formulation of a "root definition" to summarise each world view and communicate it to others. Thus, there will often be many root definitions depending on how many different perspectives there are on the problem.

At first glance, these root definitions look a little like something a lawyer would write, but on closer examination, the method used to arrive at these is very clever and can be used in many contexts outside of SSM. A root definition should be *well formulated*. Checkland (1985) stated that to be well formulated, a definition should include several different elements which are summarised in Table 9.1.

---

[2]   To paraphrase the well-known saying by Marx (Karl, not Groucho)—history repeats itself, but it plays out subtly different tragedies every time.

C	Customers	Who is on the receiving end of this transformation?
		How will they react to what you are proposing?
		Who are the winners and losers?
A	Actors	Who will be carrying out this activity?
T	Transformation	What are the inputs?
		What are the outputs?
		What is the process for transforming inputs into outputs?
W	World View	What view of the world makes this definition meaningful?
		What is the bigger picture into which the situation fits?
O	Owner	Who is the real owner of the process or situation
E	Environmental constraints	What are the broader constraints that act on the situation and this definition?

Table 9.1: The CATWOE mnemonic developed by Checkland (1985)

The mnemonic CATWOE is often used as a reminder of the elements that go into a well formed root definition. It is important to note that the mnemonic is spelt this way to make it easy to remember—it is not an indication of the relative importance of each element.

The elements of a root definition can be summarised by as follows: Who (A) is doing what (T) for whom (C) and to whom they are answerable (O); and what are the different assumptions and perspectives pertaining to the issue (W) and the wider environment (E). In our experience, the best starting point might be to consider the output of the transformation (the" T" bit)—a desired future state—before moving on to the world view and other elements.

Using an example of extra-galactic importance[3] in Table 9.2, we can see how CATWOE works to create a root definition. Imagine that you are a boutique consultancy in the Star Wars universe. Darth Sidious (Chancellor Palpatine) has engaged you to assist with developing a long term strategic plan to realise the Sith vision to rule the galaxy. You use SSM as the basis for focusing discussions around potential strategic actions. An example of a well-defined root definition from the world view held by Palpatine might be:

---

[3] There is always one person in a crowd who has never seen Star Wars. Star Wars is a terrific way to convey concepts in an interesting way. So we suggest you get with it and watch the picture.

A professionally operated death star in the Galactic Empire
which, in light of the long term career development of Anakin
Skywalker, will create the ultimate weapon, with which the Sith
will destroy all rebel scum and rule the galaxy unopposed.

Taking this apart using the CATWOE mnemonic, we can see that all
of the bases have been covered. In framing the problem via this particular
world view we have made explicit many assumptions.

C	Rebel Scum, Galactic Empire
A	Spaceship subcontractors
T	The need for an ultimate weapon → The need for the ultimate weapon met
	Rebel Scum → No more rebel scum
	Need to rule galaxy → The need to rule galaxy met
W	A death star is the best option for an ultimate weapon to meet the galactic empires strategic long term vision of unopposed galaxy ruling
O	Chancellor Palpatine
E	Whether Anakin will turn to the dark side
	Growing rebellion that threatens the empire

Table 9.2: A sample CATWOE checklist for Palpatine from Star Wars

Other root definitions could be defined, representing the perspective
of other stakeholders. Continuing our Star Wars example, "Weapons R
Us," a company specialising in planet destroying lasers, would have a very
different root definition:

A high quality laser cannon which, in light of the final design
for the Death Star, will provide the evil empire with a fully
armed battle station, and deliver sufficient profits to Weapons
R Us while also reducing the possibility of the emperor
electrocuting us.

Once this and all other root definitions have been formulated, we can set
to work on building the conceptual model of each. Where the root definition
identifies the *purpose* of the system, conceptual models focus on how the
system might *function*. i.e. what *activities* are needed to achieve the purpose.
There will be as many conceptual models as there are root definitions.

Models in SSM are relatively high level and essentially consist of a causal map with 5 to 10 activities. In Figure 9.1 we have developed a conceptual Model representing Palpatine's perspective.

Root Definition:

"A professionally operated death star in the Galactic Empire which—in light of the long term career development of Anakin Skywalker—will create the ultimate weapon, with which the Sith will destroy all rebel scum and rule the galaxy unopposed"

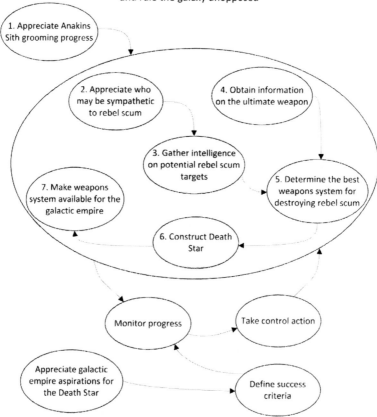

Figure 9.1: Palpatine's perspective represented by a Soft Systems Methodology conceptual model

The structure of SSM causal maps is relatively simple. They contain only one type of node and a causal relationship between the nodes. Nodes typically represent activities as part of a functioning system and are often grouped together. In the example of Figure 9.1, activities 2-7 are considered one discrete system in relation to activity 1, and accordingly have been drawn within a larger circle. This is convenient because this larger circle can be drawn as a single activity in other conceptual maps. This is also why each activity is individually numbered; it enables stakeholders to build a *hierarchy of conceptual models*. For example, Activity 6: "Construct the death star," could have a more detailed conceptual model where the sub-activities would be labelled 6.1, 6.2 and so on, listing the specific activities required to construct the death star. Accordingly, there is a great deal of flexibility and granularity here but, as you might imagine, it is easy to get carried away and lost in the bargain.

Once all root definitions representing each world view have been modelled, stakeholders can refer to them as a basis for further debate on the problem. With these models in hand, one is in a much better position to understand the parallel universes inhabited by stakeholders and thus appreciate diverse aspects of the problem space.

The act of creating and comparing conceptual models to the real world may result in reinterpretations of the root definitions and conceptual models. It may also suggest changes to the real world system being modelled. SSM does not prescribe how this process should be handled. This highlights the main criticism made of the method: it is simply not prescriptive enough.

While we have not described SSM by a long shot, we believe we have covered the gist of it. Because SSM isn't particularly prescriptive, any approach that comes close enough can be called SSM. Although Checkland and others have significantly refined and enhanced the methodology over time, there is still no objective criterion to determine whether or not a particular technique is SSM. This frustrates the hell out of critics, who argue that there is no real method behind it and that SSM doesn't actually tell you *how* to do anything useful.

The last sentence is a common criticism of any heuristic-based approach that aims to change or widen perspectives via systems thinking. For SSM advocates who actually understand the Matrix movies (in other words, the sort of academic hippies we examined in Chapter 5), the critics are simply uninformed "squares" who haven't opened their minds to the reality of the flux. Incidentally, this gives us a rather nice defence: If any hard-core SSM practitioners read this book and claim that we haven't explained it correctly, we will simply blame it on that darn flux!

Breakthrough Thinking®

If SSM was a little too far out for you, then you may want to consider our next PSM. Breakthrough Thinking (BT) was developed in the late 1960s by Gerald Nadler and Shozo Hibino (1998). Nadler and Hibino distanced themselves somewhat from classical systems theory that underlies SSM, stating that it was "a bit embarrassing to use some of the same terms that proponents of so-called systems thinking have used in their effusive flag-waving." Ouch! Academic smackdown?

Instead, Nadler and Hibino claimed to take a much more pragmatic approach, based on their study of effective problem solvers and leaders. They believed in the approaches embodied in expansionist methods like SSM but reckoned that these techniques were not effective for *detailing solutions* systematically, in the manner of reductionist approaches. Put another way, they saw the reductionist approach of problem solving as valuable and having as much validity as the expansionist approach of methods like SSM. The two were but facets of a greater truth. In their words:

> "What is called for, is a synthesis of the best of all approaches, one that recognises that each approach to problem solving, each kind of thinking, is a legitimate expression of human knowledge and experience. What is called for is an approach to problem solving that first identifies the right thing to do and then (but only then) specifies how to do things right. This is the approach of Breakthrough Thinking."

From their research, Nadler and Hibino distilled seven principles on which they based their approach to problem solving. These seven principles, taken together, form what they called a "conscious process of thinking" and a "general flow of reasoning." Each principle, with its associated tools and processes, should ideally be applied in a logical sequence. We will examine each principle briefly:

The uniqueness principle

BT assumes that no two situations are the same. Just because one organisation solves a problem in a certain way, it does not mean that the same solution will apply elsewhere. This principle recognises that despite superficial similarities, every problem is embedded in a unique context of people, culture, issues, opportunities and constraints. (Sounds very much like the SSM flux if you ask us!)

The purposes principle

The idea here is to focus and expand on the essential aim that the organisation wants to achieve and ignore all the inessential ones. This principle is predicated on the notion that the obvious solution is often not the real solution (reminiscent of the naïve simplicity stage of wicked problem "solving") and we often end up solving the wrong problem as a result.

Thus, the purpose principle is used to get a true understanding of the core elements of the problem within the widest possible context. Nadler and Hibino also state that it helps avoid what they call "analysis-first" and "technology" traps.

> "The successful people we studied avoid analytical and subdivision modelling when they first tackle what they acknowledge is a unique problem. They do not believe in launching a vast effort to collect information about a problem area before they talk about what they want to accomplish." (Inveterate data-driven managers, take note!)

The main visual artefact used in elaborating purpose is the *purposes array*. To construct it, one begins by asking all stakeholders the purpose of the project. They are then asked "expansionist" questions that seek to explore and elaborate on the underlying reasons behind their stated purpose. The purposes array is created, starting with the narrowest purpose and arranging deeper purposes in order of expanding scope. BT encourages the expansion of purpose, even beyond any practical possibility, as it helps build a broad context.

If we revisit the Star Wars universe example used in Soft Systems Methodology, a purpose array from the point of view of Palpatine might look like Figure 9.2.

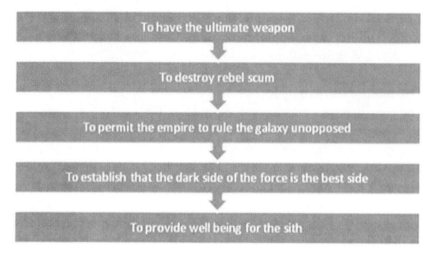

Figure 9.2: Breakthrough Thinking Purposes Array through the eyes of Palpatine

You might have noticed that the diagrammatic model behind the purpose array is a variation of the causal map, with each purpose leading on to a higher-level purpose. As with conceptual models in SSM, purpose arrays need to be developed for *each stakeholder's world view*. These provide an anchor point from which debate can be conducted. The end result of this effort is the identification and selection of a *focus purpose* together with a set of potential measures that can be used to determine if the focus purpose has been accomplished.

The "solution after next" principle

The solution after next principle is neatly summarised by Senge's (1994) first law of the Fifth Discipline "today's problems come from yesterday's solutions" and Albert Einstein's famous quote "You cannot solve a problem with the same thinking that caused the problem."

This begs the million dollar question: how can we avoid sowing the seeds of tomorrow's problems with today's solutions? While the uniqueness and purposes principles provide a means for a group to build a better, more inclusive world view of the problem, history tells us that most solutions end up biting us in some way that we did not anticipate. Additionally, innovation tends to come from *creative leaps of faith*.

Even with a well understood purpose, it can be easy to fixate on the short term, as it is the most pressing and concrete. The "solution after next" principle is all about longer-term vision. In a sense it is an attempt to gaze into a crystal ball and see what the future consequences of a solution might be. It stimulates the exploration of future scenarios with a view to providing insight into solutions currently being considered by the group. BT does not prescribe *how* this should be done—and that's no surprise because it can be hard to do. However, Nadler and Hibono suggested liberal use of techniques such as *analogy and metaphor, imagery and scenario writing.* In short, use anything that helps figure out how the current solution should be designed so as to have minimum adverse impact in the not-so-foreseeable future.

The systems principle

Breakthrough Thinking takes a more "meat and potatoes" approach to systems thinking in the sense that it is less about the trippy philosophical stuff that SSM uses and claims to be more about practical problem solving, In Nadler and Hibino's words, BT attempts to put "utility into the word *system*."

The means to add this "utility" in BT is not to use mapping techniques at all. BT's answer to the SSM conceptual model is a "systems matrix"—a 7*6 grid of various "elements" and "dimensions" of a system. We are not going to cover all of the elements in this book as it would be a chapter in itself. The best way to imagine a systems matrix is to think of a diagram that is much like an Excel spreadsheet. The idea is to make all the gory detail of a system visible by filling in all the cells of the sheet, with the aim of ensuring that all assumptions are captured and tested. Don't worry if you find this hard to visualise; we don't use the systems principle in this book and mention it here only for completeness.

The systems matrix roughly corresponds to the SSM conceptual model. In contrast to BT, a SSM conceptual model is merely an abstract representation of a system whereas the BT matrix is much more prescriptive and detailed.

Another difference with SSM is that a *single systems matrix is developed*, rather than one for each stakeholder group or world view as per SSM. This is probably a good thing, given that 6*7 means that there are 42 facets to examine. We suspect if you have to do that for each world view, you'd never finish.

The limited information collection principle

BT subscribes to the view that more data does not mean more insight. *Relevant* information is more important than *accurate* information. Further "getting the facts" data collection should not be done without "getting the purpose" first. Among other things, Nadler and Hibino warn that the quest for hard data can inhibit interpersonal collaboration, and that achieving breakthroughs depends more on *interactions* than information.

> ". . . there is an implication that the information people have in their heads is not to be trusted and must be invested with objectivity through someone else's observations and measurements. In response to this implication, those being measured become defensive."

BT suggests that when collecting data in relation to a problem, one should develop a purposes array and solution after next *first*, so that "the prospective data will accomplish needed ends." Only then should the collection of information take place. This places discipline on the reasoning process of a group.

The principle also states that information should be collected from a wide variety of sources and shared with everyone—"not just an elite coterie"—as information can be interpreted more fruitfully if all participants share their varied perspectives.

The people design principle

The notion that people resist change is regarded by BT as a fallacy. Nadler and Hibino argued that people resist when the change is not understood, is imposed or is seen as threatening to their wellbeing. You are tipping their marble boards and naturally, they darn well want to know why. This cuts to the heart of a tenet of BT and we quote:

> "Anyone has the potential to become a valuable contributor. The object is to create an atmosphere that fosters the optimal contribution that each individual can make. To do that you must first throw away any preconceptions about who is qualified to offer what solutions and really listen to what each person has to say"

In other words, create a holding environment. Need we say more?

The betterment timeline principle

The final breakthrough thinking principle is about resiliency and wraps up the other principles. It is about institutionalising the understanding that problem solving involves continual feedback.

Participants also need to internalise the process of revisiting principles, such as purposes and solution after next, to ensure that the initiative is on track and that the objectives are still the right ones. In short, this principle is about understanding that the process of managing a wicked problem is iterative, and that the solution gets better as the group's understanding of the problem improves.

Polarity Management ™

Polarity Management was developed by Barry Johnson (1992) in the mid-seventies. A book describing the technique was published much later. In essence the technique offers a simple way to frame complex problems. Polarity management is much simpler than the trippy flux and jargon-laden Soft Systems Methodology or the more prescriptive, left brained techniques of Breakthrough Thinking. For certain types of organisations or problems, it may be a better fit.

Ackoff's preference of referring to "messes" rather than problems is shared by Johnson. Johnson argued that many wicked problems should be thought of in terms of *polarities to manage, rather than problems to solve*. He differentiated between a problem that can be solved (tame problem) and a polarity that can, at best, be managed (wicked problem) through whether or not there was a well-defined endpoint to the solution process and whether or not the solution was a definitive one.

The concept of polarity is best understood through an example. As discussed in Chapter 4, Buzzbank introduced a series of best practices aimed at bringing "a level of discipline" and "an idea of professional structuring" to an IT department that was already considered to be quite innovative. In polarity management, *change* and *stability* would be the two "poles" that have to be managed. In Johnson's words:

> "Both one pole and its apparent opposite depend on each other. The pair are involved in an ongoing, balancing process over an extended period of time."

The mental model for polarity management is significantly simpler than a SSM concept map and way easier to grasp than the flux. It is essentially a two by two matrix—the kind that is often drawn on flipcharts or whiteboards in corporate meeting rooms. Each column in the matrix represents a pole—*two related but conflicting aspects, ideals or perspectives*. The rows in the matrix represent the positive and negative aspects to each pole. The positive outcomes of each pole, or in terms of the IBIS grammar—the pros, are listed in the top half of the quadrant. The bottom half contains the cons. Figure 9.3 is a polarity map for the change vs. stability aspect of the Buzzbank dilemma from Chapter 4.

L+	R+
Avoid "foolish" risks	New energy
Less mistakes	Fresh perspectives
Repeatability and consistency	Act quickly
Consistent data for analysis	Empowered individuals
Stagnation	Take foolish risks
Over-regulation	Inconsistent process
Unwilling to take risks	Lack of consistent data to make
Over-collection of questionable data	decisions
L-	Lack of sharing knowledge
	R-
Stability (structured process)	Change (unstructured process)

Figure 9.3: A sample Polarity Map

According to Johnson, organisations tended to oscillate between poles. If you accept the notion of a wicked problem as a polarity, the overall pattern traced as one moves between these poles resembles an infinity symbol. The typical path is L—to R+, to R-, across to L+ and Johnson argued that the trajectory could not be avoided. All we can do is focus on *minimizing our time spent in the lower quadrants.*

In the case of Buzzbank, perhaps management felt that the flexibility of an autonomous work culture would not scale as the organisation grew and that the risk of foolish snap decisions would increase. Perhaps the ad-hoc nature of existing process meant that management did not have the information they needed to make the strategic decisions required of them. As a result, they perceived that more predictability and process would alleviate these issues. Project management was seen as the means by which to do this.

The key issue, as Johnson saw it, is *the path we take when managing these poles*. When an organisation is close to one pole, some people will perceive the downsides of that pole, listed in the bottom half of the quadrant, more strongly than they see its advantages. As a consequence, they see the advantages of the other pole as the solution to their current problems. However, since every pole has cons as well as pros, other groups may see upsides of the pole they are on and resist change. The "crusaders" rush off in their preferred direction whereas the "tradition bearers" stay put.

Typically, a facilitated polarity management session will start out by focusing the group's attention to one of the lower quadrants, calling on participants as a group to list the downsides of that particular pole. The group then shifts diagonally upward to the opposite pole that highlights the upsides. From there, the group works its way straight down to the other negative and then through to the opposite upper quadrant. In doing so, the entire gamut of polarities is taken into account.

This method is very simple when compared to SSM or Breakthrough Thinking. A typical Polarity management session would follow these essential steps.

- Identify the polarity—determine the description or theme of each pole
- Describe the whole polarity—fill in the aspects of each quadrant
- Diagnose the polarity:
    o Which quadrant is the problem located in now? Who is crusading and who is tradition bearing?
- Predict the polarity
    o What will happen if the crusaders "win" and the concerns of the tradition bearers are neglected?
    o What will happen if the tradition bearers "win" and the concerns of the crusaders are neglected?
- Prescribe guidelines for action
    o Provide mutual assurances that the downsides of each pole are acknowledged
    o Agree on communication systems and practices to ensure that the pole is well managed going forward

Johnson stated that polarity management is not the answer to everything but in our opinion, nor are any of the methods examined earlier. Johnson also noted that a common reaction of those who have been through a polarity management session is that the problem still remains unsolved. This is based on a misunderstanding of what the technique is about. Recall that Johnson stated that wicked problems should be viewed as polarities to be managed, not problems to be "solved." This change in mindset is a core principle of the method and any facilitator using this method needs to reinforce this with participants.

Dialogue Mapping ™

We seem to be proceeding from the complex to the simple: we started out with SSM, which is conceptually dense and quite abstract and then moved on to Breakthrough Thinking. Breakthrough Thinking is, in some ways, the evil twin of SSM. Despite its apparent repudiation of the Matrix-like systems thinking that is characteristic of SSM, it is actually very much like SSM in terms of effort. We then saw Polarity Management, which is a cheeseburger compared to the double quarter pounder of SSM and BT. It uses a much simpler mental model and the supporting processes are more straightforward.

Our last PSM is Dialogue Mapping, which is qualitatively different from all the foregoing ones. Dialogue Mapping was invented by Jeff Conklin (2005). Conklin was a student of Horst Rittel and is responsible for making Rittel's 1970s era IBIS, which we described in detail in the previous chapter, into what it is today.

The philosophy behind Dialogue Mapping can be explained in two lines:

- For a project or any initiative to succeed, you need a *shared commitment* from the participants involved
- The pre-requisite to achieving shared commitment is *shared understanding* among participants

There are three elements to Dialogue Mapping: the *shared display*, the *IBIS* notation and the *mapping facilitator*. The use of IBIS has already been described in considerable detail in Chapters 7 and 8, so we will not rehash it here except to remind the reader that pretty much any discussion about issues and ways to address them can be captured using the IBIS grammar.

Dialogue Mapping essentially involves a facilitator working with a group to create, in real-time, an IBIS based issue map of the challenge the group is facing. In a typical session, the facilitator sits at a laptop, facing the rest of the group, which in turn faces a projected map on the wall behind the facilitator. The group members interact with the map as they debate various aspects of the problem. As they do this, the facilitator incorporates diverse stakeholder perspectives into the map in a way that creates a comprehensive and coherent picture of the problem space and the proposed solutions.

Unlike the other PSMs, Dialogue Mapping has no prescribed rules or principles, so there are no formal steps to follow. Further, Dialogue Mapping makes no rules as to how the conversation should proceed. Rather than impose a structure, Dialogue Mapping achieves shared understanding in an *emergent way*. It enables participants to see other world views via the shared IBIS map. Often, a group will start out with one question, and soon realise there are underlying or deeper questions that need to be addressed first. Dialogue Mapping relies on the coherence of the map to reduce the impact of tangential sub-discussions, repetition and confusion of terminology.

You might be wondering how Dialogue Mapping can improve the situation when there are no rules prescribed. To answer this, let's take a brief look at Dialogue Mapping in relation to the other PSMs.

A criticism that could be levelled at SSM and BT is that the concepts, processes and terminologies they use aren't straightforward. Participants' efforts to understand these can distract the group from the problem at hand. In other words, the cognitive overhead of understanding the methodology comes in the way of gaining a shared understanding of the problem. We note that this is a general feature of any structured methodology, be it a best practice or a not-so-good one. Conklin noted that, when following a structured approach, there is a risk that conversation is "artificially constrained." In contrast, Dialogue Mapping does not attempt to analyse the problem or get at a root cause or issue in any formal way. Instead, one just *starts* by putting up a question on the map and attempting to answer it as a group. There is no background work required in terms of understanding or explaining the PSM. One can, as the Nike catchphrase puts it, *just do it*. This, in our opinion, is a great strength of the technique.

Of course, nothing comes for free. In Dialogue Mapping, much of the onus for success lies with the facilitator. The facilitator needs to have considerable experience in using IBIS and, more importantly, building issue maps in real-time. Although the same can be said about the facilitator role in other methods, there is one key difference here. The most important people in the discussion, the participants, do not need to worry if *they* are "doing it right"; they *are* doing it right just by articulating their opinion on issues, ideas and arguments. The facilitator "translates" their contributions into the IBIS grammar and onto an integrated issue map for all to see and work with.

Dialogue Mapping has no principles, no purpose arrays, polarities or CATWOE equivalent. The technique doesn't prescribe the questions to ask, or the order in which to ask them. Instead, the facilitator listens for particular *question types* because certain types of questions will result in certain responses. According to Conklin (2005), there are seven major types of questions. These are summarised below:

Deontic questions
Deontic questions explore what is the "right course of action" or what "ought to be done." Typically they are broad questions that summarise a problem. When exploring an issue, deontic questions help to open up discussion as they often have many varied answers, reflecting several points of view. Deontic questions seek to build a broad context in which to frame a discussion and this context often has many perspectives from which it can be tackled. For this reason such questions will often be the root question in a dialogue map. Here are some examples:

- What should we do about global warming?
- What should we do about the global financial crisis?
- What should the company strategy be?

Instrumental questions
Instrumental questions seek to find the means and the methods by which a particular objective can be achieved. While deontic questions seek to build a context and framework for discussion, instrumental questions seek to find the means and methods of implementation. Often if a root question

is not deontic, it will be instrumental. Here are instrumental questions that may arise in response to the deontic questions listed above:

- How should we stop global warming?
- How do we increase liquidity in the markets?
- How do we grow the company?
- How should we cut costs?

Criterial questions

Criterial questions seek to identify the requirements, constraints or goals for a given issue. Consequently, they are generally linked to deontic or instrumental questions. They help to identify and define limits of a particular problem or its context. Some common examples are:

- What are the criteria?
- Where are our boundaries?
- What are the goals of this project?
- What do we need?

It is worth noting that criterial questions can prompt further deontic or instrumental questions which may lead to a deeper understanding of the issues under discussion.

Meaning/conceptual questions

In Chapter 1 we examined platitudes and the issue of labels and "definitionisation." The terminology that people use in discussions depends on their professional background. Consequently, even within the same organisation or department, people can have different views on what a particular term means. This may be due to differences in education, experience and their own cognitive abilities.

As you will see in the goal alignment case studies described in Chapter 12, one often finds that a group wastes valuable time arguing about an issue, without first checking that they are all talking about the same thing. "Vigorous agreement" is the phenomenon where, after thirty minutes of arguing, protagonists realise that they actually have the same viewpoint. Meaning/conceptual questions can help in fast-tracking the process of getting everyone on the same page. These questions help to define terminology used within the map. Here are some examples:

235

- What does "short term/long term" mean?
- What does "governance" mean?
- What does "structure" mean?
- What does "architecture" mean?

Factual questions

Factual questions ask the participants to articulate the facts underlying the matter under discussion. These questions are in principle the easiest to tackle. Arguments about facts can quickly be resolved by reference to a document or an accepted expert in the relevant domain. If facts are not at the group's disposal, an action item can immediately be assigned for a group member to research the answer for the next discussion. Here are some typical factual questions:

- What is the company policy on retrenchment?
- What is the current budget?
- Is X compatible with Y?

Background questions

Background questions are used to fill in the context or history of the situation. Answers to such questions tell us what is known so far and what remains open, thus setting the scene for a fruitful exploration of the problem. This helps build shared context among participants. Typically facilitators ask such questions when they notice that some members of the group lack the necessary background and context. Some examples:

- What's the background of this project?
- What is the context?
- Why are we doing this project?
- Why are we here?

Stakeholder questions

Stakeholder question ask the group to collectively consider whose ownership or buy-in is crucial to the decision they are about to make. By listing the stakeholders, the group can then identify ways to engage them. Here are some typical stakeholder questions:

- Who are the stakeholders?
- Who are the audience?
- Whose buy-in is critical for our success?
- Who should the stakeholders be?
- Who cares about the outcome?

Surprisingly, such questions can surface new criteria, new ideas, new arguments and new issues—particularly when new stakeholder groups are identified.

Asking good questions

In addition to the seven question types, Conklin points out other criteria that good questions ought to satisfy. These are:

- Questions must be simple, not compound. For example, the question "How should we design and implement the system?" is best broken up into the two constituent questions: "How should we design the system?" and "How should we implement the system?" with each question being addressed separately.
- In order to have creative conversations, assumptions should be unbundled from questions. For example, asking "What should we do to move the USA to the metric system?" presumes that moving to the metric system is a foregone conclusion.
- Questions should be open-ended rather than closed. Open questions pave the way for creativity and innovation, as well as a higher-quality conversation. For example instead of asking, "Should we implement X?" one should ask, "What should we implement?" or better yet, "What should we do?"

By understanding the general types of questions asked, a dialogue mapper can anticipate the direction of conversations and how a dialogue map may best be structured given the circumstances. There are three benefits to this.

Firstly, it prevents a dialogue map from "sprawling all over the place" and ensures that a map is not just a transcription of what is being said but a representation of the various aspects of the problem. In this respect, an

IBIS map is a mental model that shapes or frames a problem just as much as a polarity map or a conceptual model.

Secondly, knowing these question types makes it easier for the facilitator to recognise "hidden questions," where a question is implicit in statements or comments. Part of the facilitator's task is to bring hidden questions to the surface, thereby bringing more clarity, depth and completeness to the issue being mapped.

Thirdly, like CATWOE, the list of question types functions as a checklist to ensure that all of the appropriate questions have been asked. In fact, a dialogue map can be "well formed" much as a SSM root definition can. Unlike SSM though, the facilitator does not look for a root/problem definition. Instead the facilitator focuses on ensuring that the conversation is *rich,* inclusive and representative of everyone's views. One way to do this is by ensuring that all the pertinent question types have been asked.

Dialogue Mapping is both helped and hindered by its simplicity. The notion of simply *starting* with an exploration of what we know *now* can offer a lot of clarity and insight when captured and integrated into a coherent map. Instead of a long, laborious meeting where participants are prone to losing track of what's been said, there is a point of reference that everyone can see and use to focus the conversation. Furthermore, in breaking down the arguments into a simple-to-follow IBIS structure, participants are better equipped to make the kinds of connections needed to understand the viewpoints of other participants. The map is a tangible output of this collective effort, and is available for everyone in the group to explore.

Yet, because of the lack of formal structure, dialogue maps can get large and confusing very quickly. A skilled facilitator understands when the map is starting to get too unwieldy, and introduces levels of abstraction when this happens. This is done by breaking the map into more manageable sub-maps or "chunks." Referring back to "The approach" discussion from Chapter 8, a chunked version would look like Figure 9.4. Each option, as well as the criteria for decision making has been "chunked" into its own sub map. The detail of the "doing it ourselves" option is open in a separate window.

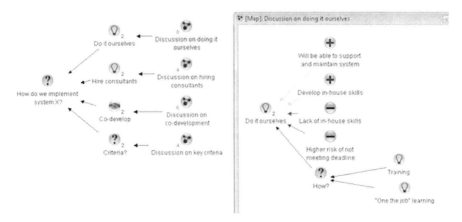

Figure 9.4. An example of a chunked dialogue map

It should be clear by now that the facilitator is the key to successful Dialogue Mapping. This person must be able to build IBIS maps in real-time, whilst keeping the discussion going and ensuring that all participants' contributions are acknowledged and recorded. The use of mapping software and a projector, as opposed to flip charts, makes map adjustment and refinement quick and non-disruptive.

While we will examine the practitioner aspects of Dialogue Mapping in Chapter 13, it is worth reiterating our observations about IBIS from Chapter 7 and 8. The IBIS grammar is particularly well suited to Dialogue Mapping because the grammar rules are simple and there are only four basic node types to worry about. The momentum and flow of discussion can be maintained without the facilitator having to stop and decide which type of node is appropriate and what sort of relationship should be drawn between the nodes. An experienced dialogue mapper can thus focus on keeping the discussion going in productive directions.

Common features of PSMs

The four PSMs we have examined represent but a fraction of those available in the research and professional literature. The ones we have looked at have different philosophical bases and provide different tools and techniques. We can imagine that a hard-core Soft Systems Methodology person would think that the polarity metaphor is not broad enough. A Dialogue Mapper may feel that the artefacts of Soft Systems Methodology are far too abstract, or that Breakthrough Thinking is far too prescribed. Similarly, a Soft Systems Methodology hippie might think that Breakthrough Thinking is like . . . "too square man."

We agree that there are differences between the PSMs, but it is more important to look at the essential *commonalities* between them.

Firstly, all begin with the basic assumption that every problem is unique. This is because every organisation has its own unique history, environment and people.

Secondly, because they encourage a manner of thinking that is expansionist, they seek *broader contexts* for the problem before jumping to solutions.

Thirdly, they all recognise that a broader shared context is hard to achieve because wicked problems are complex, messy, tangled and ill defined. Consequently, all PSMs utilise a facilitated approach with visual representations to help participants develop an understanding of the problem. Since everyone sees the same models, such approaches can help participants compare and reconcile their version of reality with those of others in the group. This helps the group develop a common understanding of the situation. Participants' insights and understanding can be fed back into the model, thereby ensuring that the models and associated representations evolve along with the group's understanding of the problem.

This brings us to our final and most important common factor: irrespective of their visual artefacts, all surveyed PSMs provide the means and methods to ask *explicit, focused questions* that are aimed at *changing the frame through which participants view the problem.* The CATWOE mnemonic of SSM could easily be used for any type of requirements gathering process. CATWOE is simply a set of focused questions:

- Who are the customers?
- Who will be carrying out this activity?
- What is the transformation taking place with this process?
- What is the bigger picture into which this situation fits?
- Who is the owner of the process?
- What are the broader constraints of the process?

BT achieves a similar end via its seven principles that provide a basis for frame-changing questions. Taking the uniqueness, purposes and solution-after-next principles as examples, we can ask the sort of questions listed in Table 9.3.

Uniqueness	What is unique about this project?
	What stakeholders, organisations, cultures make this unique?
	What is different about this project from previous efforts?
Purposes	What business are we in?
	What larger need caused this problem/requirement?
	Who are our "customers"? What are their needs?
	What is the right solution?
Solution After Next	What future problems might occur if we proceed?
	If we were totally unconstrained, how would we solve this problem?

Table 9.3: Questions arising from Breakthrough Thinking principles

Similarly, a core tenet of Dialogue Mapping is to use IBIS to extract the *implied* question in the conversation and make it clear and explicit. Dialogue Mapping also seeks comprehensive coverage of an issue by ensuring that all *question types* have been asked where relevant. This ensures that the resulting IBIS map is complete in the sense that it covers all aspects of the root question.

Clearly, regardless of the tools and methods used, asking the right question at the right time in the right way makes a big difference. In contrast to the QOC or DRL maps of the last chapter, where the *notation frames a discussion*, problem structuring methods use a more open palette of questions that can surface hidden issues and assumptions.

For example, consider the obvious question that arises from the uniqueness principle of Breakthrough Thinking: "What is unique about this project?" The question is a great way to elicit many of the divergent views on the project in the one hit. This means that most of the assumptions underlying stakeholder positions are addressed at the start, rather than in dribs and drabs over time (and often in a negative way). From a cognitive point of view, this is a very clever question to ask. Unlike asking about risk, asking about uniqueness doesn't have positive or negative connotations and is thus more likely to generate a considered response.

Dialogue Mapping facilitators have a different job in this respect. They know about different question types and are careful to word their prompting questions in such a way that elicits rich dialogue. This leads to a good, comprehensive dialogue map. That said, one can easily create an IBIS template to guide a conversation that uses CATWOE questions or BT principles (see Figure 9.5).

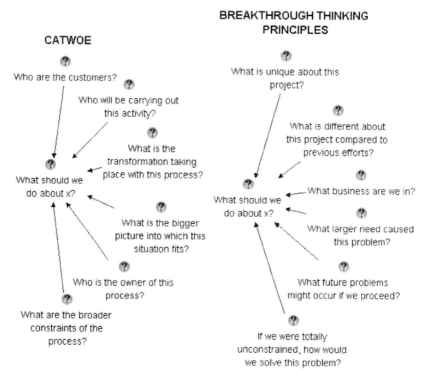

Figure 9.5: Soft Systems Methodology CATWOE and three Breakthrough Thinking principles captured in IBIS notation

Abstraction revisited

The first four problem structuring methods discussed in this chapter use abstract mental models to represent different views of a problem. However, the debate or the *rationale* behind the views is not captured explicitly. Such abstraction is in theory, a good thing because it helps participants let go of their preconceptions. However, abstract models are necessarily incomplete, and can result in pointless arguments over the interpretation of what something means. Two forms of pointless arguments are particularly common in meetings: *death by repetition* and *grenade lobbing*.

Death by repetition occurs when someone holds an opinion which they feel compelled to air in a million and one different ways, all in the same meeting. It is characterised by a participant offering the same answer over and over again, regardless of what the question is. This type of behaviour may be displayed by a person who feels that he or she has *not been heard*. Although the intent may be noble, this behaviour has the opposite effect to the one intended. The more such people persist, the less the group listens to them.

Grenade lobbing happens when someone challenges the basis or context of the conversation in some way. This is very common with wicked problems and diverse stakeholders. The grenade lob usually starts with a statement along the lines of "That's not what this is *really* all about . . ." Such statements are indications that all participants' world views have not been addressed adequately.

You will notice that PSMs such as SSM attempt to handle death by repetition and grenade lobs via high level and abstract mental models. SSM practitioners will create additional root definitions and construct contextual models for each additional world view. Each conceptual model would then need to be compared to the real world. However, although the conceptual models shape and inform the debate, the problems of repetition, tangents or grenades will continue to occur, though possibly at a reduced level if the models are representative of all viewpoints.

Dialogue Mapping, however, trumps death by repetition in a simple manner. Once an idea is captured by the dialogue mapper, it is visible along with all the other ideas. If repetition continues, all the dialogue mapper needs to do is ask the person if they have *anything more to add to the point that's already been captured on the map*. This is surprisingly effective as the disruptive behaviour becomes very obvious to the serial offender and the rest of the crowd.

Dialogue Mapping tackles grenade lobbing in an entirely different and dare we say, more elegant way. When the grenade is launched and the frame of the conversation challenged, the dialogue mapper simply captures the point made as a new issue and restructures the map to accommodate it. This restructure is referred to as a *left hand move*, because it usually involves shifting the existing map to the right and adding the new, deeper issue (the grenade) to the left. The dialogue mapper will work with the group to get at the unarticulated question that generated the grenade. This can sometimes lead to the group realising that the issue under discussion is broader than was originally envisaged (a deeper purpose in BT speak). In this way, disruptive power of the grenade lob is nullified and the map now has a broader scope and reach than it did before. On the other hand, if the grenade is irrelevant, the node will remain unconnected to the rest of the discussion. In this way, the grenade lobber and the group will see the point for the non sequitur that it is.

Thus Dialogue Mapping is unique in that it can be used to capture discourse *regarding* a PSM mental model whilst being a PSM mental model *at the same time*. Dialogue Mapping creates a representation of the *rationale* that emerges from dialogue between participants, while also representing the problem in a visual way. One can consider the highly abstract visual methods of the first four PSMs as *top down* approaches. Dialogue Mapping, on the other hand, constructs rationale from the *bottom up*. As you will see in the case studies of Chapter 12, an appropriate *combination* of top down and bottom up approaches can be very useful indeed.

Power, politics and choice

At the end of the last chapter, we noted that mapping dialogue does not, by itself, guarantee that the right questions will be asked or that the discussion will cover issues that are important. We suggest that the answer lies not in more complex notations, but in using problem structuring methods to frame problems in such a way that the right questions are asked, combined with using IBIS as a means to capture rationale as it emerges in the discussion.

The use of a problem structuring method together with visual reasoning can enable a group to reach shared understanding or a solution of principled simplicity. This is, effectively, a holding environment in action. If you do get to this stage, it is a terrific outcome, especially since many groups do not get past the roadblocks to rational dialogue.

That said, we still aren't quite done because there is a major issue we have not addressed. You can do all the above and still have poor participation. Essentially, no mapping technique or PSM, however elegant or well designed, can force someone to engage in open and transparent dialogue if *they don't want to*. What we have outlined thus far, are techniques to create *some* of the conditions necessary to improve shared understanding. But none of these methods address the issues of *power neutrality* and *empathy;* two of the five requirements required for open dialogue in the sense of Habermas (see Chapter 6).

Authority and the unwillingness to listen to others can still come in the way of a holding environment. In fact, this problem has been noted by critics of certain PSMs. For example, Dr Jim Underwood (1996) from the University of Technology Sydney made the following observations of SSM.

> "Some say that SSM assumes that all members of the enterprise have choice, in fact equal choice. The idea that managers and workers can openly discuss their problems and needs is fanciful and that SSM ignores issues of power. SSM supporters would reply that the very act of open discussion changes the organisational culture and empowers workers."

This observation holds true for other PSMs discussed in this chapter too. M C Jackson (1991), who was influenced by Habermas, made a similar observation of "subjectivist methodologies."

> "The kind of open participative debate, that is crucial for the success of the soft systems approach and is the justification for the results obtained, is impossible to obtain in problem situations where there is a fundamental conflict between interest groups which have access to unequal power resources when power is distributed unequally"

The issue of power is not a simple one, and has been explored at length by the French philosopher Michel Foucault (see Gutting 2005 for a simplified introduction to Foucault's ideas on power). Drawing on the work of Foucault, Flyvbjerg and Richardson (2002) pointed out that the theory of communicative rationality actually hampers an understanding of how power shapes discourse. So it's all easy to say "be transparent" and "allow all viewpoints," but typical organisational reality often comes in the way of such openness.

In the next chapter, we will examine what it takes to address issues of power and lack of empathy. Be warned though, it is our cue to move away from new age academic hippiedom of problem structuring methods to the sometimes scary world of contracts and lawyers.

10

Rationality and Relationships

"It has been said that man is a rational animal. All my life I have been searching for evidence which could support this." (Bertrand Russell)

Why hawks win

According to Hollywood teen movies, American high school is characterised by a strict social order where jocks and cheerleaders, who are collectively about as smart as a box of potatoes, reign supreme over nerds. Being lower down the social ladder, nerds, despite their superior intellect, have to scurry around hallways dodging nipple twisters, wet willies, atomic wedgies and the dreaded royal flush—much as mammals did when dinosaurs roamed unchallenged.

Of course, nerds and mammals have one thing in common: both got the upper hand in the end. But sometimes nerds actually turn into jocks, albeit in a different form. Often politicians are described as *hawkish* and while we both doubt that certain pollies were jocks at school, when it comes to talking tough, they sometimes act like they were. We suspect that hawkish politicians were victims of many wedgies at school and therefore, spend their adult life over-compensating for schoolyard injustices.

Daniel Kahneman and Jonathan Renshon (2007) compared political jocks and nerds in an article called "Why hawks win." In their paper they asked the following question:

> "Why are hawks so influential? The answer may lie deep in the human mind. People have dozens of decision-making biases, and almost all favor conflict rather than concession. [here we] look at why the tough guys win more than they should"

We already spoke of Kahneman and his contributions to our knowledge of cognitive bias in Chapter 2. This particular paper applied ideas from behavioural studies to understand characteristics of hawks and doves. Kahneman and Renshon described hawks as those who:

> ". . . favor coercive action, are more willing to use military force, and are more likely to doubt the value of offering concessions; when they look at adversaries overseas, they often see unremittingly hostile regimes who only understand the language of force."

Doves, on the other hand, are described as:

"skeptical about the usefulness of force and more inclined to contemplate political solutions."

They concluded their comparison by stating that:

"where hawks see little in their adversaries but hostility, doves often point to subtle openings for dialogue."

There is that "dialogue" word again. Clearly to the hawks, the authors of this book must be a pair of those wussy types who want to talk all day and never get anything done. To hawks, a holding environment would be seen as a means to facilitate a talkfest. Once this characterisation has been made, it is clear that anyone who has gotten this far into this book might be labelled as having strong dove-like tendencies. As self-admitted doves, Paul and Kailash suspect that hawks may lose interest in this book once they realise that it has no pop up pictures.

On a more serious note, human decision-making appears to be wired for hawkish behaviour: Kahneman and Renshon pointed out that the cognitive biases discussed in Chapter 2 *favour hawks*. As they put it:

"In fact, when we constructed a list of the biases uncovered in 40 years of psychological research, we were startled by what we found: All the biases in our list favor hawks. These psychological impulses—only a few of which we discuss here—incline national leaders to exaggerate the evil intentions of adversaries, to misjudge how adversaries perceive them, to be overly sanguine when hostilities start, and overly reluctant to make necessary concessions in negotiations. In short, these biases have the effect of making wars more likely to begin and more difficult to end."

In particular, *optimism* and *illusion of control* are often the basis of aggressive decisions based on misjudgements of situations. Again, quoting from Kahneman and Renshon:

"A hawk's preference for military action over diplomatic measures is often built upon the assumption that victory will come easily and swiftly. Predictions that the Iraq war would be a "cakewalk," offered up by some supporters of that conflict, are just the latest in a long string of bad hawkish predictions."

From the perspective of our discussion however, the point is that *hawks in organisations also tend to win*, just like their political counterparts.

Why dove tools aren't popular

Our focus on dialogue and our exploration of visual argumentation and problem structuring methods to this point, indicates quite clearly that these techniques are suitable for the "dove" tool box. But no matter how good a dove tool is, you still have to get past the defence mechanisms of the hawks. We note that there are many problem structuring methods to choose from, yet despite the veritable smorgasbord, none are commonly used in organisational life. Why is this so? Is it because hawks pre-empt their use?

While it's easy to take cheap shots at hawks, especially as they are none in sight as we write these lines, we feel that this is not the full story. In the Introduction, we spoke of the "elaborate rituals" clothed in terms such as management strategies, best practices, methodologies and frameworks that give us the illusion of predictability. These encourage us to gloss over inconvenient and difficult issues relevant to the problem at hand, which leaves us with an incomplete, or worse, incorrect understanding of the problem. We then discussed how problem structuring methods can help in overcoming this.

We think it odd that these powerful techniques have not gained mainstream acceptance. Certainly, some PSMs are elaborate and fail the "beer test"—that is, the methods cannot be explained and understood over a single beer. As a result, they are too complex, have steep learning curves and are overloaded with jargon and new concepts. We also think a subtle memetic effect is at work here; the techniques are not accepted because they threaten the very basis of certain popular management techniques. Hence the reluctance of individuals trained in the mainstream techniques to give the new tools a fair go. Moreover, they may even actively dissuade others from using them.

. . . **Furthermore**

In Chapter 6, we noted the five conditions Habermas listed for communicative rationality. As a reminder, they were:

- **Inclusion:** all affected parties should be included in the dialogue
- **Autonomy:** all participants should be able to present and criticise validity claims independently
- **Empathy:** participants must be willing to listen to, and understand claims made by others
- **Power neutrality:** power differences (levels of authority) between participants should not affect the discussion
- **Transparency:** participants must not indulge in strategic actions, i.e. lying!

When we look at this list in the context of the argumentation and problem structuring methods, it is clear that we cannot guarantee that *any* of these conditions will be satisfied. For example, would the use of Soft Systems Methodology or Breakthrough Thinking have convinced Buzzbank management that their new "best practice" methodology was not worth the price of the book it was written in? Would Buzzbank have even allowed a technique such as Soft Systems Methodology to be used when discussing the rationale for introducing the new practices? Of course, we can only speculate on the matter but it seems from Hodgson's description of the case study in Chapter 4, that such a discussion would have been "out of bounds." People were not consulted prior to the decision—they were simply told what was going to happen.

It seems that a mature best practice memeplex (as discussed in Chapter 3), will beat out any fledgling concept, particularly if it has a whiff of dovish-ness. Therefore, a problem structuring method, or a visual tool like IBIS, will not be enough to foster and develop the sort of holding environment that we need for these techniques to work their magic. It seems that if you want to tame a hawk, you might just need to learn some hawk kung-fu. However, we take a different tack—one in which hawks tame themselves, so to speak. As it turns out, if one wants to learn about collaborative project delivery and gain insight into what is needed to structure and maintain a holding environment, the best place to begin is in an industry that has a long, painful history of being *non-collaborative* . . . the construction industry.

What can we learn from construction guys?

If you ask people to describe construction industry stereotypes, they often come up with things such as excessive rear end flesh exposure due to ill-fitting pants, language laced with expletives, wolf whistles and most important from our point of view, a long history of adversarial relationships with customers. In the words of Graham Duff (1994), the construction industry was "the last bastion of the knucklemen where conflict has been for such a long time accepted as a normal, and indeed even perversely comfortable, element in our way of doing business."

One of the major causes for adversarial situations occurring in construction projects is the nature of the legal contracts that formalise the agreement between the party wanting the work done (the owner) and the contractors doing the work. Owners have a budget that is not unlimited. In their view, "value for money" consists of getting the work done to scope with a defined, predictable cost. Accordingly, contractors who tender for the work are required to offer a fixed price and, more often than not, the one with the lowest bid is awarded the work. For tame projects in which the work can be specified in detail, this method works well. However, for many construction projects, especially large, unique or complex ones, this is simply not possible. For one, there may be a number of contractors or subcontractors involved because of the multitude of specialist skills required. This makes the whole notion of responsibility and accountability hard to contractualise. Darryl Whiteley (2004) summarised this point as follows:

> "The conventional approach to the procurement of construction services was characterised by single point accountability, a stratification of services, (where each phase is discretely separated and carried out by different service providers), with little or no integration between the service providers from one phase to the next, led to a fragmented procurement process . . . The result is procurement processes with many interfaces, not only between the client and the key service providers, but between the service providers themselves. The management of these interfaces proved to be difficult and the conventional

> contracting strategies used did not provide mechanisms for the development of shared goals and objectives or effective communication. The contracting relationships used in these transactions focussed on selecting service providers on price with clients prescribing rigid processes and specifications that are to be followed by the service providers. Clients also unfairly assigned risk and liabilities and did not always clearly define the nature and scope of the services to be provided."

The really important thing about contracts is that they are legally binding and enforceable. Therefore, even if contract terms are unfair or cause severe hardship to one of the parties, courts will determine the outcome of disagreements in accordance with the fine-print of the contract terms and conditions. This, in combination with Whiteley's point about value for money being judged on price (and with that often a fixed price, with a fixed end date and penalties for late completion), the *majority of the risk is transferred to the contractor.*

Does this story sound familiar so far? It may, given that this style of formalising agreements is very common beyond the construction industry. For example, in this day and age of outsourcing, it has become particularly popular in IT projects. Many organisations issue a request for contractors to tender for work, even though the project may be little more than a platitude with some vague requirements hanging off it. To make things worse, such requests for proposals often mandate a fixed price, with any variations borne by the lucky contractor who wins the bid.

The perverse logic offered to justify this approach is that a fixed price contract awarded to the lowest bidder provides an opportunity for the contractor to *work smarter* to maximise profit. Supposedly, by working smarter, contractors develop all sorts of wonderful innovative outcomes while at the same time, saving money. Sounds like a winner when put that way.

Although this approach appears to offer certainty to the customer, the reality is that the lowest bidder runs on small margins and will be the most affected by unexpected or unplanned aspects of the project. Contractors have to turn a profit too and the deck is stacked against them even before the game has begun. What's important, but rarely considered, is that any adverse impact on the contractor will affect both parties.

The painful history of construction projects tells us what typically happens as a consequence of this perversity. Contractors do not come up with "innovative outcomes." Rather, the "contract-variation form" becomes the blunt weapon of choice. Among other things, this causes a great deal of argument over interpretation of what's in scope and what's not. Owners and contractors know this, so they attempt to word contracts in such a way that ensures a degree of protection for themselves, while ignoring the legitimate concerns of the other party. In other words, by its very nature, the relationship as formalised in these contracts is *adversarial*. A party enters into a contract at their own risk and therefore contracts are drafted to protect their own interests. This leaves little flexibility for addressing problems encountered in the course of the project. Relationships inevitably break down when there is a dispute. The end result, quite often, is litigation.

A vicious cycle

Over time, a vicious cycle takes hold. Cost overruns become normal on large construction projects. In an attempt to protect themselves, clients incorporate complex clauses into contracts, which make them even more difficult to administer. As a consequence, contract arbitration becomes an expensive and adversarial process. Paradoxically, this leads to even more complex contractual clauses as owner and contractor attempt to safeguard their own interests.

The long term effects of treating the other party as an adversary extends way beyond complex contractual arrangements. Some of the other features of such traditional contracts are that they:

- Foster short term views
- Do not encourage alignment of objectives between client and vendor
- Do not define accountabilities clearly
- Place responsibility for risks on those unable to influence or manage them
- Do not ensure that skills are recognized and/or efficiently used

By the late 1980s and early 1990s, cost overrun and expensive litigation were depressingly common in the construction industry. This resulted in entrenched dysfunctional behaviours that contributed to self-interest, mistrust and adversarial behaviour. The large cost overruns on these projects were, however, accepted as normal . . . "the way things are done around here." Thus came about the reputation of the construction industry as the "last bastion of the knucklemen."

Hawks turned doves

After setting this scene readers might wonder if there is any hope of recovery from such a situation. If we look at the traditional construction scenario through the lens of bureaucracy vs. post bureaucracy from Chapter 4, we can see that the construction industry operates pretty much at the bureaucratic end of the spectrum. A look at the comparison reproduced from Chapter 4 suggests this is so.

Bureaucracy	Post-bureaucracy
Consensus through Acquiescence to Authority	Consensus through Institutionalized Dialogue
Influence based on Formal Position	Influence through Persuasion/Personal Qualities
Internal Trust Immaterial	High Need for Internal Trust
Emphasis on Rules and Regulations	Emphasis on Organisational Mission
Information Monopolised at Top of Hierarchy	Strategic Information shared in Organisation
Focus on Rules for Conduct	Focus on Principles Guiding Action
Fixed (and Clear) Decision Making Processes	Fluid/Flexible Decision Making Processes
Network of Specialized Functional Relationships	Communal Spirit/Friendship Groupings
Hierarchical Appraisal	Open and Visible Peer Review Processes
Definite and Impermeable Boundaries	Open and Permeable Boundaries
Objective Rules to ensure Equity of Treatment	Broad Public Standards of Performance
Expectation of Constancy	Expectation of Change

Table 10.1: Comparison of bureaucratic and post-bureaucratic organisations (from Hodgson 2004)

But as the old saying goes, one can fight fire with fire. If there is one thing that even hawks fear, it is lawyers. For even for the most hawkish of hawks, litigation is generally undesirable. Thus both hawks and doves realised that there had to be a better way to do things. Again quoting from Whiteley (2004):

> "The high levels of disputation and intra-party claims being experienced by clients and contractors using the conventional forms of contract was seen as the catalyst that led project sponsors and contractors to look for more productive ways of delivering their projects. Parties on both sides of contracts began to realise that the "zero sum mentality" (one parties loss is the other parties gain), is counterproductive and that a change in approach was needed"

. . . and so from the ashes of adversity arose a more collaborative approach to running construction projects. While it didn't solve the problem of poorly fitting pants or excessive profanity, it did mark a change in areas that matter.

The emergence of Partnering

In the late 1980s *Partnering* emerged as a new contracting philosophy, designed to return to the "old way" of doing business by putting "handshake" back in the process. Partnering, in this context, is essentially an informal understanding between the owner and contractor as to how they will conduct business in a traditional "risk transfer" contract.

In Partnering, the principles of commitment, equity, trust, mutual goals, implementation, continuous evaluation and timely responsiveness *overlay* a conventional contracting arrangement. The parties sign a *Partnering Charter* that sets out a framework that will govern the behaviour of the parties to the contract. Typical principles set out in a Partnering Charter include commitment to the charter; equity through joint mutual goals; trust via personal relationships and timely communication; agreed techniques for conflict resolution; and continual review of progress of goals and objectives.

It is clear that a Partnering Charter emphasises some elements of a post-bureaucracy (such as "high need for internal trust," "emphasis on organisational mission," "strategic information shared in organisation," for example). It is just as clear that Partnering attempts to foster a holding environment that is necessary for truly collaborative project work.

Nevertheless, it was found that the results obtained in Partnering projects *were mixed.* It turned out that contracts still got in the way. The collaborative approach as defined by a Partnering Charter *cannot always be maintained within a contractual regime.* As Jim Ross (1999) explained:

> "Partnering tries to impose a culture of win-win over the top of a commercial and contractual framework that is inherently win-lose. The verbal commitments during the partnering process, even if genuine at the time, cannot withstand the stress imposed by gross misalignment of commercial interests."

Essentially, a Partnering Charter is *not always enough* to create a holding environment that can override the self-interest that is implicit in contractual arrangements. The underlying issue of risk transfer—the question of who is responsible for managing a risk—*still remains unresolved.* An adversarial relationship is the most common symptom of this difference in perception of risk responsibility. As a result, Partnering addresses the symptoms but not the root cause. Quoting from Whiteley (2004):

> "The Partnering agreement is superimposed over a conventional risk transfer contract where risk is generally shed from the client to the contractor and the rights, liabilities and obligations with respect to time, cost and quality are generally unfairly assigned to the contractor. The Partnering agreement and the contract are generally not aligned in their intent and processes and this creates tensions between the underlying contractual arrangement and the Partnering agreement. It is the opposing obligations, one legal and one voluntary that has led to Partnering being seen as a management tool that is used to regulate the conduct and attitudes of the participants."

The phrase about Partnering being a "management tool that is used to regulate the conduct and attitudes of participants" is reminiscent of the Buzzbank case study covered in Chapter 4. In particular, Buzzbank management termed employee resistance as being "natural growing pains" to the "next stage of evolution." Similarly, in the case of Partnering,

256

resistance to the fairness of the underlying contractual arrangements can also be seen as being in conflict with the "being nice" aspect of the Partnering Charter. Contractors were painted as not holding up their end of the Partnering bargain when they made such complaints.

It should therefore come as little surprise that Partnering had a whiff of Chapter 1's BOHICA about it. For example, Jim Ross (1999) pointed out that while there are numerous examples where Partnering is acknowledged to have improved the standard of project administration and delivery, there are just as many examples where the opposite occurred. In particular, he mentioned:

- Situations where both parties expressed great cynicism about the genuineness of the process based on their experiences
- A few notable cases where Partnering seemed to do nothing to alleviate adversarial conduct but served to *greatly increase* the associated level of bitterness

Towards Alliancing

Clearly, Partnering is not always enough to tame those pesky hawks. A Partnering Charter that asks all participants to shake hands and "play nice" does not provide a strong foundation for a holding environment that can counter a legal contract that legitimises self-interest and unfair distribution of risk. Partnering can fail when self-interest can thrive, regardless of the principles enshrined in a Partnering Charter.

The next stage of evolution in construction contracting occurred in the late 1990s, when a new form of project delivery took shape. The interesting thing about this model was that the aforementioned ideals of trust, integrity and a more cooperative relationship were *enshrined into the contract itself* and therefore legally enforceable. This was a game changer because the very tool that allowed the hawks to be hawkish and act in self-interest was now employed as a means to counter it. The big stick for not playing fair thus becomes both tangible and difficult to dodge. Imagine a contract that penalises a party for not operating in an open, transparent and collaborative manner; one in which risks and rewards are accepted equally among parties.

This mode of formalising relationships between stakeholder groups came to be known as *Relationship Contracting* or—in its strongest form—*Alliancing*. It is not hard to see that such an inclusive or win-win approach is consistent with the concepts we have discussed in earlier chapters. Rittel and Heifetz get a look in, but the key lies with Ostrom through her ideas of cooperative action through communication, reciprocity and innovative governance.

The anatomy of an alliance

Alliancing is underpinned by principles similar to Partnering but expands on them in several areas. Whiteley surveyed the principles used on many alliances and noted those common to most Alliancing arrangements. These are listed in Table 10.2.

Common Alliance Principles
Joint management of risk
Commitment at all levels
Equity for all parties
Trust
Strive for Innovation
Best for project decisions
No blame
Open book approach
Open and honest communication
Integration
Empowerment
Mutual support
Cooperation
Fairness
Collaboration and shared commitment
Have fun

Table 10.2: Whiteley's list of common alliancing principles

The similarity between these principles and those of a post-bureaucratic organisation are obvious, as are the connections to Habermas principles of inclusion, autonomy, empathy, power neutrality and transparency. Furthermore, we suspect that Umpa Lumpas would be particularly delighted with the "have fun" principle.

At first glance, some might see these as platitudes. However, since lawyers are involved it should be pretty clear that these will be defined in legally unambiguous terms. After all, this is still a contract we are talking about. Note that alliance contracts do not have any less legalese than any other contract (so lawyers still make lots of money). Nevertheless, the framework of alliance agreements turns some aspects of traditional contracting on its head. In the next few pages, we examine how this comes about.

It is not about price

The first key aspect of an alliance is the way in which participants are selected. Unlike most other approaches, the commercial aspects of the competing proposals are not discussed until later in the process, thus ensuring that participants are chosen on the basis of selection criteria other than price alone. This ensures that selection process is not distorted by commercial game play. While contractors might rejoice about not having to come up with a low fixed price for a vague requirement, the selection criteria are still very stringent. These include:

- Financial capacity.
- Technical and management expertise.
- Capacity to carry out the project.
- Track record in incorporating innovation.
- Track record on similar projects.

In addition to these criteria, one of the most important factors in selecting alliance partners is whether the partner has a corporate culture that is compatible with the alliance approach and a team that has the commitment and skills to work in such an environment. In other words, members are selected based on their *predisposition to collaborating*. This is a critical point and we will return to it later in this chapter.

Early involvement and shared objectives

Readers who feel that omitting price as a selection criterion is unusual, may find the contractual requirement around shared objectives and its implications for the project even stranger. Alliances advocate the *early involvement of the contractor and other key contributors (consultants, sub-contractors and suppliers)*. This enables the development of a joint statement of mission, principles, shared objectives and commitments for the *whole alliance team.*

The statement of mission and shared objectives is therefore much more than the desired outcome for the owner alone. Other viewpoints are also taken into account. Moreover, performance and flexibility comes from a "best for project" focus where all decisions are made for the good of project objectives and deliverables, transcending politics and corporate or personal interests.

Among other things, Alliancing recognises that contractors must make a reasonable profit so they are able to continue in business and provide a service in the future. Essentially, each partner must recognise and respect the other's *fundamental objective.* Implicit in this is the requirement that partners *understand* each other's need to achieve their respective objectives. Traditional contracts recognise the fundamental objectives of owners alone and this generally leads to the transfer of risk to the contractor.

The shared understanding mentioned in the previous paragraph is required because it forms the basis for sharing risks and formulating joint key performance indicators (KPIs) that monitor performance. The implication for owners is that they have to work to achieve KPIs that include contractor objectives—not just their own. The owners, contractors and all other stakeholders thus build a collective comprehension of what the project means to the team as a whole.

It has been said that projects are social constructs (see Cicmil et. al. 2009 for example). Alliancing makes such a social construction a deliberate and conscious process.

But there is more. If you think that the notion of owners having to weave contractor objectives into the performance framework prior to project start is a stretch, you haven't seen anything yet!

Open book approach, flexibility to deal with scope change and "no blame"

To deliver on the statement of mission, principles, shared objectives and commitments, an alliance is formed under a joint board comprising equal representation from each alliance participant. This is usually referred to as an Alliance Leadership Team (ALT). The ALT is an integrated team comprising of the best people for the project, drawn from each of the alliance participants. This ensures unbiased oversight to ensure that the project is run in a cooperative and consultative manner. It is important to note that the owner is of course on the ALT but does not have a majority vote. In fact, there is no voting in alliances. All decisions must be unanimous or no decision is made. The implication is that the ALT has to continually work towards finding a solution that all participants will support!

To ensure that project objectives are not only met but exceeded, project scope can be changed to improve project outcomes, providing all parties agree. This is done without the constraints that are normally encountered on more traditional contracting arrangements. For example: rigid, time consuming change management processes are done away with. (As the old project management saying goes, "the function of the change approval board is to reject all changes").

Participants are discouraged from litigating. This is achieved by the use of "no blame" and "no dispute" provisions that are written into the contract. All issues are resolved within the alliance, with the Alliance Board being the final arbiter[1].

Further, to ensure transparency, it is *mandated* in the contract that all accounts, processes, procedures and correspondence that relate to the alliance are available *to all parties at all times*. This is known as an *open book approach.*

Since Alliancing contracts weave contractor objectives into the performance framework prior to the start of the project, we have a situation in which owners' decisions are not necessarily final. On the other hand, contractors cannot play with contract variations or cut corners. Indeed, this is starting to look like that mythical Habermas machine we described in Chapter 6. But wait, there is even more . . .

---

[1] There are some exclusions to the "No Litigation" provisions. These relate to circumstances that are (i) wilful default by a party to the contract and (ii) insolvency of a party.

Risks, rewards and shared KPIs

One of the first things that an alliance must do is determine a *target cost* for the project. Unlike traditional forms of contracting where risk is allocated to different parties, under a true project alliance, the participants take *collective ownership* of all risk associated with delivery of the project. This is achieved by creating a mechanism that links participants' profits to delivery against the project objectives and KPIs.

Therefore exceptional performance on an alliance project is highly likely to deliver profitable outcomes for all parties. On the other hand, the pain of cost overruns is *shared* by the participants. This commercial alignment is consistent with the "no blame/best for project" philosophy that focuses on achieving joint objectives and mutually accepting risks so as to attain a "win-win" result for all.

The above indicates why such high importance is placed on selecting alliance members based on their *predisposition to collaborating*. Alliances routinely use organisational development professionals to make these assessments of potential partners as part of the selection process. However, as we shall now see, maintaining a high performing team goes beyond selection.

Behaviour modification therapy

In the movie "A Clockwork Orange," there is a famous scene where the protagonist Alex (played by Roddy McDowell) is strapped to a chair with his eyes forced open and subjected to the fictitious Ludovico technique. This is a drug-assisted aversion therapy where a patient is forced to watch violent images while under the effect of drugs that cause a near death experience. The idea is that a patient who is forced to watch the acts of violence while suffering from the effects of the drug will develop an aversion to performing such acts.

Things are similar, although not quite as drastic, in the case of Alliancing. Firstly, the concepts behind Alliancing can be a serious shock to those who are used to working with traditional modes of project delivery. Many aspects of traditional project delivery are turned on their head to make the environment conducive to collaborative behaviour. The scale of the adjustment required for all participants—from owners to contractors to other stakeholders—cannot be overstated. Certain patterns of behaviour, learnt through years of working with business-as-usual project delivery techniques means that adversarial habits are firmly entrenched. As a result, it can be difficult for some participants to accept and adopt the philosophies associated with contracting by alliance. In short, the incubation of a culture of collaboration often requires a deprogramming of old habits. Stiles and Oliver (1998) noted that the effort associated with making alliances work should not be glossed over, but the end makes it worthwhile:

> "Sounds simple? Well, in theory it is, but in practice it requires patience, determination, attention to detail, a measure of self-effacement and an unparalleled commitment on both sides of the alliance to challenge the paradigms which are so prevalent amongst operator and contractor. Just because your revered rotating machinery engineer has always used cast steel when specifying a particular compressor casing, it may not suit the project's minimalist design criteria. The result is cast iron, a cost saving to the project and a disaffected engineer who feels his integrity has been called into question. Such situations must be managed for the alliance to be effective."

The deprogramming of old habits is done through training, ongoing coaching and facilitation. At the start of a project, alliance members are often shipped off to team building courses. This is backed up by ongoing reinforcement of Alliancing ideals through coaching and training. Accordingly, alliances also typically include a dedicated coaching role of "Relationships Manager" or "Alliancing Manager" whose job is to ensure that the cogs of collaboration are kept well oiled. Relationship health is a key focus area and is regularly measured via the KPI framework.

Alliancing as a holding environment

Alliancing represents a governance-centric approach to creating and maintaining a holding environment. As is evidenced by the anatomy of an alliance, maintaining this holding environment for complex projects with many uncertainties requires considerable up-front and ongoing effort, backed up by the clout of a relationship-based contract.

After reading through the ins and outs of Alliancing, you are probably thinking that it would be impossible to run all organisational projects as alliances. This is correct: Whiteley (2004) noted that alliances are designed to be used on very large construction projects that:

- Involve significant complexity
- Have optimistic or overly challenging schedules or budgets
- Require flexibility in design and implementation
- Involve new or emerging technologies
- Require innovation in the early stages of development to make the project viable
- Require expertise that is spread over a number of organisations, including the owner

Essentially, we are talking about large, complex problems with strong "wicked" elements to them.

The above list begs the question as to when Alliancing is not suitable. Alliancing is counter-indicated in many situations including when (Queensland Government 2008):

- The personnel involved are not experienced at working together and unwilling or unable to adopt the attitudes and corporate cultures necessary to work as a team
- The owner is not prepared to invest the resources required to participate in a relationship contract and accept a risk sharing arrangement
- The project is relatively small, and the additional implementation costs are disproportionate with the cost of the work and the likely benefits
- The owner judges that the budget and financial risks are too great to enter into a commercial arrangement where project costs or schedules are uncapped
- More conventional contracts will achieve the outcomes required, since the project is not complex, risks are well understood or there is little room for improving outcomes or issues can be resolved without contractor involvement early in the design process

The lessons gained from alliances have encouraged practitioners to use similar approaches in other types of projects and domains. Further, it is also interesting to note that many existing project management methodologies incorporate elements of Alliancing. We'll discuss one such approach next as it provides a hint as to how Alliancing might be adapted to smaller projects in domains other than construction and infrastructure.

Beyond construction—the journey to scrum

Around the same time that Partnering began to be taken seriously in the construction industry, Hirotaka Takeuchi and Ikujiro Nonaka (1986) wrote about new approaches creeping into the world of commercial product development. They labelled the traditional waterfall approach to project delivery (familiar from Chapter 3) as a "relay race" and claimed that this approach conflicted with the goals of maximum speed and flexibility that are so critical to getting a new product to market.

> "Under the sequential or relay race approach, a project goes through several phases in a step-by-step fashion, moving from one phase to the next only after all the requirements of the preceding phase are satisfied. These checkpoints control risk. But at the same time, this approach leaves little room for integration. A bottleneck in one phase can slow or even halt the entire development process."

Instead, they recommend that a holistic or "rugby" approach should be used, that is, an approach in which the "team tries to go the distance as a unit, passing the ball back and forth."

> "Under the rugby approach, the product development process emerges from the constant interaction of a hand-picked, multidisciplinary team whose members work together from start to finish. Rather than moving in defined, highly structured stages, the process is born out of the team members' interplay . . . The shift from a linear to an integrated approach encourages trial and error and challenges the status quo. It

stimulates new kinds of learning and thinking within the organisation at different levels and functions."

Four years later, nerds started getting in on the act. Peter DeGrace and Leslie Hulet Stahl (1990) wrote a book on the problems of the "software crisis," referring specifically to poor quality and productivity in software projects. Apart from challenging the waterfall model (who isn't?), many alternate project delivery approaches were examined. DeGrace and Stahl cited the work of Takeuchi and Nonaka and their "rugby approach" and extended the metaphor by labelling the team on these types of projects as a "scrum."

"Suppose you have a software development project to do. For each traditional phase, you can draw from a pool of experienced people. Rather than have several designers do the design phase and have several coders do the construction phase, etc., you form a team by carefully selecting one person from each pool. During a team meeting, you will tell them that they have been carefully chosen to do a project that is very important to the company, country, organisation or whatever. This unsettles them somewhat. You then give them a description of the problem to be solved, the figures for how much it cost in time and money to do similar projects and what the performance figures for similar systems are. Then, after you have gotten them used to the idea that they are special, having been specifically chosen and challenged to do an important job, you further unsettle them by saying that their job is to produce the system in say, half the time and money and it must have twice the performance of other systems. Next, you say that how they do it is their business. Your business is to support them in getting resources. Then, you leave them alone."

The really interesting thing about this description—beyond its obvious similarities to the ideals espoused by Alliancing—is the title of DeGrace and Stahl's book: "Wicked Problems, Righteous Solutions." This hat-tip to Rittel is one of the early indications of a realisation that the wicked problem metaphor is relevant to organisational problems.

The next step in this journey came from the work of Ken Schwaber and Jeff Sutherland (2004). Inspired by the works of those described above, Schwaber and Sutherland formalised "Scrum" as a methodology for software development projects in the mid-nineties. In the years since its formulation, Scrum has gained considerable mainstream success and consequently, the status of a best practice. Indeed, as the first few lines of the "definitive" Scrum Guide state (Schwaber and Sutherland 2010):

> "Scrum is based on industry-accepted *best practices*, used and proven for decades. It is then set in an empirical process theory. As Jim Coplien once remarked to Jeff, 'Everyone will like Scrum; it is what we already do when our back is against the wall.'" (italics ours)

Scrum and Agile

Scrum is one of a family of software development techniques that come under the banner of "Agile Methodologies." Agile techniques are based on iterative and incremental development, in which requirements are not defined upfront in exquisite detail, but are allowed to evolve and emerge as the product takes shape. These methodologies share the following common characteristics, specified in the *Agile Manifesto*[2]:

- Individuals and interactions over processes and tools
- Working software over comprehensive documentation
- Customer collaboration over contract negotiation
- Responding to change over following a plan

When we compare the principles outlined in the Agile Manifesto with those of Alliancing examined earlier, it is clear that the two have much in common. We list the major overlaps below:

---

[2] Scrum and related Agile techniques are signatories to the *Agile Manifesto*—a statement of core values and principles developed in 2001 by a group of software industry representatives who were sympathetic to the need for an alternative to documentation driven, heavyweight software development processes. See http://Agilemanifesto.org/ for a statement of the manifesto.

- "Individuals and interactions" in the Agile world corresponds to commitment at all levels, equity for all parties, no blame, empowerment, cooperation and collaboration, shared commitment and have fun in the Alliancing world. Traditionally software development has aimed to de-emphasise the role of individuals and interactions. Agile methodologies, much like Alliancing, bring these principles to the centre-stage of projects.
- "Working software" in the Agile world corresponds to strive for innovation, best for project decisions and excellence in the Alliancing world. The connection becomes clear when one notes that many projects produce unusable software because the developers were not creative, made poor decisions or did not otherwise strive to develop the best software they possibly could.
- "Customer collaboration" in the Agile world corresponds to trust, open and honest communication, open book approach, integration, cooperation, fairness, collaboration and shared commitment. Note that the Agile manifesto uses the word "customer" to qualify the collaboration because traditionally software development rarely involves the customer except as an upfront provider of requirements and recipient of the final product. Agile methodologies emphasises continuous collaboration in exactly the same way as Alliancing.
- "Responding to change" in the Agile world corresponds to flexibility, cooperation, open and honest communication, equity for all parties and mutual support. To see this, note that changes in a project are typically initiated by one party (usually the customer). Generally such changes have an adverse effect on the project variables of scope, time and cost. Hence, most project methodologies tend to treat changes as things to be avoided. In Alliancing, however, the principles of open communication, cooperation, support and risk/reward sharing (equity for all parties) serve to rid change of its negative connotations.

From the above, it appears that the construction and software development industries evolved in similar ways. The Agile Manifesto reminds us very much of the notion of a Partnering Charter—a framework that guides behaviours and decisions on projects. The manifesto encourages collaboration over contract negotiation, which is basically the essence of Partnering.

Yet, despite its promise as a means to tackle the wickedness inherent in software development, there is a problem at the heart of Scrum and other Agile methodologies. From this, it may come as no surprise to our readers that we think Scrum is not the answer—well, not the whole answer at any rate . . .

The fragility of agility

Despite the noble intent behind Scrum and other methods of the same ilk, the benefits advertised sometimes fail to materialize. The main reason for this was described by Ken Schwaber in a 2008 interview (AgileCollab 2008):

> ". . . Many CIO's still think of Agile as more, faster. However, as organisations and projects flee the existing controls and safeguards of waterfall and predictive processes, they need to recognize the even higher degree of control, risk management and transparency required to use Scrum successfully. I estimate that 75% of those organisations using Scrum will not succeed in getting the benefits that they hope for from it . . ."

The success of Agile methods depends, rather crucially, on the principles outlined in the Agile manifesto. Schwaber ascribed the failure of Agile methods—and Scrum in particular—to the failure of organisations to adhere to those principles. The fragility of agility lies in the ease with which implementing organisations can bypass, or completely ignore, the principles that are absolutely critical to its success. The reason they do so is because they *can*: adherence to the principles is neither enforced nor necessarily monitored.

This is akin to the situation in Partnering vis-a-vis Alliancing. However, in contrast to the software business, the construction industry recognised that without a governance model that incorporates strong reciprocity (see Chapter 6) via mutual acceptance of risk, a charter does not offer a holding environment that can counter the negative effects of unbridled self-interest. The key point is that a charter that consists of warm, fuzzy notions simply cannot survive when risk is not accepted in an equitable manner. Consequently, the Agile principle that espouses

"Customer collaboration over contract negotiation" as a principle remains just that—a principle.

A lot of the IT industry it seems, is still running with the Partnering paradigm whereas construction has moved on. This may come as a surprise to those who work in high-tech areas—but it appears that the construction industry has pioneered a means to create a much more robust holding environment than the IT industry has.

To be fair, this is an apples-versus-oranges comparison. Alliance projects tend to be very large whereas IT projects are usually much smaller in scale. Accordingly, many of the characteristics of alliances are unlikely to be appropriate or applicable in an IT context. Nevertheless, the striking similarities between Agile principles in software development and Partnering principles in construction, offer hints on how Agile outcomes can be improved by incorporating elements of Alliancing.

When is an Alliance not an Alliance?

To understand how one might incorporate elements of Alliancing into methods such as Scrum, it makes sense to begin with a more fundamental question. When is an Alliance not an Alliance? Put another way, what elements can one remove from Alliancing and still have in place the spirit of an alliance?

This is not an academic question. In recent years the construction industry has developed and used hybrid contract models that modify the notion of the pure alliance as described earlier in this chapter. For example: some hybrid alliances re-introduce direct price competition models for selecting alliance members; others allow the owner to retain the right to overturn decisions that would be made jointly in a pure alliance.

Paul asked the "When is an alliance not an alliance?" question to Mike Kapitola and Darryl Whiteley—both individuals with considerable experience at setting up and working in alliance-based projects.

As it happened, Mike Kapitola had been pondering this very question for a number of years. According to him, even if one applied some of the elements of Alliancing to other project delivery methods, it would not magically make them Alliances. For example: one could mandate that a fixed price project must use an open book approach or that it must involve contractors at an early stage. However, Kapitola asserted that these would not make the project an Alliance. Similarly you could take these elements away from a pure Alliance, and *still* have it function as an Alliance would, provided that one key requirement is met. That requirement is . . . (drum roll please).

According to Mike Kapitola (2011), the key element of Alliancing is the paradigm of *mutually accepted risk*. One simply cannot have an alliance without the mutual acceptance and joint management of risks, where the fate of each party is intimately entwined with that of the others. He put it this way:

> "The essential principle is that the owner is inside the alliance with the non-owner participants and as such is also responsible—along with all other participants in the alliance agreement—for delivering the outcomes. This leads to a shared risk paradigm where the fate of each party is entwined with that of the other, since there is a mutual and joint management of risks. 'No Blame' and 'Open Book' are subsets of this principle as they both naturally follow. That is, courts cannot apportion blame since the owner is entwined with the other participants in acting on the risks. Open book is obvious because the owner is part of the team delivering the alliance outcomes."

Darryl Whiteley (2011), on the other hand, took a more purist view. He agreed that the equitable sharing of risk is a fundamental requirement of alliances, though it is not the only fundamental element. According to Whiteley, the other fundamental elements are;

- Full commitment to the alliance approach and alliance principles by the top levels of management in the *participating organisations*. After all, the people participating in an Alliance are usually still employed by their participating organisation. If those organisations operate under a business-as-usual management structure and project delivery approach, then this might conflict with Alliancing principles.
- Integrated governance structure and management structures that operate under the principles of trust, transparency, integrity, unanimous decision making, open book and best for project.

- Mutually agreed objectives, commitments and principles of behaviour that are bound into the Alliance Agreement (the contract).
- The inclusion of the alliance principles of trust, no blame, no litigation, best for project, win-win outcomes.
- A fully integrated project team collocated in one office.
- Risk reward schemes that include both cost and non-cost Key Result Areas that include outcomes beneficial to the parties to the alliance, external stakeholders and the wider community.

The need for structure

In Part 2 of this book, we have tried to provide practical tools to create, augment, and even challenge the mental models we use to make sense of wicked problems. The Alliancing-inspired discussion thus far has been around the notion of providing an *operating structure* that fosters the right environment for visual tools, problem structuring methods and their underlying philosophies to take root and flourish. While we do not claim that an alliance based contract is necessary for this to happen, there is ample evidence that it is a sufficient condition for the development of a holding environment in large, complex projects.

While other management texts have described the ideal of a holding environment using different metaphors (Senge's (1994) "The Learning Organisation" from The Fifth Discipline has sold him a million books), few, if any of these books, have looked at governance structures like Alliancing as part of the solution.

When you think about it, the notion of structural governance takes away some of the romanticism that other books espouse—the perfect, post bureaucratic organisation that runs on benevolence and goodwill, under the stewardship of an inspiring leader. To be sure, we share the idealistic aspirations of the heretics whose work we have examined. However, we cannot ignore the fact that although people have been writing about this stuff for many years it still has not taken root in mainstream organisational practice.

Peter Senge argued that the structures we put in place influence our behaviours. As he stated:

"Different people in the same structure tend to produce qualitatively similar results. When there are problems, or performance fails to live up to what is intended, it is easy to find someone or something else to blame. But more often than we realise, systems cause their own crises, not external forces or individuals mistakes"

We couldn't agree more. As an example, we note that Winston Royce's influential paper on the waterfall methodology (discussed at length in Chapter 3) was written when the government contracting models of the 1960s were in vogue. His ideas were very much a product of that time.

Another way to see historical context of waterfall is to have fun messing with people who are passionate about Scrum and other Agile methods. Scrum fans are intensely passionate in a cultish kind of a way, so they are an easy target. Moreover, Scrum users tend to hate waterfall approaches to software development and some of them will lose no opportunity to launch into a tirade about its evils. Yet, some Scrum adherents treat any negative press about their own favoured methodology as being due to a lack of understanding of what Scrum is "really about."

Such reactions make us wonder how methodology adherents who state that critics "don't get it" can be so blind to the fact that they can often be guilty of treating other methodologies in exactly the same way as the critics they criticise. Our blatantly unscientific method of assessing this is to ask the following question to a hard core Scrum fanatic:

"Would waterfall work if one could create an environment where all parties—as soon as they become aware of something that might affect a project materially—communicate it to all other parties involved in the project?"

You will likely get one of three typical answers. For some, especially the hard core fanatics, it is hard to answer "Yes" to this question, which in itself is quite telling. Some will grudgingly concede that it might work, while others may argue that in such an environment, *waterfall would actually not exist in the first place*. This answer has a lot of truth to it, especially when one keeps in mind that waterfall methodologies arose from 1960s era government contract models that required vendors to quote fixed prices upfront.

Note that our question simply articulates the essence of a holding environment in which open communication as suggested by Habermas can occur. Whether you agree that waterfall can work in this environment, or that "waterfall isn't waterfall any more" is actually beside the point. The question that all methodology, framework or best-practice adherents should be asking is:

> "What can I do to create an environment where all parties, as soon as they become aware of something that will materially impact on the project, communicate that fully to all other parties?"

We think that the answer to this question is what is missing from many methodologies and frameworks (and to Scrum fans who may have taken offence: we aren't just picking on Scrum here—it is merely a convenient straw man to illustrate a more general issue). While we don't know the answer to the above question for sure either, our explorations thus far offer some ideas.

Given that relationship based contracting is designed for really, really big projects, it is not exactly practical for say, your $200,000 IT system upgrade. This begs the question: *Is it possible to extract the essence of Alliancing and apply it to smaller projects and get similar results?* We will round out Part 2 of this book by indulging in some speculation about that question.

Upfront alignment of expectations

The key differentiator between Alliancing and other approaches to project delivery lies in how risk is handled. In Alliancing, risk is not transferred; it is mutually accepted by all parties in a way that acknowledges the fact that each participant's fate is intertwined with that of others: "all for one and one for all." To achieve this, we need some upfront alignment of expectations among participants and subsequent commitment to meet those expectations.

What difference would such upfront commitment make? One insight comes from Dan Ariely (2008), whose book "Predictably Irrational" is a hilarious and at times, disturbing account of how damn *predictable* our cognitive biases are. Ariely was interested in the all too common problem of procrastination. As an experiment, he gave three of his classes, on the same subject, different deadlines for handing in three papers during the semester. The papers were identical for each class—the only difference was in the way the deadlines were set.

For the first class, he *mandated* that the deadlines would be week four, eight and twelve. Students in the second class were allowed to nominate the date for each paper but were told that once nominated, the deadline could not be changed. The third class had no deadline. All they had to do was hand in their papers at the end of the semester. The first two classes would lose 1% of the grade for each day past the deadline. The third class did not face this penalty since they had the entire term to finish their work.

Now, you might conclude that the second and third groups would have the advantage, since they have the benefit of more time and flexibility in how they managed their deadlines. But that's not what happened.

The first group—the class with the mandated deadline—did the best quality papers, followed by the class with the choose-your-own deadline, with the end of semester group bringing up the rear. The difference between the second and third groups appeared to be that many students in the second group, when they self-set their deadlines, paced them evenly throughout the semester. Others in the class nominated the end of the semester (in effect the same scenario as the third group). As a result, the second group grades averaged lower, brought down by those who set their deadlines to be the end of the semester!

One of Ariely's conclusions was that offering students a tool to control their procrastination by up-front commitment to a deadline was just as effective as mandating a fixed deadline.

> "... the biggest revelation was that simply offering students a tool by which they could precommit to deadlines helped them achieve better grades"

Ariely went on to repeat the experiment in self-control scenarios and concluded that

> "We find ourselves again and again in the same predicament as my students—failing over and over to reach our long term

goals. Why? Because without precommitment, we keep on falling for temptation."

In Chapter 6, we noted that Habermas referred to actions based on rational dialogue as *communicative action*. Such actions are a result of commitments that are based on shared understanding arising from deliberations. In the context of projects, such commitments could be formal or informal agreements to perform actions ranging from recurring, operational tasks to resolving one-off issues—essentially the things that make a project tick. We feel that projects are a network of such commitments (Culmsee and Awati 2012), but where exactly are those commitments? If you ask a project manager, he might reply that these commitments are on a schedule with names assigned to tasks. However, given the way schedules are drawn up, it is questionable that that really denotes commitment. Perhaps then, we should look at how *initial commitments* are made in projects?

Imagine if you will, an "I told you so" clause, where all stakeholders articulate their fears or concerns about a project. In doing so, stakeholders place their "marble onto the table" for all to see, so to speak. All other stakeholders then have to explicitly challenge or accept this "I told you so" and also state the commitments they will make to ensure it does not eventuate. The result would be mutual acceptance of risk with the added bonus that all stakeholders would have a shared understanding of their collective concerns.

It took the Ariely book for Paul to realise that he knew how this sort of commitment could be solicited. He had dialogue mapped such "I told you so" workshops with Darryl Whiteley—who we cited earlier in this chapter. Let's look at some of the tools that were used in those workshops.

Stakeholder alignment workshops

Stakeholder analysis is a tool used to identify the groups that will affect, or will likely be affected by a project. It is commonly used in project management and business analysis (Project Management Institute 2008). The basic idea is to identify each major stakeholder and collate information such as their impact on the project, current and future commitment levels, and what is needed for their buy-in. Once each stakeholder group has been assessed, the project team develops approaches to address the concerns of each group.

Stakeholder analysis seems like a good thing to do—and it is, for the simple reason that it helps a project team understand who they are dealing with and what their concerns are. Nevertheless, it misses a subtle, yet critical aspect of project delivery. While the project team might feel that they have identified stakeholders and know how to engage with them, in a project that requires learning and adaptive change it is still quite likely that stakeholders have *misaligned expectations of each other*. In other words, by performing stakeholder analysis alone, the project team may have fallen back into the "back-room" analytical modelling trap of Rosenhead and Mingers described in Chapter 9.

An alternate approach is to conduct a stakeholder *alignment* workshop. Such a workshop crystallises the notion of commitment while also surfacing assumptions about expectations among parties *up front*, before any work is done.

A stakeholder alignment workshop typically occurs after the key objectives of a project have been agreed to. In other words, when we have enough shared understanding to delve into the expectations and commitments required to see things through to fruition. The basic idea of the workshop is to split stakeholders into homogenous groups. Each stakeholder group then works independently to list the things they can be *counted on to provide*, as well as any *concerns they have* in the context of the project and the outcomes required. These commitments and concerns are captured on flip charts or a tool such as IBIS based dialogue maps. Once complete, each group reads out their undertakings and their concerns to the other stakeholder groups. Typical output of such a process would look like Figure 10.1.

Program Management Office	What we can be counted on for	What our concerns are

	• Ensuring that scope aligns with other projects in this program of work
	• Provision of key staff that are available and have decision making authority
	• Help manage budget and accountabilities
	   • Provide inputs for reports to the finance department
	• Executive liaison
	• Manage the implication of program staging
	   • Ensuring that no projects are overlapping
	   • Ensuring that projects are adequately resourced
		• Manage end users and communication of project outcomes
		• Availability of suitably skilled contractors to start scope of work on time
		• We feel we are at arms length to the process
		• Overly simplistic expectations around scope and timing have already been communicated to the user base without adequate up-front planning
		   • Budget may be too low to deliver scope expected
		• Not sure if the communication process is in place for matters related to:
		   • Scope
		   • Design
		   • Function
		   • Budget
		   • Ongoing development

Figure 10.1: A sample output of undertaking and concerns from a stakeholder alignment workshop

The other stakeholder groups are encouraged to take note of whether those commitments are appropriate (for example: whether they are adequate or not), using the project objectives as a guide. At this stage things get really interesting. After each group articulates their commitments and concerns to the others, they generate a list of the expectations they have *for each of the other groups* as shown in Figure 10.2.

Program Management Office Expectations of	IT Infrastructure team	Business Systems Team
	• Deliver on what you said you can be counted on for • Be enthusiastic and responsive in collaborating with other stakeholder groups on the project • Have a clear understanding of scope to be delivered and budget we have for it • Ensure that all hardware and infrastructure risks have been identified and mitigation steps have been collectively agreed upon • Maintain and operate the system in a responsive manner in accordance with agreed serice levels • Procure and install all hardware and supporting infrastructure accordance with the project timeline • Minimise any disruption to delivery of the project • Remain engaged in the project for the life of it	• Deliver on what you said you can be counted on for • Be enthusiastic and responsive in collaborating with other stakeholder groups on the project • Have a clear understanding of scope to be delivered and budget we have for it • Leverage the strategic planning work that was done last year - don't reinvent the wheel • Ensure that all stakeholders have been identified and develop an overall communications strategy with departments • Innovate where possible – be flexible and responsive to change and where efficiencies can be made, they should be made • Be available for open discussions on any aspect to the delivery of this project • Minimize any disruption to the delivery of this project

Figure 10.2: Sample output of one stakeholder group expectations of other stakeholder groups from a stakeholder alignment workshop

To "seal the deal," so to speak, the stakeholder groups negotiate these expectations. Alignment is reached by one group reading out the list of expectations it has of another group and asking the target group *if they can support them*. If the group does not support an expectation, they clearly state the reasons why and *make a counter offer*.

If agreement cannot be reached on an expectation there may be a need to renegotiate the expectations. In these instances the *expectation stands* until the negotiation is completed at a later date. But once an expectation is agreed, it becomes a *commitment* to the other stakeholder groups. The commitment means that the group will deliver on that commitment, no matter what.

The intention of this process is to create an *agreed and accepted list* of each stakeholder group's expectations of other stakeholder groups, while at the same time surfacing concerns that may not have been addressed. Surfacing these expectations up front, using project objectives as a guide, reinforces the outcomes required of each group. Furthermore, commitments are made and documented, providing a baseline to which we can compare behaviour on the ground over time.

In Chapter 6, we noted Ostrom's (1998) point that designing a governance structure to support the collective work of problem solving should be *done by the group itself.* Thus, whether you go the simple route and create a database of "I told you so" clauses, or go through a rigorous stakeholder alignment exercise, the notion of upfront commitment is a powerful tool for achieving a shared understanding. It also offers a means to compare actual behaviour to what is espoused. Unlike Partnering Charters or Agile Manifestos, where we agree to "higher level" guiding principles or values, expectations are *aired directly between stakeholders* and *tested via the negotiation process* before being committed to. The world view that arises from this negotiation process helps all stakeholders to collectively create their own manifesto—one that all have contributed to, rather than have it thrust upon them by a framework or methodology.

Strong reciprocity, incentives and penalties

While we think that upfront, documented commitment takes the ideal of a high level charter or manifesto and turns it into something that is much more deeply understood and owned by stakeholders, we are still not done.

Sure . . . up front commitments make a difference to behaviours, but the issues of mutual acceptance of risk and shared incentive remain. The fate of Partnering in the construction industry shows that upfront commitments are not enough to survive a misalignment of interests and risks between parties. Without shared, mutually accepted risk, you can accept someone else's "I told you so" till the cows come home, but it may not matter a whit. When push comes to shove, stakeholders could simply choose to ignore their commitments.

If this is not recognised, people will often blame the tool that was used to create these initial commitments if things fall apart. However, it isn't the tool as much as it is human nature. What is needed is a means to encourage behaviours that *honour* commitments through the long term.

Unfortunately, typical incentive schemes reward self-interest. Economist Steven Levitt, the co-author of the book "Freakonomics" (Levitt and Dubner 2005), explained the power of incentives via the story of his three year old daughter Amanda, who was going through the stage of potty training. After some initial success, Amanda had decided, for reasons known only to her, that she would not use the toilet anymore.

In order to encourage his daughter to use the potty, Levitt provided her with an incentive that she couldn't resist. Like the vast majority of three year olds, Amanda was a huge fan of M&Ms. Levitt told Amanda that if she used the potty, he would give her a bag of M&Ms. This did the trick—for a couple of days at least. Amanda would dutifully use the toilet and collect her chocolaty reward. Mother and father were happy that they were back in business . . . so to speak.

However, by day three the law of unintended consequences began to manifest itself. Amanda would pee for a few seconds into the potty and cut off mid-stream to collect her prize. Soon afterwards, she would announce that she needed to pee again. This allowed her to amass a much larger quantity of M&Ms as well as develop some very impressive bladder control for a three year old.

This story highlights the very common problem of "gaming the system." The question is: How can we incentivise a group in a manner that avoids the side-effects illustrated by the story?

We think that some insights may lie with the notion of reciprocity that we explored in Chapter 6. There we demonstrated, via a simple example of the red-blue game, how self-interest can be beaten if the group has the power to punish those acting outside the mutually accepted norms. But the kicker is that this works only if the *entire group is also punished.* In the case of the red-blue game, Paul's team were happy to take down the opposite team and demonstrated their willingness to do so even at a cost to themselves. When faced with this realisation, the other team altered its behaviour and acted in the collective interest of all those in the game.

In other words, everyone in the game has the power to deny gains to each other but in doing so, denies themselves as well. This is the notion of *strong reciprocity.*

We speculate that if one could combine the notion of up-front commitment, with some sort of incentive mechanism that incorporated mutual acceptance of risk via strong reciprocity, we just might have the means to help organisations go beyond best practices in their endeavours. Although these ideas remain speculations, relationship contracting provides us with a tested approach that could be leveraged to incorporate these notions into other frameworks.

Herding marbles

In the introduction to this book, we spoke of the folly of trying to "herd the marbles" of individual and group wellbeing. We then spent the remainder of Part 1 traipsing through a world of platitudinal goals, BOHICA, cognitive bias, memeplexes, tacit knowledge, Willy Wonka and wicked problems. We concluded Part 1 by arguing that best practices alone are not enough; that the secret sauce to getting best practices to work lies not in the practices themselves but in the holding environment surrounding them, predicated on the notion of shared understanding and commitment.

With wicked problems, the issue is often less about finding the right answer but asking the right questions. Thus in Part 2, we started to flesh out the notion of a holding environment by exploring visual tools to represent diverse viewpoints regarding wicked problems and clarifying arguments regarding them. We then turned our attention to problem structuring methods, which help surface questions we really should be asking. By combining visual reasoning with problem structuring methods, we have a much greater chance of developing shared understanding—and with it, a lasting holding environment. Such a construct is more likely to develop and flourish than an arbitrarily imposed best practice, mainly because all stakeholders have participated in its creation.

In this final chapter of Part 2, we have attempted to outline governance structures that can help in creating the conditions necessary for a holding environment to take root. We have specifically focused on structures that make the environment as conducive to meaningful collaboration as possible, using the lessons learned from the construction industry as an example. Now that we are done, we urge you *not* to run off and form an Alliance for your next project. If you did, you would actually be herding marbles—even if your heart is in the right place. Remember that it is impossible to prescribe a one-size-fits-all process for the implementation of such structures; what works in your case may not work in ours and, as should be evident by now, there is no best practice for it.

Before we move on to the case studies in Part 3, it is worth making a rather obvious point that is discussed in Glass' (2003) book "Facts and Fallacies of Software Engineering": *people matter more than processes.* Although most managers would say they agree with this, their actions often belie their alleged beliefs. A couple of lines from the book are particularly apt in this regard:

> ". . . Nearly everyone agrees, at a superficial level, that people trump tools, techniques, and process. And yet we keep behaving as if it were not true. Perhaps it's because people are a harder problem to address than tools, techniques and process"

We believe this to be true not just of software development but any kind of work that involves a hint of creativity. Until this is *truly* understood, organisations will continue to be seduced by superficial best practices that are far from best, hawks will keep winning, memetic smackdowns will be common-place . . . and people will continue to write books yearning for something better.

Interlude:

From theory to practice

"In theory there is no difference between theory and practice. In practice there is."—(Yogi Berra)

Now that Part 2 of this book is behind us, we expect that your mind is awash with concepts like IBIS, CATWOE, Umpa Lumpas, Breakthrough Thinking, Agile, Alliancing and a whole lot of stuff between. We also expect that you will sleep very well tonight! Nevertheless, we hope that our exploration of these rather eclectic ideas and concepts have given you some insights on approaches you can take to achieve and maintain a holding environment—one that enables you to leverage the wisdom of a diverse crowd and get the best out of best practices, free of the debilitating dysfunctions explored in Part 1.

But there comes a time when one must leave the cloistered realm of theoretical possibilities and get out into the real world where marbles of wellbeing roll in confusing directions and tilts of the board are unexpectedly steep. Paul, through his Dialogue Mapping and problem structuring work, has a number of interesting case studies to draw upon, and here in Part 3 we will examine some of them. Two of the case studies come from the area of urban planning which, as it happens, was the focus area that Horst Rittel used to illustrate his concept of wicked problems in the first place. The final case study is an IT project, which had proved to be a difficult nut to crack using standard "best practice" approaches.

At this point it is worth emphasising that the methods we discussed in Part 2 are not incompatible with any best practice methodologies. On the contrary, they fill critical gaps that the methodologies either do not touch, or pay platitudinal lip service to. To that end, it is also important to note that all of the case studies operated within the framework of various best-practice standards.

Finally, to round out Part 3 and the book, we take a detailed look at what it takes to be a practitioner of the approaches that we advocate.

PART 3
From the field

11

Planners and Precinct 5

"He who fails to plan, plans to fail"—(we think, the Sphinx)

As we stated in the interlude, Rittel came up with the concept of wicked problems in the context of urban planning. The case study we are about to examine is a classic example of what Rittel was referring to. Of course, the thing about wicked problems is that some context setting is required because of the scale of the wickedness! Thus, Kailash will step back while Paul gives his take on both how urban planning works in general, as well as specifics of the situation and the problem he was called in to help with.

Planners have it tough

If there is one job in the world where you can never please anybody, it has to be that of a town planner. No matter what you do as a planner, someone is always going to be unhappy with you. Whilst IT tech support people might think they have it bad in terms of dealing with difficult users, planners definitely have it worse, especially since they do not have recourse to the solution of last resort: telling the user to "reboot and see if that fixes the problem."

Planners have to deal with as diverse a range of stakeholders as you could get: local residents who are spread widely over a wide socio-economic and ethnic spectrum, community and environmental groups, small business owners, the odd property baron, one or two multinational organisations that own the shopping precinct as well as assorted government agencies.

As we learnt in our exploration of rationality, stakeholders are boundedly rational, so it is unsurprising that such a diversity of parties means that there are many agendas and world views among stakeholders. In addition, the planner will, by virtue of their job title alone, be held responsible for every dodgy planning decision of the past that negatively affected someone. Even if the planner had nothing to do with the previous decision, it will still be their fault. By the law of averages alone, this means that there is always someone who is smarting from a decision that didn't go their way sometime in the past and are still mad about it.

If that wasn't difficult enough, the planner is also constrained by a mysterious document known as a *scheme*. The scheme is there to guide planners so that the plans they create are in keeping with the vision for the area. Schemes are great for planners because they combine acronyms and jargon known only to planners, while at the same time being ambiguous enough that two planners can have diametrically opposite interpretations of the same information. Thus, while a planner can out-argue a resident on an issue of road or land use, a commercial property developer who knows planning kung-fu can often get their own way. In fact, many former planners work for property developers for this reason.

An unfortunate consequence of the two factors—schemes and stakeholders with long memories—is the pathological fear that planners have of an event called "the town hall meeting." It is unsurprising that such meetings leave planners in a cold sweat. It is the same fear a boy-band would have if they were the support act for Metallica. This is no different from the reaction of a CEO who has to sell an unpopular corporate policy to the rank-and-file. CEOs avoid these sorts of meetings, despite being paid way more and having better behaved constituents than those that planners have to contend with. In short, the town hall meeting is not exactly the ideal holding environment for communicative rationality in the way our philosophical friend Jurgen Habermas envisioned.

Like CEOs, clever senior planners wise-up fairly quickly and rope in someone junior to do the dirty work of town hall meetings. Of course, the very fact that a town hall event is called implies there is a contentious and/or complex issue that is causing some stakeholders some angst. So, what better way to handle it than to put the person least capable of dealing with it in front of the mob?

As we described in Chapter 6, no-one likes stress and conflict, so the instinctive reaction to it is avoidance. Hence, the development of the culture of avoidance we see in many organisations. Over time, this process becomes a negatively reinforcing cycle seen both in the public and private sectors alike. Whilst many public sector agencies are criticised about attitudes to and process for community engagement[1], just as many corporations have appalling customer service too. For example, those answering service calls are usually the least empowered to do anything about customer grievances.

The irony, of course, is that most often town planners and other public servants are actually trying to improve the wellbeing of the community as a whole. After all, no-one is *deliberately* out to make a place worse than it already is.

---

[1]   Many public sector agencies world-wide are trying to change culture under the banner of Government 2.0—which in itself is a wicked problem.

The planning process—business as usual

When a new planning initiative kicks off, planners will do what planners do best—plan stuff. This will usually take place in the confines of the planners' work cubicle and generally involve the planner, and occasionally, the planner's boss. Other stakeholders are avoided because they have this annoying tendency to push their own agendas, which creates arguments. Things are much easier when you work with a small team that is completely isolated from reality.

Planners will try their best to balance the vision for an area, juggling things such as amenity, traffic, population diversity and the balance of commercial vs. residential property. This is laid out in what is often called a *structure plan* for the area. Since planners do not have the specialist expertise to deal with all aspects of the plan, other consultants and relevant government agencies are commonly called into a process called a Charrette (Lennertz et. al. 2008) or "Enquiry by Design" workshop. (We will describe what this workshop looks like a little later). This workshop is not always a smooth process because every public sector agency has its own, unique mission statement that directs its focus. Each agency mission will be different from, and may even conflict with the mission of another. Thus, an agency that maintains the road network might look at traffic flow patterns, do some projections and decide that a six lane highway is required. This will be a very different plan than a local government agency whose mission is to serve the community of the area. According to the latter, a six lane freeway might be the worst thing to do.

The planner will spend months putting together their masterpiece and when it is finally ready, it will be made available to the public via a notice in the classified advertisement section of the local paper. The public will be given two weeks to respond to the plan. Being conscious of the importance of engaging with the community, the council will upload a PDF of the plan to its web site and provide a URL pointing to it in the advertisement.

Around thirteen days into the mandatory fourteen day public consultation phase, the general public will get wind of the new plan, not through the formal notice but through the neighbourhood grapevine. Moreover, the original message has likely been distorted as it passed from person to person. Consequently, no matter how well intentioned the plan is and no matter how pressing the need for the plan, the community will absolutely hate it. With a day left, it is too late for stakeholders to make any formal submission outlining their concerns or oppose the plan. As a result, they will begin to band together and sign petitions lobbying their elected local government representatives (the councillors) to oppose the plan.

Councillors, like all other politicians, generally want to be voted back in. Sensitive as ever to negative community reaction, they will start to get cold feet about any planning changes that are copping serious community heat. Thus, if enough phone calls, letters and emails convince them that they may be voted out at the next election, they will likely strike down the plan.

The residents, having defeated those faceless bureaucrats in their ivory towers, settle back to business as usual and vote their councillors back in. However, in the longer term, the underlying problems that necessitated the plan will continue to fester and residents will complain that nothing ever gets done in the neighbourhood. A junior planner will be assigned to develop a plan to alleviate the problem and the cycle starts all over again.

There you have it folks: the strategic planning cycle. While we are deliberately exaggerating here, we are sure some readers will see similar patterns in other forms of complex project delivery. Like the town hall meeting approach, the business as usual consultative process is also not exactly conducive to communicative rationality!

The two processes, the town hall meeting and business as usual consultation, usually do not work the way they ought. One is too chaotic and the other too prone to sabotage, both by planners and self-interest driven community members.

Now that we all understand the planning process, let's take a mile-high view of the area to be planned and then progressively zoom in.

Western Australia—mine is bigger than yours

Western Australia is the largest state of Australia, covering nearly one-third of the entire Australian continent. Ever since Crocodile Dundee famously asserted that Australian spiders are deadlier than American spiders because they "can kill you just by looking at you," Australians delight in telling you fun-filled facts about their sunburnt land that are designed to feed their "mine is bigger than yours" ego. Being a proud native of Western Australia, Paul cannot help himself with a few of these ego feeding facts.

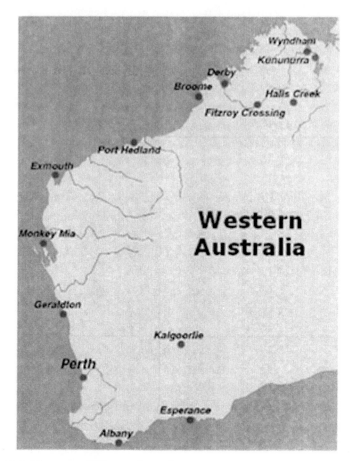

Figure 11.1: The state of Western Australia
with its capital Perth and major regional centres

Western Australia is bloody big! In land area, the state is almost five times the size of Texas, albeit with one of the smallest population densities in the world. Believe it or not, with less than 1 person per square kilometre, Western Australia is density-wise on par with Mongolia.

Western Australia has considerable mineral resource assets, particularly in the remote north of the state. It has benefited greatly from these assets, more so in recent years with the significant increases in the prices of commodities such as gold, iron ore and natural gas. The main customer for Western Australia's bounty is the economic powerhouse of China, which lies in relatively close proximity and happens to have an overlapping time zone. Australia, being politically stable, is seen as a reliable supplier.

Despite the size of the state, the majority of Western Australia's population is based in Perth, its capital city in the south west of the state. One consequence due to the size of the state is that Perth is one of the most isolated metropolitan cities in the world. The nearest city to Perth with a population of over one million is Adelaide in South Australia, which is 2,100 kilometres away. (That's further than London to Berlin and back). Despite this isolation, the population of Perth is growing at a higher rate than most other Australian cities.

Of the 2.2 million people who live in the state, 1.7 million live in the Perth metropolitan area and the rest are scattered far and wide. In terms of population, there are no other major cities in Western Australia. The next most populated town outside of Perth is Mandurah with some 83,000 people.

Because of its economic prosperity, Perth is one of the most expensive cities to buy a home in Australia. According to a report by the Council of Australian Governments Reform Council, only 5.5 per cent of dwellings are considered affordable[2].

Yearnings for the quarter acre block

With the economic and geographical backdrop thus painted, we take a quick peek at some aspects of the cultural history of Western Australia. To use a fairly broad brush, it is fair to say that Western Australians like their space—after all, they have had oodles of it for generations. One of the cultural effects of this space is that it has instilled a certain type of lifestyle centred around the "quarter acre block" and the car. This is an Australian ideal that revolves around a single freestanding brick and tile home in the middle of the largest possible land area that one can afford, surrounded by a garden, patio, barbecue and two cars in the garage. This trend has resulted in a large urban sprawl that has seen Perth become more dependent on private motor vehicle travel than most other cities around the world. As a result, local attitudes towards public transport have traditionally been lukewarm compared to other cities.

Although this cultural ideal has slowly been eroded over recent years, mainly due to the economic realities of population growth and affordability,

[2]   Affordable defined as a dwelling where the purchaser does not have to spend more than 30 per cent of pre-tax income on mortgage repayments.

many Western Australians still yearn for this ideal that their parents and grandparents enjoyed. They are dismayed at the direction that Perth is heading in, as they sit in peak hour, snail-paced traffic on the clogged freeway, looking at the bumper of the car in front of them, cursing the price of petrol and how small blocks of land are becoming. An additional consequence of the dependence on cars is that more carbon dioxide is generated in Perth than in cities of comparable size and population.

Yet, despite the changes taking place, Perth is still a small city by world standards. Many of the broader constraints and challenges faced by bigger cities in terms of physical services like traffic, public transport usage and social infrastructure are yet to really bite hard. Due to the isolation of the population, there is an understandable lack of appreciation of the extent of lifestyle changes to come.

Whether people like it or not, things are changing rapidly.

Directions 2031—setting the wicked scene

One key statistic causing concern is that the population of Perth has been forecast to rise from 1.7 million in 2010 to somewhere between 2.2 and 2.8 million by 2031. In order to accommodate this level of growth it is estimated that Perth will need, at minimum, another 328,000 houses and 353,000 jobs. If we stretch the horizon out further, it is estimated that the population of Perth will be 4 million by 2050.

You do not have to be an Einstein to realise that this sort of growth is unsustainable if infrastructure, planning and cultural attitudes were to continue as is. The pace of change affecting the community will be significantly more dynamic than it has been up till now.

These projections spurred the West Australian government to develop a planning framework called "Directions 2031"[3], aimed at setting the direction and shape of the future of Perth. Given the population growth statistics, the report makes an understatement when it states:

> "Planning for these extra residents, along with the housing, infrastructure, services and jobs they will require presents a significant challenge to Government."

---

[3]   http://www.planning.wa.gov.au/Plans+and+policies/Publications/2224.aspx

One of the major components of Directions 2031 was the notion of a network of "strategic activity centres"; in effect, satellite cities surrounding Perth, to offset the growth of the Perth city and provide overflow and better use of the infrastructure and resources. Each strategic activity centre would accommodate a much denser population than it does at present. Directions 2031 sets an ambitious target of 47 per cent or 154,000 of the required 328,000 dwellings state-wide as *infill development*—i.e. using land within an already built-up area, focusing on the reuse and repositioning of obsolete or under-utilized buildings and sites.

Towards a new city centre in Stirling

The area of Stirling, just north of Perth, was an obvious choice as one of the strategic activity centres because of its proximity to Perth city and an availability of under-developed land around a well-connected transport hub (freeway and train station). In this respect, Stirling is unique in Perth. No other proposed strategic activity centre has the combination of land availability, proximity and transport connectivity. In terms of Directions 2031, the Stirling City Centre area has a population target of a minimum of 25,000 people and 12,500 dwellings.

While the Stirling City Centre has some aspects that make it a prime candidate for a strategic activity centre with an increased population density, it is also beset with some wicked problems. Previous planning had not been well thought through and, as a consequence, the entire area lacks cohesion, amenity and heart. Traffic-wise, the area is a nightmare. A significant flow of non-local traffic is forced to pass through what you would call the "city centre" because there is no real bypass to allow through traffic north/south. This traffic snarl is exacerbated by a major shopping centre that contributes to traffic congestion. This results in Stirling City Centre being one of the most congested areas in Perth.

Pollution is another major issue. Of particular concern are a contaminated stream, now a drain, and an old rubbish tip, closed and covered years before. The tip is leaching contaminants into the nearby soil and groundwater. Cost estimates for remediation run into the hundreds of millions of dollars. (It turns out that some golf courses in Perth are former rubbish tips with a nice bit of turf on them—these may eventually face similar problems). Some local residents are unable to use groundwater for reticulation as it is so contaminated that it would kill plants in their garden.

On top of these wicked problems, the local community were particularly leery of their local government, thanks to a previous town planning scheme that delivered some very poor outcomes for them. (We will return to this aspect in a moment).

The City of Stirling and the Western Australian Planning Commission recognised that a strong collaboration between all stakeholders offered the best approach to resolving the complex issues facing the Stirling City Centre. It was in this context that the Stirling Alliance was formed in July 2008, as a collaborative partnership between the community, several government agencies and the private sector. Borrowing extensively from the construction oriented alliances outlined in the previous chapter, the Stirling alliance was dedicated to achieving "best for community" outcomes by working together towards a shared vision for a completely new and revitalised Stirling City Centre, incorporating a significantly increased local population. The vision was to:

"Create Stirling as a sustainable 21st century city—a place for everyone. It will be a hub for a diverse and prosperous community offering wellbeing for all."

Given that we are talking about an entire city, you would expect the vision to be fairly aspirational and therefore high up on the sort of platitude scale we spoke of in Chapter 3. Yet, this vision avoids outright platitude status by virtue of the fact that it offers, quite explicitly, what Stirling will be (a place for everyone, diverse and prosperous) and in doing so, makes it measurable. Contrasting this with previous redevelopments in Perth with investment in amenity and innovative forms of land use, projects of a similar nature had created high priced suburbs which *reduced* the diversity of the population. Yuppies ended up usurping families, retirees and students. As a result of a largely homogenous population, these areas looked terrific but were about as exciting as a tomb. There was no buzz of diversity and certainly no soul. Therefore, the Stirling vision enshrined the fact that a *diverse population* was critical to the long term success of the area.

But there is the rub. We are talking about an entire city, so the vision for it has to be carried down from lofty ideals into a strategic plan, right down to the day to day activities of planning and subsequent development. To achieve density as well as diversity of population (both ethnic and socio-economic), housing affordability had to be addressed. But as stated earlier, Perth is one of the least affordable cities in Australia and is one of the most isolated in the world to boot.

This is where things started to get considerably more difficult. Balancing the competing interests of stakeholders against the sometimes conflicting demands of economic, environmental and social constraints is a tricky balancing act. How do you ensure that, say, a multinational commercial property owner who wants to redevelop does so in a manner that is consistent with the vision and is also profitable? How do you plan for social cohesion? How do you increase population, reduce demand for resources and, at the same time, remediate contamination going back decades? How do you inspire a BOHICA-like cynical community that has suffered from poor planning outcomes for years to engage this time around?

Developing such a strategic plan is a classic mess of wicked problems. In developing a brand new city that is sustainable, cohesive and prosperous, we have to try and redeem the sins of the past, whilst accommodating a wide variety of stakeholders, often with particular interests and world views that invariably conflict with those of some others in the group.

Precinct 5

Although the vision for Stirling is a single, cohesive, mixed use centre, the area is defined by a variety of "neighbourhoods" or precincts, each having qualities or emphases that differentiate them from one another. Precinct 5 is an area to the west of the city centre, adjoining the existing train station and retail precinct (Precincts 1 and 2).

Precinct 5 is a suburban, residential area with very little commercial activity. Residential subdivision and development in the area began in earnest from the late 1940s in the classic single residential, quarter acre block format as previously described. Over time, subdivisions occurred and a significant number of lots now accommodate grouped housing of two or more dwellings. A large, yet under-utilised, park forms a central recreational location for residents. In other words, Precinct 5 is your typical Australian suburb from the 1940-1950s era.

However, surrounding Precinct 5, things have changed significantly. The present day shopping centre was one of the first suburban shopping centres in Perth and over the years it had expanded considerably and other retail developments had sprung up around it. As you can imagine, a residential suburb bordering this scale of commercial activity is problematic.

But if that wasn't enough, years before, many residents in this area had been asked to pay an additional levy as part of a town planning scheme that promised them better zoning (and in theory better property prices), to enable the expanded development of the nearby commercial precincts. What they got, in hindsight, are a number of problems. Rat running (shoppers taking short cuts through the suburb, via the park to avoid traffic snarls) had become a major problem for local residents making the area both noisy and more dangerous for children. Furthermore, the surrounding traffic generated by the commercial/retail activity made it difficult for locals to get into and out of their own suburb—even on weekends. The amenity of the area has been affected by the surrounding commercial activities. In fact, the commercial activity was so disruptive that, for some residents, the evenings were not night as such, but a strange kind of Avatar-like blue hue, due to the spotlights on a particularly large blue retail building nearby. Residents were routinely woken to the distant noise of supply trucks unloading and loudspeakers blaring "Price check, aisle 4" first thing in the morning.

This is the present state of affairs, yet irrespective of what Precinct 5 look and feels like now, even bigger changes are underway. Massive development will occur in the surrounding precincts as they form the heart of the new Stirling City Centre. An entire new city centre will be within close proximity which will bring new commercial activity, jobs and increased pressure on transport and associated infrastructure.

Given the close proximity of such a dense city centre adjacent, the broad plan for Precinct 5 is to turn it into Stirling's "inner city" neighbourhood, characterised by high quality, medium to high density residential buildings focussed around the existing park. According to the vision, there will be excellent accessibility to the city core, retail and associated activities via high quality, pedestrian friendly streets designed to discourage through traffic.

Phew! Of course, all of this is well and good but the residents of Precinct 5, as well as various other stakeholders, have to buy into this vision and plan for their area. The Alliance asked a diverse community group (with no formal planning, traffic or land use expertise) to think about what their area would look like in 15-30 years' time. Unsurprisingly, this is something people are not really used to doing. Add to this the pent up cynicism and resentment from the negative effects of rapid development to this point and you can imagine that residents were not overly impressed with their local government. From their perspective, this all sounded eerily like the previous zoning change which they not only had to pay for via levy but then had to pay an additional price in terms of their wellbeing.

Given the futility of the town hall style of meeting and the required alliancing principles of trust, transparency, fairness, mutual support and best for project outcomes, a different approach to business as usual was needed. An approach that turned the traditional planning model on its head; one in which residents and the broader community would be *directly and intimately* involved in a genuine collaborative planning effort; where planners and discipline experts would work together, confronting complex and difficult issues, to create a win-win solution for all stakeholders.

Rather than devise a plan, advertise it and solicit feedback, the aim was for the group to evaluate existing road and land-use options, and identify and develop new options *together*. The end goal was to create a final precinct plan that worked within the constraints of the surrounding area while incorporating local knowledge and "the wisdom of a diverse crowd" to deliver the vision for the city. In this way, the option development from start to finish would involve all stakeholders. It was also understood that advertising of the plan to the broader community would only happen *after a final option had been developed and ratified by this group* and distributed to the broader community via collaborative means.

In short, a heck of a challenge! A robust holding environment was definitely going to be needed.

A hybrid approach

The basic approach to this challenge was to hold a series of weekly workshops that in the urban design field would be described as a hybrid between an *enquiry-by-design* (Lennertz et. al. 2008) and a *value management* (New South Wales Treasury 2004) workshop, using Dialogue Mapping as the means to capture rationale.

Enquiry-by-design workshops, also known as Charrettes, are common in urban planning. They are used to bring together major stakeholders at one time and place to discuss, develop and draw possible urban designs and planning solutions to specific, place-based problems. Participants typically meet for anywhere from a half day to several days, working together in an interactive and iterative way, designing a plan to meet community and planning objectives.

Value management workshops, on the other hand, are used to discuss identified options from an enquiry-by-design effort and thus gain a shared understanding of what options provide the best balance across social, environmental, economic and engineering issues. Criteria to assess each option are identified and agreed. Each option is then rated by the group to narrow focus to preferred options.

Paul had previously worked with the Stirling Alliance as a dialogue mapper, assisting in the development of plans for the transport problems of the broader area in the longer term. This particular issue had been contentious, difficult to progress and had essentially stalled. Dialogue Mapping had proved its usefulness in these sessions, enabling the group to get back on track to develop and rate options before settling on a final road network design.[4]

In the case of Precinct 5, the model was altered in that the vast majority of the participants were from the local community, with *very few technical professionals* initially involved. The exceptions were Daniel Heymans, a senior strategic planner, working for the Stirling Alliance in the role of co-facilitator and subject matter expert, Paul in the role of co-facilitator and dialogue mapper, and Marie Verschuer as a community consultant.

Although residents had to apply in order to participate, an open-door policy was instituted. This meant that any local resident could participate and that the vast majority of participants were not planning or urban design professionals. As mentioned earlier, this also meant that most participants had a limited knowledge of the technical aspects of the problem and had little expert knowledge. On the other hand, they had something that the professionals lacked—local knowledge of the area. After all, they lived there.

This model reflected Rittel's symmetry of ignorance that we covered in Chapter 7. To quote Rittel (emphasis ours):

> "The knowledge needed in a planning problem, a wicked problem, is not concentrated in any single head; for wicked problems there are no specialists. The expertise which you

---

4   For a description of the long term transport issue and the context by which the Stirling alliance was formed, see http://www.ictcsociety.org/papers/heymanns.pdf

need in dealing with a wicked problem is usually distributed over many people. *Those people, who are the best experts with the best knowledge, are usually those who are likely to be affected by your solution. Hence, ask those who become affected but not the experts. . . .*You do not learn in school how to deal with wicked problems. The expertise and ignorance is distributed over all participants in a wicked problem. There is *symmetry of ignorance* among those who participate because nobody knows better by virtue of his degrees or his status."

Paul's task was to use the IBIS grammar to capture the argumentation of the group using Dialogue Mapping as the group worked through the pros and cons of each identified road and land use option, the determination of evaluation criteria and the identification of any other important or pertinent information. Through Dialogue Mapping, the basis of participants' judgements was made transparent, explicit and easier to communicate to others.

No hard limit was set on the number of workshops, although it was initially estimated that six to eight would be required and eventually twelve were conducted. The basic breakdown of the overall process was to:

- Set the scene by explaining to stakeholders the current state of affairs, the broader state-wide challenges, Direction 2031 vision and the effect it would have on their precinct
- Identify possible road and land-use solutions that would enable Precinct 5 to integrate with the changing environment around it (the enquiry by design bit)
- Identify additional critical information relevant to identified options
- Develop a series of evaluation criteria, clearly define them and weight them (the value management bit)
- By consensus, rank each of the road and land-use options and discard low ranking options
- Identify refinements to remaining options or create hybrid options where necessary
- Arrive at the option that will, within reason, generate the highest level of value for the greatest number of stakeholders (a solution of principled simplicity)

- Take that option to the broader community via an inclusive event
- Take the option to council for advertising and the standard review and approval process

Figure 11.2 shows the original IBIS map of the process that was captured on that first day as Daniel described the process for the first time to participants.

Figure 11.2: IBIS Map from the first Precinct 5 workshop

How NOT to create a holding environment

Step 1 of the process, scene setting, took two workshops in itself. Daniel found out the hard way just what it takes to establish a holding environment for a wicked problem.

As mentioned at the start of this chapter, many residents of Stirling carried long memories of frustration from previous planning decisions that had impacted their lifestyles negatively. Further, because of their lack of specialist knowledge about urban design, they did not always appreciate the reasons why certain things were the way they were. As a result, they were suspicious of the process, the intentions of various government agencies and of other stakeholders, such as commercial property owners. Further, there was a lack of trust in Daniel, primarily because he was a planner and therefore represented all the planning ills of the past.

Daniel started by explaining the background to the present situation, including the backdrop of the alliance and the long term challenges for the area. He outlined the workshop goals and the process that would be used to take it forward. After that, he found it hard to get a word in.

The community used the first workshop, as well as a chunk of the second, to vent their frustrations. Daniel initially countered this by, in his words, "thinking like a planner." When a participant asked why certain decisions were made, suggested options that were clearly not going to fly, or why certain options were not on the table, Daniel unconsciously switched to "planner mode" and would try and close off the option with an answer like "That would never work" or "We looked at that but it was not feasible." By around halfway through the first workshop, Daniel realised that this was a mistake because, instead of shutting down that avenue of conversation to move things forward, the opposite happened. Participants challenged the basis of the closing down of the thread of conversation and became frustrated with Daniel's answers and challenged them. In short, Daniel's attempts at giving technical answers fell on ears deafened by frustration.

From a Dialogue Mapping perspective, Paul was very busy in these early sessions. Although he captured rapid-fire rationale, the quality of the dialogue was not rich. The conversation was attack and defence and not real dialogue as such. After some time, Paul stopped mapping because it was clear that participants were not interacting with the map. Although they could see the rationale being captured as it happened, they were no more trusting of the process than when they started.

The key to changing this pattern of behaviour and the first step in the establishment of a lasting holding environment lay with Daniel. In his own words, when faced with a naïve statement or an idea that had serious problems with it, he had to stop thinking like a planner and "let it go." In doing so, he was entrusting the validity of ideas to the issue map and ultimately, the wisdom of the crowd. This is a huge change in perspective—from a technical view to a socio-technical or even purely social one.

Horst Rittel, of course, figured this out back in 1970, but neither Paul nor Daniel were aware during the workshops of Rittel's work beyond his role in inventing IBIS. In Rittel's terms, Daniel switched from being a doctor to the mid-wife role that we spoke about in Chapter 7. Quoting from Rittel:

"This planner is not an expert and he sees his role as somebody who helps to bring about problems rather than one who offers solutions to problems. *He is a mid-wife of problems* rather than an offerer of therapies. He is a teacher much more than a doctor. Of course, it is a modest and not a very heroic role that such a planner can play"

Why can't it stay the way it is?

The next thing that Daniel had to endure was the establishment of trust—one of the key elements to a holding environment. When we say endure, participants continued to vent their frustrations and Daniel continued to be the lightning rod. However, now he ceased to try and answer all the criticisms as a planner. Instead, he accepted all criticisms and did not dismiss any ideas, regardless of what his planning instincts told him. In actual fact, participants knew full well that Daniel had nothing to do with their present frustrations, but he was the representative and venting was part of the engagement process.

In effect, Daniel took on the role of punching bag, taking shots that were not really aimed at him but allowing that pent up frustration to find an outlet. Soon, the venting changed from the sins of the past and its impact on the present, to the present and its impact on the future. We were asking participants to make value judgements based on a vision for the broader area in 20-25 years' time.

One particular challenge that Daniel had to overcome was the effect of the naïve simplicity stage of coping with wicked problems, characterised by the "Why can't it be the way it is?" type question or "Well, I won't be here to worry about it anyway" comment.

Daniel patiently answered all the questions that were asked. He also let naïve statements pass and, over time, participants began to grasp the true scale of the challenge and the map started to reflect its context. In essence, Daniel shifted the frame of conversation from telling participants what would work and what would not, to letting it emerge from the conversation itself, sometimes challenging the group to the dilemmas faced by planners by asking *them* to take on the same questions he and his colleagues faced.

This shift in dialogue actually continued all the way through the workshop sessions, although in a diminishing fashion, as the group learned more about the problem and started developing their own solutions. The solutions were then examined and rated by the group.

The very act of examining and rating various options often raised more questions. These had to be answered, but this was often not straightforward because the background and context to answer the question was not known to everyone. Thus, the main discussion of option development had to be parked while the side questions were answered. Discussions thus traversed unexpected terrain and more shared learning took place. In this process, previously answered questions were often raised again by participants. Here, the IBIS maps were very valuable. Paul could point to the previous discussion of the issue, thus saving a lot of needless repetition of previously discussed issues.

Figure 11.3 show some of the contextual aspects captured in dialogue maps

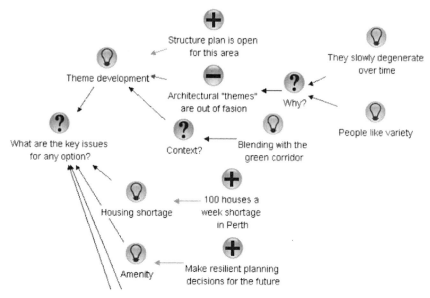

Figure 11.3: An IBIS map capturing contextual discussions on Precinct 5

Options aplenty

Once the first option was discussed, a cadence emerged and the group got into a groove in which options were examined in a consistent fashion. An option would be displayed on projector or poster and participants would discuss the characteristics for the option. After context had been set by documenting characteristics, pros and cons were solicited, followed by a debate on these. Paul captured all of this in detail into IBIS maps.

The first option that was considered was the "Do nothing" option. Figure 11.4 shows the map for this option. Note that the rationale was accompanied by a spatial image of the area in question. Via mouse-over, Paul was able to zoom the image to allow participants to understand the topographic changes that each option would require (in this case, no change).

Figure 11.4: An IBIS map of a Precinct 5 road option

The use of Dialogue Mapping ensured that all contributions were heard and acknowledged and the group did not have to spend excessive time on repetition and the sort of disruptive "grenade lobbing" that make meetings a burden for those involved. Participants went from an arms folded "Why can't we leave it the way it is" mentality to having a very deep understanding of the interlocking issues that they had to confront. They may not have been entirely happy about some of the discussions but it was no longer about Daniel or the Stirling Alliance. The group had taken ownership of the problem.

The holding environment takes root

The process of developing and rating options became quite clinical once participants started to trust Daniel and the process. In fact, after a while, participants solicited Daniel's guidance on planning guidelines and scheme constraints when debating particular points. Between meetings, some participants were out in the streets with tape measures, designing potential options to take back to the group at the next workshop. Often, these solutions were hand drawn over a basic road map of the area. Irrespective of the format or quality of the diagram, each option was scanned, inserted into a dialogue map, with characteristics fleshed out and pros and cons discussed by the group. Figure 11.5 shows a map created from this process.

Paul jokingly told Daniel at the time that he was breeding a precinct full of urban planning experts—such was the development of their understanding of the long term goals, constraints and the magical ingredient of local, on-the-ground knowledge. Daniel was taking to his planning mid-wife role with relish. Horst Rittel would have been proud!

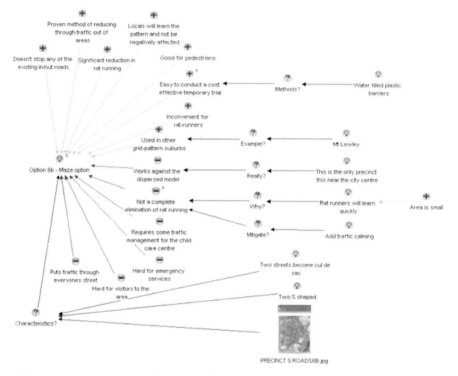

PRECINCT 5 ROADS6B.jpg

Figure 11.5: An option with topographic map, characteristics, pros and cons captured in IBIS

As the option development process continued, suspicion diminished. Such was the trust in the process that some options involved the compulsory acquisition of participants own houses. Given the impact to wellbeing that this obviously has, it was a testament to the participants' belief in the process and their collaborative maturity that they were prepared to see those options listed on the maps and rated at all.

Mapping rationale via IBIS for each option was a key to the success of the process. This rationale demonstrated the openness and transparency required. Further, because participants had the means to make their thought process visible, they were able to demonstrate their logic to the rest of the neighbourhood. In fact, on occasions during the process where rationale wasn't being captured, some participants indicated a reluctance to discuss issues without using Dialogue Mapping. They *wanted* the rationale captured so that any decisions made would be transparent and defensible in the future.

This process also resulted in considerable cost savings. Under normal circumstances, any plan put to the local residents would be professionally designed and developed by a consulting firm. The process followed here did not require it. Even better, an examination of the rationale captured revealed recurring patterns: it was evident that the outlines of a final plan were starting to emerge from the workshops.

Breakthrough moments

As previously stated, by this time some of the participants were really engaging with the process. With guidance from Daniel, they would work during the week on alternative options and bring them for the group to discuss.

One resident, Gary, had been thinking about the shortcomings of many of the options and arrived with a design that no-one else (not even the planners or road engineers) had considered. Based on what he had learned via Daniel, Gary had ensured that his design met all the planning guidelines in terms of set-backs and required distances between infrastructure. Gary's plan alleviated several issues, but best of all, it was very cheap to test out: all the road reconfigurations he suggested could be achieved with temporary water filled plastic road barriers.

Another interesting outcome came from an option that was identified as a great longer term option but considered infeasible because it required a new road to be constructed over some private commercial property in one of the other precincts. The property in question was leased by a nationwide chain of hardware stores and it was assumed that this meant that the option was not feasible.

The owners of that property, who had not been a part of the first few workshops, were invited to join. Upon examining the rationale for the option in question, the owners indicated their support for the idea. After all they reasoned "It's just a big shed." Once the current lease expired for the premises, the owner would likely redevelop the site in any event. Therefore, incorporating the long term road usage needs into a redevelopment plan was supported by the owner of the site and this option was a great medium to longer term strategy.

Another particularly powerful experience was dubbed "The magical mystery tour." Before Dialogue Mapping one afternoon, a bus was hired and the residents were taken to an area where a similar urban transformation had occurred ten years before. All participants walked around the area for an hour, soaking in the vibe, learning its history, how the area was redeveloped and how certain planning challenges were overcome. As stated earlier, as was the case with many previous Perth urban transformations, the area looked great and was a beautiful balance of multipurpose land use. Yet, it was lacking heart and felt somehow sterile, due principally to the high property prices that resulted in a lack of diversity of residents.

This tour allowed the participants to get a real sense of the issues they needed to confront, and they felt it with all senses, sight, sound and tactile, rather than in some cold, detached room with a projected map on the wall. Later when they returned to the meeting room and discussed issues, the quality of the rationale captured was much richer and faster, possibly because of the sensory immersion that took place before the mapping process began.

Developing the criteria

Eventually the identification and examination of road and land use options were exhausted and focus switched to the value management side of things where criteria for scoring each option had to be developed. Dialogue Mapping was used to determine the criteria that would be used to rate the developed options.

Different criteria were used for land use options versus road options. Previous work performed at the alliance had identified several criteria across a triple bottom line basis (social, environmental and economic criteria). The group took these criteria as a base-set and then determined which ones were relevant to Precinct 5. They also checked if there were any considerations overlooked by the base criteria. As a result of this, some criteria were added and others were removed. Once again, Dialogue Mapping was used to capture the process of criteria selection and the process was relatively straightforward.

From this process, ten criteria for roads were chosen, broken down to four relating to community and social aspects, two across environmental and four under economic criteria. Table 11.1 lists the criteria chosen and Figure 11.6 shows a snippet of the IBIS map with the rationale underpinning the criteria.

C1: Local residential street connectivity does not encourage rat runs
C2: Traffic speeds and volumes are managed to suit the local community
C3: Accessible safe walkable precinct
C4: Accessibility in around the precinct for motor vehicles by residents and visitors
ENV1: Improve safety and amenity in and around the precinct.
ENV2: High quality streetscape, public spaces and parklands
EC1: Implementation can be staged for timely delivery
EC2: Preserve or enhance the economic value of the existing community
EC3: Preserve or enhance the economic value of existing businesses
EC4: Cost of option

Table 11.1: Option evaluation criteria determined by the Precinct 5 working group

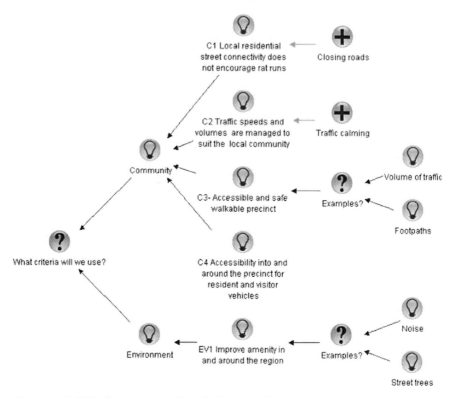

Figure 11.6: IBIS discussion on identified criteria for evaluating options

The next step was to rank the identified criteria from the most to the least important. For the probability experts who might be squirming at this point, remember that this ranking and scoring method is, by design, a *values based assessment*; subjectivity is assumed.

The group had to choose between splitting the weights of criteria evenly or ranking each individual criterion. The group chose the latter as, in their eyes, the different criteria did not merit equal weighting. The process of weighting criteria was interesting because it surfaced some additional assumptions. As an example, criteria EC2: "Preserve or enhance the economic value of the existing community" essentially means that no resident should be any worse off from any new plans. This was ranked 3rd most important by participants, based on the assumption that compensation paid to residents who would lose their homes would be *adequate in the eyes of the affected resident,* as opposed to the state. Clearly these sorts of assumptions are critical to the validity of the scoring. IBIS was an excellent vehicle to capture this key information that formed critical context.

Table 11.2 shows the final rankings along with the specific weightings applied to them. For example, a score of say, six out of ten for criterion C1 would have more weight than a similar score for EC4 due to the significant difference in weighting.

Criteria	Rank	Weighting
C1: Local residential street connectivity does not encourage rat runs	1	18%
C2: Traffic speeds and volumes are managed to suit the local community	2	18%
EC2: Preserve or enhance the economic value of the existing community	3	16%
C3: Accessible safe walkable precinct	4	14%
C4: Accessibility in around the precinct for motor vehicles by residents and visitors	5	10%
EC1: Implementation can be staged for timely delivery	6	8%
ENV1: Improve safety and amenity in and around the precinct.	7	6%
ENV2: High quality streetscape, public spaces and parklands	8	4%
EC3: Preserve or enhance the economic value of existing businesses	9	3%
EC4: Cost of option	10	3%
Total		**100%**

Table 11.2: Final rankings of criteria for ranking options

Once the scoring criteria were agreed to and ranked by participants, it was time to score each option. Each option was displayed on screen in the format of Figure 11.7, where an Excel spreadsheet replaced the dialogue map. Scoring of each option was done as a group, with an optional scoring by individuals (if an individual disagreed strongly with the group score, they could rate the option individually). The combined individual and group scores were averaged to create a final derived score for each criterion. This process took into account the criteria ranking displayed in Table 11.2.

Road Options

CRITERIA/GUIDING PRINCIPLES	1	2	3	4	5	6a	6b	7a	7b	7c	8a	8b	8c
C1 local residential street connectivity does not encourage rat runs	1	4	1	1	5	9	5	5	5	5	4	4	3
C2 Traffic speeds and volumes are managed to suit the local community	1	3	3	2	4	7	5	5	5	5	4	4	3
C3 Accessible safe walkable precinct	4	5	4	4	5	8	6	5	5	5	5	5	5
C4 Accessibility in around the precinct for motor vehicles by residents and visitors	7	5	8	5	5	2	4	5	6	7	7	7	7
ENV1 Improve safety and amenity in and around the precinct.	4	6	2	5	5	7	5	5	5	5	6	6	6
ENV2 high quality streetscape, public spaces and parklands	4	4	4	5	4	4	5	5	5	5	5	5	5
EC1 implementation can be staged for timely delivery	8	7	3	7	7	7	5	2	5	4	1	2	3
EC2 Preserve or enhance the economic value of the existing community	6	7	3	6	7	6	6	5	6	6	5	7	7
EC3 Preserve or enhance the economic value of existing businesses	5	5	4	6	6	5	5	6	6	6	1	1	1
EC4 Cost of option	9	7	2	6	7	8	6	2	4	3	1	1	2
Total	404	502	326	398	535	669	523	470	516	515	434	474	455

Scores 1 = worst, 9 - best

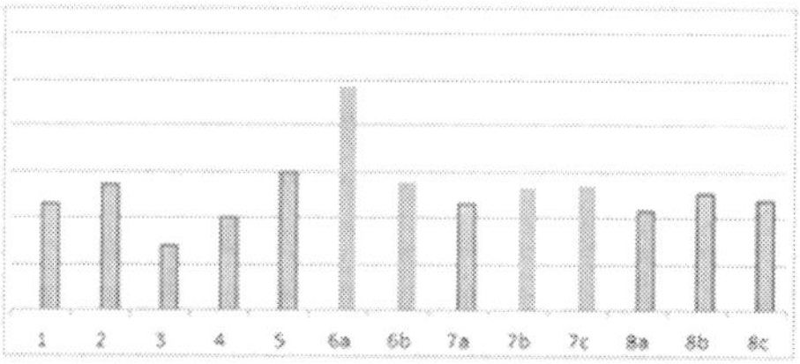

Figure 11.7: Precinct 5 road options ranked according to weighted criteria

Options were scored via a 1 to 9 scale where 1 was worst and 9 was best. Some of the low scoring options were retired fairly quickly. Retired options were flagged in the issue map along with the core reason why they were retired. Figure 11.8 is a snapshot of the map at the point where four options had been retired.

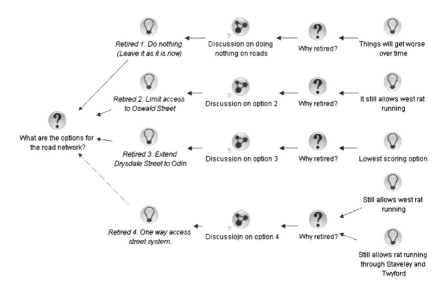

Figure 11.8: An IBIS map illustrating options as they were retired

Synergise

Over time, most options were discarded due to their low scores. A final larger workshop was held to synthesise a solution from the few road and land use options that remained. This workshop was a classic enquiry-by-design/Charrette process with large maps, plenty of marker pens and the addition of discipline experts in traffic, urban design and place building.

By this stage, the residents had a deep understanding of the problem and were much better informed in various areas of planning and urban design. Daniel, in particular, found that this stage of the process was considerably smoother when compared to many of his previous experiences.

In the workshop, three hybrid solutions were considered and a final solution was agreed upon. Some additional strategies to complement the design were also agreed to and some additional legwork was identified. From here, the final option was drafted into a detailed report with designs, illustrations and supporting arguments. All discarded options were included in the report, along with the rationale captured, a map showing the details of the option and how it rated according to the criteria. An example of a discarded option is shown in Figure 11.9.

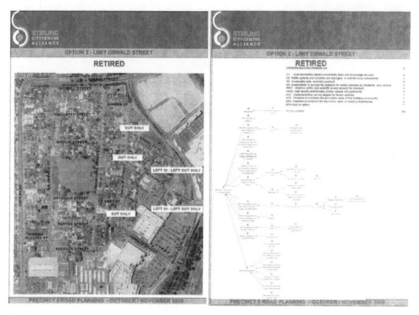

Figure 11.9: A sample page from the Precinct 5 road and land-use options report

Preliminary consultation

Soon after the final option had been synthesised, a community BBQ was held in order to consult and communicate with the wider community. Invitations were dispersed through a door to door letter drop. Additionally, individually addressed invitations were sent by mail to every person who owned a property within the precinct.

250 people from the community attended, many concerned and suspicious about any planning work. The folks were surprised to see their fellow community members sitting at the desk and welcoming them in ("What are you doing here?"). Of those 250 attendees, 57 completed a feedback sheet. The responses showed the majority of respondents felt comfortable with their knowledge about the general concepts of the plan. The majority of respondents were supportive of the traffic and movement measures being undertaken in the plan (Gary's solution).

Although the road option proved popular, there was more concern with the final land use option that the group came up with. Some attendees did not want to live in a higher density area as the plan proposed. This highlights the wickedness of planning. Despite the participants in the process having developed the plan via the shared learning of the process among participants, conveying that learning to others remained difficult.

Conclusion

This case study covers the early stages of a large and ambitious project over a long timeframe, one that is aimed at changing the face of a large urban area. Rittel and Webber's (1973) original formulation of the term "wicked problem" was made in the context of urban planning—exactly this kind of problem.

The outcome outlined above could not have occurred without the underlying alliance structure and its principles of fairness, trust, best-for-project decisions, no blame and open and honest communication. This structure provided the opportunity to utilise problem structuring methods, along with various visual methods to create a shared understanding among participants. Further, this combination of governance, problem structuring (and with it, facilitation, shared display and shared notation) helped establish the conditions for rational discourse in the sense of Habermas. In reviewing the conditions listed for communicative rationality, we see how they were achieved—albeit, approximately—in the workshops:

- **Inclusion**: This was formalised in the Alliancing agreement and was implemented "on the ground" through facilitation techniques that encouraged participation.
- **Autonomy**: Once they saw that their views mattered, participants—particularly those from the community—felt free to articulate their opinions in the workshops.
- **Empathy**: The planner listened to the concerns of participants from the community, thereby gaining their trust.
- **Power Neutrality**: The planner's attitude ensured that as far as the workshops were concerned, all opinions had equal value, and that his formal position as town planner did not give his views more weight.
- **Transparency**: Once trust was established, difficult questions were dealt with openly (consider the discussion about the option that involved building a road through private property). Participants

actually indicated a reluctance to participate in deliberations that were *not* captured into IBIS maps.

Of course, it would be a stretch to suggest that the conditions persisted through the entire course of the workshops. However, the fact that they were clearly on display at times when it mattered, indicates that the governance structures and tools described here can help in fostering dialogue aimed at achieving shared understanding and subsequent commitment to action.

All in all, Paul was glad to have been a part of it.

12

Taming Definitions, Bywords and Platitudes

"It's easy to agree with something the meaning of which is completely vague" (Russell Ackoff)

Navigating the corporate jungle

Imagine you and your project team are stuck in a thick jungle, like the ones from those war movies where soldiers hack away at tangled undergrowth with machetes. Progress is painful, sweaty and laborious. To make matters worse, the team is being stung by swarms of insects as it finds itself being surrounded by yet more vines and undergrowth.

Now, if you have spent your days simply hacking away at the undergrowth, where everything is dense and tangled, you would not know if you have strayed off course. Thus, every so often someone has to find a tall tree, climb above the jungle and look out to the horizon to figure out where the group is and where they need to go. Atop the tree, we look into the distance and make sure that the direction is still the right one, before climbing back down to advise our troops where they should be heading.

In Chapter 1 we made fun of those trite, platitudinous vision and mission statements intended to provide us direction and guide our behaviours individually and as a team. We lamented the difficulty with such statements in terms of the mirages they create. Such statements provide us little guidance when we are up that metaphorical tree, trying to find some clear direction. Without this direction, how can we provide some guidance to our tired, machete-wielding troops below? How are we to motivate and reassure them that their relentless hacking will amount to something?

If we switch from the jungle to our utopian world where everyone implicitly understands each other, we would all have complete understanding of our organisation's vision and mission. We would know what the end looks and feels like. This, in turn, would allow us to define strategic goals which would be unambiguous to all. Therefore, we would all collectively understand where we should be headed: these strategic goals would inform programs of work undertaken within our organisation and the individual projects within those programs.

When the system is defined thus, it is a thing of beauty. Each and every worker, from the executive in the top floor to the guy who fixes the photocopier, performs their tasks with a clear knowledge of the organisation's purpose and their role in it. The tasks they perform all fit seamlessly into a larger program of work that meets the strategic goals, thus realising the vision and mission of the organisation.

Sounds simple, right? After all, take the example of the Apollo missions in the 1960s. With a vision of going to the moon and a mission to successfully land a man on it and return him to Earth, an unbelievably ambitious program of work was undertaken, resulting in one of humanity's greatest achievements. It boggles the mind when one thinks of the myriad individual projects and all the complicated interdependencies that went into making that "one small step for a man." One of the reasons this program was so successful was that the vision was clear and unambiguous; it is likely that every one of the thousands of mobilised people involved knew and understood the significance of what they were undertaking, and their role in it.

The wickedness of aligning goals

The two case studies presented in this chapter illustrate two very different problems that were ultimately tackled in a similar manner. One is a large scale project in urban planning and the other is in the world of corporate IT.

The first is the same alliance from the case study in the previous chapter—the Stirling Alliance. It is an example of trying to align a broad vision with what happens at all levels: from the coalface right up to the echelons of political leadership. If you think it is hard to get consensus on where your organisation's next Christmas party should be held, imagine the difficulty of envisioning an entire city and aligning several large organisations with diametrically opposing viewpoints (think residents and property developers for one)!

The second case study illustrates the long term damage of chasing a giant platitude; how the platitude was recognised for what it was, and the road back from the brink.

Case Study 1: How do you measure a city?

Envisioning a city centre is actually not an overly difficult task. People know cities intimately and have seen enough Discovery Channel documentaries to know what their ideal city would look like. The Stirling Alliance conducted a multi-day Charrette-type workshop entitled "The Festival of Ideas" where the community directly contributed their ideas on what the city ought to look like in twenty five years (see Chapter 11 for more on the Stirling Alliance and Charrettes). Among the many outputs of this process was the city vision outlined in the previous chapter:

> "Create Stirling as a sustainable 21st century city—a place for everyone. It will be a hub for a diverse and prosperous community offering wellbeing for all"

The next step was to ensure that the eventual program of work would be governed by key performance indicators (KPIs) to realise this vision. Without these, it would be impossible for the Alliance to ensure that all projects and initiatives, large and small, were aligned with the vision of the new city.

If you have taken anything away from this book by now, it is that things are rarely as simple as they seem at first. While the vision came easily enough, the first attempts to come up with KPIs got bogged down in a tangle of definitions and ambiguous terminology. The very nature of Alliances meant that participants came from different organisations, that had their own strategic objectives and governance structures in place. One result of this was that people used differing terminology. One person's vision was another person's "noble purpose." Was it a KPI (Key Performance Indicator) or a KRA (Key Result Area)? Was it a guiding principle or a strategic objective?

It did not help that the tool used in developing this framework was Microsoft Excel. While Excel is a great tool for many scenarios, it is not so great for unpacking a performance framework, essentially because a blank spreadsheet needs descriptive labels on each column and row to clarify meaning. Participants, therefore, tended to focus attention on the definitions of the labels, rather than the empty cells below where the focus needed to be. This, in combination with the ambiguity of terminology, ensured that workshops became long winded discussions about what terms meant. This stymied efforts aimed at making progress.

Attempts to clarify the meaning of various words were made but got nowhere. As we indicated in our chapter on platitudes, attempts to gain clarity via definitions are generally doomed as there are always situations or contexts in which a particular definition is inadequate. The essence of what was being defined seemed to "wriggle out" of the grasp of the words used to pin it down.

Nevertheless, genuine efforts were made to create a performance framework. As the process wore on, frustrations boiled over, and the push to "get it done already" was high. As typically happens when there are looming deadlines and pressures for results, push came to an almighty shove, and a goal and KPI framework was developed by a small subset of Alliance staff members who put in one of those "above and beyond" efforts.

But any sense of relief that the job was done was short-lived. The key problem was a lack of buy-in from those who were not directly involved with this effort. The attempt to tame "wickedness" of the problem by reducing the number of participants in the process did not work. It seldom does, and even in cases where it *seems* to work, the result tends not to survive the test of commitment. It was therefore no surprise that many felt that the framework had not been consultative enough and did not represent input from the entire spectrum of stakeholders. This was disheartening to those Alliance members who had made a heroic effort to complete the framework.

The visible effect of this lack of shared commitment manifested itself via differences of opinion on priorities and the importance and priority of particular projects. It exposed gaps between vision, values and behaviours among participants. When stakeholders with particular interests rattled their sabres, there were long and heated arguments about the validity of their claims.

To return to our jungle metaphor, the people on the ground were hacking away but were not confident that those up the tree looking out to the horizon of the vision were pointing them in the right direction.

A new initiative

Spurred by the success of the precinct planning sessions outlined in the last chapter, a wider, more inclusive working group was formed to nail this issue of aligning goals. This working group had a varied make-up, ranging from community members to a variety of discipline experts across the public and private sector. As part of this, Paul was engaged to map the dialogue of the kick-off meeting. Another consultant, Darryl Whiteley (who figured in Chapter 10's discussion on Alliancing) had also been engaged to steer and facilitate the process.

Darryl has an extensive background in Alliancing, project delivery, project contract management and goal alignment. Paul and Darryl had worked together before in various collaborative workshops aimed at shared understanding. Despite having very different backgrounds and skill sets, Darryl and Paul had a lot in common. Although Darryl's long career in the management and delivery of large scale infrastructure and construction projects around the world was light years away from Paul's IT based background, both recognised the importance of shared commitment for project success.

During the kick off meeting, Darryl suggested to the working group that a combination of Dialogue Mapping and a problem structuring framework he had studied a decade prior, might help in achieving what had eluded the team thus far . . . shared understanding and commitment to an integrated set of goals and measures. The framework Darryl suggested was the "Breakthrough Thinking" method that we examined in Chapter 9. This was accepted, and Darryl and Paul formulated a hybrid approach that married the Breakthrough Thinking process of problem structuring with the issue-based, conversational approach of IBIS and Dialogue Mapping.

Cherry picking . . .

Darryl's belief of the suitability of Breakthrough Thinking stemmed from the method's focus on ensuring that the true purpose of a project or program is fleshed out in sufficient detail before commencement of work. Darryl argued that conventional thinking focuses on data collection and analysis, finding out what is wrong, identifying facts and truths and applying *past solutions*. Here we were working to create a crystal ball for a vision that was set twenty five years into the future. The problem was not at the vision end, nor at the KPI end (as it is easy to come up with measures), but all the mushy stuff in the middle that linked the two. In effect, here was no clear chain of reasoning linking the two ends.

The Breakthrough Thinking approach is based on the seven principles described in Chapter 9. But like most of the authors of such problem structuring methods (and best practice methodologies for that matter), Nadler and Hibino did not advocate rigidly sticking to the rules that are laid out. Darryl and Paul cherry-picked what they needed and used only *three* of the seven principles: the uniqueness, solution-after-next and purpose principles. To refresh your memory:

Uniqueness is used to put a problem into context. It assumes that no two situations are the same and therefore no two problems are the same. For the goal alignment task at hand, the fact that no-one could agree on performance framework was testament to the truth of this claim. Each attempt to transplant a solution that had worked for one agency in another completely different situation ended up widening the gap between the agency and all others involved in the process.

From a practical viewpoint, uniqueness is about asking a simple question. "What is unique about this city?" This question happens to be a great way to collect many of the divergent views on the project in one hit. This means that most of the context is fleshed out at the start, rather than in dribs and drabs over time—often in a negative way.

From a cognitive point of view, this is also a very clever, if obvious, question to ask. Asking about uniqueness doesn't have a positive or negative connotation. In the case of Stirling for example, it was considered that the area was the most congested traffic area in Perth. Equally, unique was the fact that the alliance model that was set up had never been tried before and participants were proud and felt privileged to be involved in something truly ground-breaking on a national scale. (A planning alliance of this type and scale had never been attempted before in Australia).

Solution-after-next is the principle that today's solutions do not solve tomorrow's problems. As Albert Einstein once said, "The problems that exist in the world today cannot be solved by the level of thinking that created them." Solution after next is about clarity of vision, using methods to stimulate creativity while looking into the crystal ball. It challenges participants to think beyond their initial solutions, by a process of iteratively asking questions such as:

- What future problems may occur if we were to choose the proposed course of action?
- If we were unconstrained, how would we solve those problems now?

By framing questions in this way, we often find emergent solutions to potential problems that were originally not on the radar.

Purpose principle is predicated on the notion that many interrelated problems are separated, in space and time, from their causes. Thus, the connection between the two isn't always evident. The classical approach to addressing purpose in Breakthrough Thinking is to create an array of purpose statements, ordered from most specific purpose to the most broad or fundamental purpose. Figure 9.2 from Chapter 9 illustrated a basic example of this idea.

Darryl and Paul, however, did not use this method. The *Kapitola Pathway* map, described in Chapter 7, was chosen instead. Daryl and Paul found that the Why/How structure was the ideal visual means to create an interactive view of purpose expansion that could easily be evolved over time.

As you may recall from Chapter 7, a Kapitola Pathway diagram is a variant of a causal map that utilises a relationship based on direction. Any node that you focus on is a "What" node. The two questions that are asked from any given "What" node are "Why" or "How." The former addresses the reasoning behind the goal described by the node and the latter, how it will be achieved. A "Why" answer is drawn to the *left* of the current node and any "How answer" is drawn to the *right*. Therefore, the diagram is bi-directional, with the idea being that as you add more and more nodes to the right, you should see things that are *measurable* (i.e. lower level goals) and as you move to the left, you are getting to the *underlying purpose* (or vision) of the project or program.

If we left it at that, some readers may argue that the Why/How ontology is simply a reworking of other cause/effect type models such as the Results Chain (Figure 8.5). There is some truth to this, but there are four aspects of the Kapitola pathway that made it particularly suitable for this goal alignment effort.

1. **Avoiding definitions:** The beauty of Kapitola's approach is that it focuses solely on the goals and purposes of the project *itself*. It avoids two forms of myopia that comes with this sort of work. Firstly, there is no need to define fancy terminology to focus the discussions. There is no "KRA," "KPI" or "noble purpose." Just a goal that is expanded on by asking why or how. This sidesteps the issue of terminology arguments by focusing participants on core purposes and the actions required to make those purposes a reality.

2. **Simplicity**: The structure of the Kapitola Pathway is about as simple as it gets. Most other diagrams of this type, such as results chains, have different visual symbols to represent different aspects of a problem. Thus, a result chain might use a square for an "initiative," a circle for an "outcome," a hexagon for an "assumption" and so on. The Kapitola why/how ontology, on the other hand, is even simpler than IBIS, in that there is one type of node (goal) and one type of relationship (why/how). It is, therefore, very easy to use. One can just put it down on paper or computer without having to worry about rules of grammar involving different types of nodes.

3. **The ultimate left hand goal:** Another interesting aspect of the Kapitola Pathway comes from an observation that Mike Kapitola made when he first showed it to Paul. Unlike any parent who has had to deal with their toddler asking "Are we there yet?" with a Kapitola map, there is a limit to how far *left* you can go. In other words, asking "Why" and then "Why" again and again does actually come to a stop. Mike argued that for any project, if you keep asking "Why?" you will invariably end up at "wellbeing" as the ultimate goal. Once you arrive at wellbeing, there is no further "Why." Try it yourself:

   - Question: Why do we want wellbeing?
   - Answer: So we can have wellbeing

   It is the ultimate reason we embark on any organisational initiative—and now you know why we started our book with the wellbeing marble board analogy in the Introduction.

4. **IBIS Coexistence:** When Mike originally showed Paul his map, he drew the map on a napkin at a cafe. Unfortunately (or perhaps fortunately), Mike and Paul only had one bar napkin at the table so ran out of space as they worked through Mike's hand-drawn model. With no spare napkins within the vicinity, Paul grabbed his laptop and tried out Mike's model using the Dialogue Mapping software, Compendium. The simplicity of Mike's ontology meant

that within a minute or so, he was able to reproduce it in software as shown in Figure 12.1.

Utilising Compendium meant that one could adjust the map quickly and very easily on the fly—something that is hard to do on paper. Thus, if a new goal arose, it could easily be added to the map and the consequent on-the-fly adjustments of relationships between the nodes could be just as easily managed.

As an improvisation, Paul opted to use Compendium map nodes to represent each goal. This was an important enhancement because each of the goal nodes *could have an IBIS map inside it*. In other words, we could *dive down* into a dialogue involving goal details *within the same map*. The top level map was the Kapitola Pathway and the sub maps could then use the IBIS structure within them. Thus, if we wished to discuss the context around a given goal, argue the validity of the goal, we could click on the map node, and within it, start to use IBIS rationale to do so.

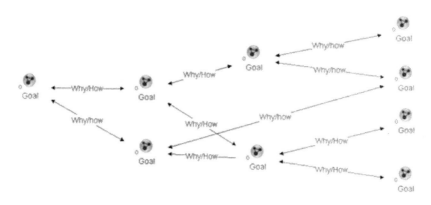

Figure 12.1: A Kapitola Pathway map utilising Compendium

The process

Armed with this recipe of Breakthrough Thinking, IBIS, the Kapitola Pathway and Dialogue Mapping, we set to work. Six workshops were held in all, each with a diverse group of participants—ranging from community representatives from the Stirling area to planning and delivery professionals from various government agencies and private industry.

The first workshop was held the week after the kick off meeting. The initial focus was on the uniqueness principle. From a Dialogue Mapping point of view, it was a fairly standard affair: IBIS was used to capture answers to the root question of "What is unique about this project?"

Participants were encouraged to put anything they felt contributed to the project uniqueness onto the map. Due to the diversity of the participants, the final uniqueness map was large—much larger than any of the participants had expected it to be.

After the meeting, a copy of the raw uniqueness map was taken and restructured via categorising each unique element in terms of economic, governance, social and environmental uniqueness. The map also incorporated photographs to augment the rationale collected by participants (see Figure 12.2).

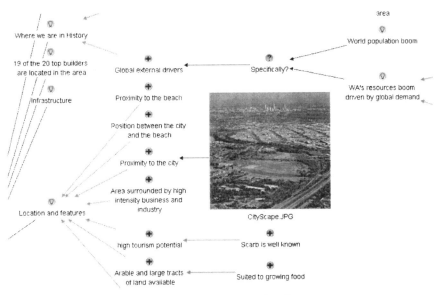

Figure 12.2: An excerpt of an IBIS map augmented with imagery

With context set via the uniqueness principle, the group moved onto the purpose expansion phase of Breakthrough Thinking. This was where we utilised a combination of the Kapitola Pathway and IBIS together. We began with a very simple and obvious top level map. All it listed was the core objective for Stirling and how the Alliance's vision related to it. We also enshrined Mike's principle that wellbeing was the ultimate "Why."

This was the area where previous attempts to create a framework faltered. However, in contrast to the past difficulties of arguments over labels at this stage, participants did not take very long to get into the groove this time. Fairly early in the meeting, participants realised that by asking "Why," the context of Stirling harmonising with the greater Perth area had not been taken into account. Accordingly, an additional left hand node was added as shown in Figure 12.3.

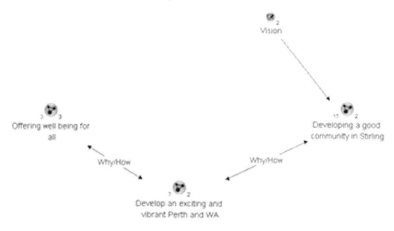

Figure 12.3: An early stage of the purpose expansion

The rest of the workshop continued in this fashion, mainly asking "How" questions and working from left to right. Conversation was not constrained, and Paul would switch between using the top level Kapitola Pathway to capture key purposes and lower-level IBIS maps to capture the dialogue on specifics. The IBIS sub-maps contained context, assumptions and facts to do with each top level "purpose."

By the time the workshop was over, the map had expanded in various directions as directed by the conversation. Figure 12.4 shows a bird's eye view of the pathway map from the second workshop. It is clear from the figure that the higher purposes on the left and specific initiatives on the right were taking shape.

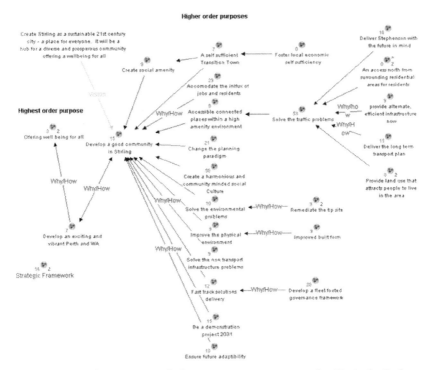

Higher order purposes

Figure 12.4: Bird's eye view of the purpose array using the Kapitola Pathway notation

During the third workshop, the evolving map was categorised in terms of "areas of focus," KPIs and KRAs. In other words, with context built, the labels that had caused so much argument initially were now added back in. This time, definitions of the labels were not controversial. With context now built and a shared understanding of it, the group avoided terminology myopia and had a very solid structure to work with.

Figure 12.5 shows a section of the pathway, now starting to take on an emergent structure as the purposes were grouped according to logical areas. By the fourth workshop, several broad focus areas, labelled as "areas of strategic focus" had emerged and the KRAs and KPIs under each area were taking shape. This was an important milestone because it allowed the third principle of Breakthrough Thinking to be applied—the solution after next.

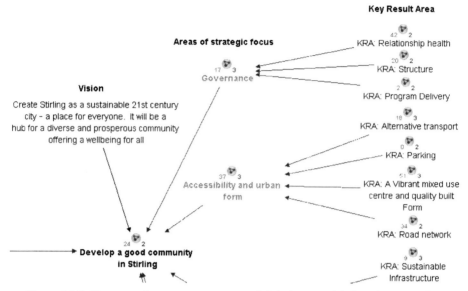

Figure 12.5: Near complete purposes array with labels now added to the rationale

Like uniqueness, the "solution-after-next" phase was a straightforward Dialogue Mapping exercise utilising IBIS. This exercise was specifically aimed at identifying and working through the potential consequences of identified strategies to deliver the vision, and coming up with measures to avoid any undesirable side-effects.

For each area of strategic focus identified, a new map was created to represent each solution-after-next discussion. Thus, for a given area of strategic focus, several key questions were asked:

- What are the objectives of this area of focus?
- What future problems would we have if we implemented the actions that we have come up with?
- What will we change now to stop these future problems from happening?

These are all unashamedly expansionist questions, deliberately designed to change the frame of reference to the future impact of potential actions. Figure 12.6 illustrates a small section of the actual solution after next discussions.

Figure 12.6: Solution after next IBIS maps for an area of strategic focus

The answers to the "What will we change now to stop this problem from happening?" questions proved to be the most useful. On occasion, participants would discuss a particular solution-after-next and come up with an answer that, on reflection, was a potential KPI or KRA in the making. As a result, that idea would be *lifted* back out to the top level Kapitola Pathway as a *Why/How* node in *its own right*.

The importance of this process of *emerging* KRAs and KPIs cannot be understated. As well as refining and improving the top level array of purposes, each top level node contained deep reasoning as to why a particular KPI or KRA was chosen.

By the end of the sixth workshop, the areas of strategic focus and many of the KPIs had been nailed down in detail. The group had developed a rich array of performance measures and how they related to the vision, with very detailed rationale as to why they were chosen and how the group arrived at them. There was a clear chain of logic from the KPIs, back to each KRA, area of strategic focus, right back to the vision for the area of Stirling and the city of Perth beyond it.

The final product

Interestingly, many people will never see the underlying maps that were used to come up with the final strategic framework. Figures 12.7 through

335

12.9 illustrate different ways in which the vision and focus areas together with the underlying key result areas (KRAs), objectives, KPIs and targets were presented to a wider audience. Although the images are not the best, we show them here as examples of how the outcomes of discussions can be presented to a general audience within a couple of pages, or even on a web site (Stirling Alliance 2011). Each higher level has less detail (to make it more digestible), but has a lot of rigour behind it. We emphasise that although the final product (web page of Fig 12.9), is designed for general consumption, it is much more than a bunch of platitudes because each point can be traced back to a section of the map that provides the detailed rationale behind it.

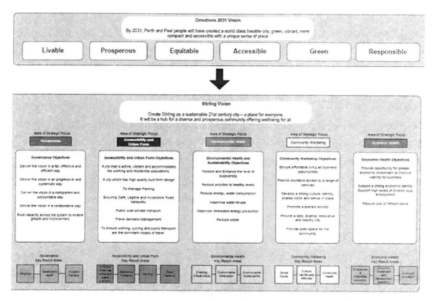

Figure 12.7: A one page overview of the Stirling performance framework

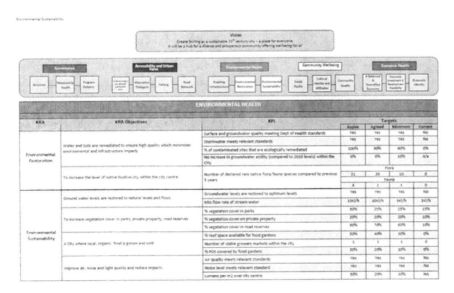

Figure 12.8: The specific KRAs and KPIs for one area of strategic focus

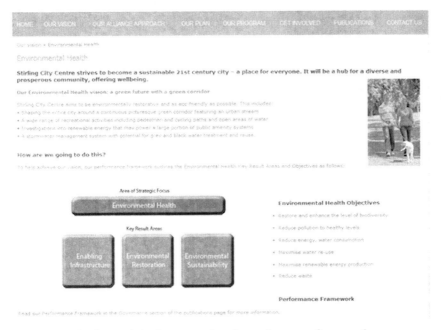

Figure 12.9: Stirling website incorporating the performance framework

Like the Precinct 5 workshops outlined in the last chapter, the performance framework was a result of the collective learning of the varied participants involved. Despite the sheer scale of the task at hand and the diversity of stakeholders, this process allowed the Alliance to finally develop a performance framework that, until that time, had been exceedingly difficult.

It is worth emphasising that there were no complex procedures or formal methodologies used in this process. No-one had to learn a new role or be trained up on how to utilise the method. Indeed, the working group contributed by simply being there and participating. They were able to put aside the need to define labels such as KPI or KRA for a while, simply by asking carefully framed open questions and focusing on building a coherent map of rationale from vision to measures of success. This switch in focus was the key to success, as was the fact that the process made good use of participants' time by facilitating shared learning and allowing all voices to be heard.

That was all that was needed for collective wisdom to emerge.

Case study 2: Chasing knowledge management

"Knowledge management" is a world-class platitude by virtue of the fact that it has probably had more people looking up the term on Wikipedia before they go into a meeting to discuss it than any other platitude (. . . and yes, we've done it too). Sometime after Paul's work with the performance framework for the Stirling Alliance, he encountered an organisation that had been chasing this mirage for years without anything to show for it.

The client in question was an organisation that, for privacy reasons, will remain nameless. Paul's company was initially asked to demonstrate a software system to them. The stipulation was that Paul and his colleagues would get just one meeting to gather requirements, followed by a single opportunity to demonstrate their solution. This is a fairly typical approach used in the IT industry for product evaluation. Each vendor receives equal air-time, which ensures that no potential vendor is disadvantaged over another.

But from the perspective of those who were charged with choosing a product, it made things difficult and ultimately put the project at risk. How on earth could a project team or focus group possibly understand the details and nuances of what a vendor offered, as well as how it related to a platitudinous goal in a single demonstration?

This became clear in the initial requirements gathering meeting that Paul's team had opted to dialogue map. As Paul and his colleagues unpacked the requirements of this organisation into an IBIS map, it became patently obvious that "knowledge management" had different meanings to different stakeholder groups in the organisation. As a result, there was simply no shared understanding of what the term meant. The effect of this was that the scope of this project was massive in terms of functionality, audience and success factors.

It turned out that history contributed to the confusion as well. The project had been an on again, off again affair for a couple of years. Staff had come and priorities had changed over time. In short, the problem had very strong wicked characteristics.

During the mandated single session, Paul explained the nature of wicked problems. To some team members the concept of wickedness was a revelation. He also encouraged staff to think of knowledge management, not in terms of what the Internet told them what it was, but instead what the organisation would be like if this thing they termed "knowledge management" was successfully implemented. This exercise in reframing the problem further demonstrated that depending on the stakeholder group, the term "knowledge management" could mean a customer facing employee being able to give a straight answer, right through to complex software that scanned a legal document, such as a sales contract, for the number of times the word "shall" or "must" existed (In the scary world of lawyers this sort of stuff makes a big difference!).

As a result of the complexity of the problem and the detail which Paul's team was able to capture in an IBIS map, participants also took a keen interest in the power of Dialogue Mapping. This was the first time that they had seen their project dissected in an integrated display which allowed them to explore the problem space visually.

What was the product again?

Paul and his colleagues did eventually demo their solution, and sometime later they were contacted by the project team and engaged—only in a different capacity. The team had decided to put aside product evaluations for the time being and use Dialogue Mapping to help them and their stakeholders get alignment on what knowledge management actually meant to them and the wider organisation; why they were embarking on this initiative and why it mattered to the organisation.

Paul realised that the hybrid Breakthrough Thinking/Dialogue Mapping method that was used for the Stirling Alliance might be suitable in this case. While this project could not be more different in terms of goal, vertical market, scope and timeframe, the core problem was still one of goal alignment. In the absence of any clear and coherent reasoning as to how this knowledge management initiative fitted into organisational strategy, the project team had found themselves floundering in the quicksand of vague and varied interpretations of a platitude.

The platitude of knowledge management had led to many fluid and conflicting requirements. In the IT world, such a big list of pseudo-requirements invariably results in huge "enterprise" systems being considered as potential solutions. This is exactly what happened here. However, such systems tend to be very complex, so it was no surprise that the evaluation of these systems created a negative feedback loop due to evaluators being daunted by the complexity. Further, enterprise systems typically take vastly different approaches to solving problems. This had the effect of further fragmenting the project team's understanding of what needed to be delivered. Finally, there was the question of cost: enterprise systems also come with huge enterprise price tags. How could one demonstrate that value for money was going to be achieved?

Paul explained how the Stirling sessions were conducted to create an integrated performance framework to deliver on a vision for a city, twenty five years into the future. The process had resulted in KRAs and KPIs that aligned to this vision, which allowed the city to track and measure success. He explained that the knowledge management project might benefit from a similar expansion of *why* and *how*, to help the project team work out where the key focus areas were and ensuring that they aligned this initiative to strategic organisational goals. The project team decided it was worth trying out and a block of 20 hours was committed to.

Starting in the middle

Unlike Stirling, where the team started on the vision, this group started with the initiative that had come to be known as "knowledge management." From a map point of view, the process was started placing a single node in the centre of the map called "Implement a Knowledge Management System" as shown in Figure 12.10

Figure 12.10: The starting point for the knowledge management goal alignment sessions

The project team had a lot of information available that had been collected over the last few years. This included user questionnaires, old functional specifications, risk workshop outputs and so on. Nevertheless, the one document that was missing from the work was the most important one of all. Paul asked the team for the organisation's five year plan outlining high level strategic objectives (this organisation operated in an industry sector where such plans are mandatory).

The plan outlined a mission, purpose and five strategic key result areas that had to be satisfied in order to deliver the mission. Each of these elements were entered onto the map in the Kapitola Pathway form. These (in anonymised form) are shown in Figure 12.11. Note that the node for knowledge management is detached from the strategy. This was done deliberately.

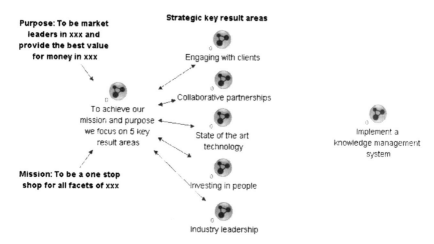

Figure 12.11: A strategic framework drawn using the Kapitola Pathway

Right away, the project team saw an issue with the strategic plan. Even before the purpose expansion was performed, the team honed in on the objective of "State of the art technology." Technology, they reasoned, was the means to an end—not the end itself. The team realised that when framed this way, "state of the art" implied that the organisations strategic goal was to have technology for technology's sake (not to mention the risk of "bleeding edge" technology). This didn't feel right at all.

The team opened up the "state of the art technology" node and used IBIS to examine the sub objectives of technology. In the ensuing discussion, it became clear that "state of the art" was actually a proxy for something else: "Timely business-goal decision making." The latter was the real strategic goal and "state of the art technology" was an *enabler*. This observation was fed back to the right channels within the organisation and the view of the team was supported. The strategic plan was summarily altered by the organisation to better fit reality. No longer was state of the art technology the strategic goal. It was replaced by "timely business-goal decision making" as shown in Figure 12.12.

Thus, even before the group had undertaken the Breakthrough Thinking process or IBIS mapping, the effect of *visually displaying the strategic plan had highlighted a flaw.* When you think about it, this basic application of IBIS and the Kapitola Pathway is a form of *validation* of a strategic plan. By framing the strategic plan in a causal fashion, the weaknesses in the chain of logic became apparent[1].

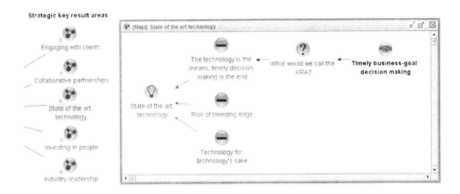

Figure 12.12: The IBIS examination of "state of the art" and the rationale for changing it

Dialogue Mapping and Breakthrough Thinking

Like Stirling, the first step for this organisation was to examine the *uniqueness* of the organisation as well as the present situation. Also like Stirling, there was a lot of uniqueness! For some of the project team members, many of the outputs from mapping this dialogue represented context that they were not aware of. Due to staff changes and the long history of the project, this process filled in many contextual gaps for them. Many "aha" moments were shared during these discussions.

In the *purpose expansion* step, the group attempted to link the knowledge management initiative (the orphaned node on the right of Figure 12.11) to the strategic plan on the left side of Figure 12.11. This exercise was initiated by asking *why* the knowledge management project was conceived in the first place. Once again, the Kapitola Pathway was the perfect tool for capturing rationale.

Given the sheer scope of the project, as established via examining uniqueness, the initial why/how expansion resulted in a messy map with

---

[1]   As it happens, this pattern has repeated itself in other organisations that Paul has worked with. The Kapitola Pathway is a handy way to test the validity of a strategic plan.

many links and many reasons for implementing the new knowledge management system. Nevertheless, it did not take long for some interesting insights to emerge. An example of this was when one project champion was pushing hard for the knowledge management system to "Track all occurrences of non-conformance."

The answer to the "Why" this was needed was that it was necessary to ensure that the organisation was compliant with a quality management regime that it operated under. While this was a perfectly valid reason to implement knowledge management in some shape or form, there was one minor hitch—*there was no matching strategic objective to link this to.* In other words, the five year plan made no mention of or reference to the importance of compliance at all. How was the project team going to prioritise this requirement, given that other requirements directly satisfied strategic objectives? Figure 12.13 illustrates how this key point was captured.

Like the "state of the art technology" example discussed earlier, the attempt to validate the strategic plan by aligning a project to it resulted in an apparent gap in the strategic plan being identified. Once again, this was fed back to the team developing the strategic plan and they set about making changes to ensure this gap was closed. Meanwhile the knowledge management team soldiered on.

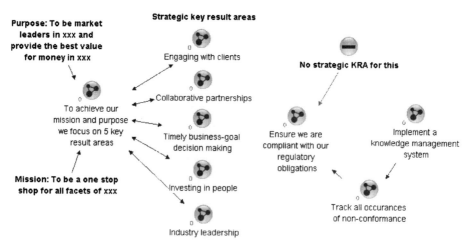

Figure 12.13: An example of a project justification with no strategic basis

Building the picture

By the end of the first two workshops, a detailed pathway was emerging. Via the use of purpose expansion and solution-after-next, the linkages between the planned knowledge management "system" and the organisation's strategic plan were further fleshed out and solidified.

As this work continued, one particular "Why" emerged as especially important to the success of the new system. In the past, there had been several instances in the organisation where credit for work was not given to whom it was due. This lack of recognition and reward for effort had created resentment, which in turn led to a culture of secrecy and knowledge hoarding. The project team realised that the single biggest challenge to their project was this fundamental problem of organisational culture. The team was being asked to implement a knowledge management system in an environment where knowledge was not freely shared.

During the *solution after next* discussions, with their focus on "what future problems may happen if we take this action?" type questions, the group examined this issue and the very likely future scenario of the culture problem persisting after the knowledge management system had been implemented. The outputs of this and other discussions resulted in a new *emergent purpose* that the new system had to somehow address. That purpose was to "Regain reputation for how we manage knowledge."

It was realised that this purpose in turn addressed the organisations strategic goals of "collaborative partnerships," "investing in people" and "timely business-goal decision making"—three of the five core strategic focus areas from the organisation's five year plan. There was now a clear why/how linkage.

The group then asked themselves *how* to regain reputation for how knowledge was managed. The answers were quite unsurprisingly multipronged. The interesting thing was *none of the answers were to "implement a knowledge management system!"* The four identified strategies for "regain reputation for how we manage knowledge," as shown in Figure 12.14, were to:

- Improve the mode of delivery of information to stakeholders
- Close the gap between credit of authorship vs. ownership of content
- Make information easier to find
- Provide a feedback loop for continual improvement

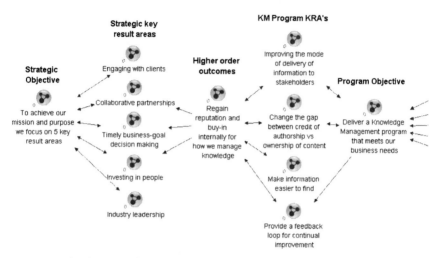

Figure 12.14: The Kapitola Pathway showing strategies for regaining reputation for how knowledge is managed

At this point the group realised that they were dealing with a broader program of work, not just implementing a new tool or system. This was because some of the "How" strategies were beyond the scope of the starting goal of "implementing a knowledge management system" (See Figure 12.10).

The initial focus on evaluating and selecting enterprise software was just one aspect of a multifaceted challenge. It became clear that this initial focus on technology evaluation had blinded the group to the most critical success factor—to "regain reputation for how we manage knowledge." When faced with that realisation, as well as the strategies that would be needed to achieve it, the initiative that the group started with: "Implement a knowledge management system" now seemed incomplete. Instead a new initiative was added, "Implement a knowledge management *program* to meet our business needs." Implementing a knowledge management system was one of several things that had to happen in order to deliver on some of the strategic objectives of the organisation. Other initiatives would be needed to support the system.

Conclusion

By the end of the final workshop, the team had mapped out several other key objectives for the knowledge management program. All of these objectives were aligned to the now *validated strategic plan*. Further, the team had identified several additional initiatives that would need to be delivered to make the vision for the knowledge management program a reality. As it happened, existing projects running in parallel to the knowledge management program of work were already addressing some of the identified gaps. These projects were incorporated into the program and in some cases, were explicitly aligned with the knowledge management objectives. The organisation was able to realign these projects a little and in effect, kill two birds with one stone. Those projects satisfied their original objectives, while addressing the needs of the knowledge management program of work as well.

With this newfound context, together with clear goals in hand, the project team went on to develop a phased delivery plan that made sense and incorporated the broader perspectives. Needless to say, technology was simply one facet among several to be considered, not the "be-all and end-all" of the initiative.

Like the Stirling case study earlier in the chapter, there were no complex, formal processes followed beyond asking expansionist questions and framing the problem in terms of the positive difference a knowledge management system would make. The realisations, outputs and outcomes from the process were *emergent*, as evidenced by the critical evaluation and adjustment of the strategic plan to which the initiative was trying to align to. No one would have imagined that the organisation's strategic plan would be challenged and improved as part of this work, yet the process served to help participants better understand, and as a result improve, the communication of the strategic aims of their organisation *in both directions*. To hark back to David H. H. Diamond's "the plan" from our introduction, the gap between the executive vision and coalface reality was reduced through this process, and significant shared learning took place.

The approach of Dialogue Mapping with IBIS, the Kapitola Pathway with a dash of Breakthrough Thinking, combined to provide a holding environment that enabled participants to explore the problem and break through the trap of naïve simplicity and the frustration of overwhelming complexity. Finally, after years of going in circles, the team was able to develop a shared understanding of the knowledge management challenge and shared commitment to doing something about it.

All in all, not bad for 20 hours of work, eh?

13

The Practice of Dialogue Mapping

"I really thought I was pretty good before I saw Hendrix, and then I thought: Yeah, not so good." (Brian May)

Remember that one guitar lesson you had?

Just about everybody has had romantic notions of being a guitarist, banging out the blues like Clapton or blistering solos like Kirk Hammett or Brian May. A surprisingly large number of people have actually bought a guitar at some stage in their lives and have tried to live the dream. Most give it up once they find that the gap between their ability to play a G chord and their dream of playing the solo to Hotel California stretches to the moon and back. Inevitably, many guitars end up collecting dust in the attic, along with the home gym set and many other items that were bought from late night infomercials.

Given that IBIS and Dialogue Mapping has been the technique we have spent the most time on in this book, we felt that we needed to spend some time talking about the practice of the craft: the ins and outs, the things books never tell you and practitioners are reluctant to reveal. This is because learning how to use IBIS, or indeed any of the visual notation tools in a facilitated scenario, is a *craft based skill*. In other words, like the aforementioned guitar skills, one improves with practice. While we can't make you an expert in one chapter, we hope that a few lessons learned by practitioners might take you a part of the way.

Furthermore, there are a number of insights we have gleaned from Dialogue Mapping engagements that we haven't discussed in the book. These engagements, for one reason or another, did not warrant a chapter on their own. We give them some airplay here.

IBIS in the reptile brain

IBIS is the core grammar that you use to map group dialogue. When mapping rapid-fire contributions from a group of people, they do not want to sit and wait for you to mull over whether their statement was an idea followed by a pro or an inferred question with an idea. Interpretation costs time and time costs momentum in the conversation.

In a way, this is like trying to play a song on guitar and having to consciously think about how to play that G chord. Consider how much you'd enjoy a rock concert if the guitarist stopped proceedings on a hard bit of a song because they had to think through the chords—with a "Wait!

Oh, sorry . . . I will get this . . ." scenario, familiar to beginner guitarists. Experienced players know how to play without thinking about it.

In much the same way, the process of translating dialogue into IBIS needs to be burned into the mapper's reptile brain so that it is automatic. To achieve this level of proficiency, you need to get plenty of practice with the IBIS grammar before getting up in front of a group and mapping live. A good way to begin is by mapping the rationale behind a prose piece, such as an article or a position-paper. Start with topics that you are familiar with but resist the urge to overlay your opinions and biases on those of the author. You need to ensure that you are mapping the author's rationale faithfully, whether or not you agree with what's written. As a test, you may want to map a political piece written by someone whose political leanings you do not share.

By mapping written prose, you learn to recognise argumentation patterns and map them to IBIS rapidly. Be warned though, mapping this way is performed *at your own pace*. Although this is a stepping stone to live mapping, it is not reflective of a live situation. To test your ability to map in real-time, try mapping a live interview on the radio or on television. You will find very quickly that it is near impossible to do, as the conversation will always go faster than your ability to keep up with it. Don't worry: not even Jeff Conklin, the inventor of Dialogue Mapping, could pull this off. In a real mapping situation, you will likely be facilitating the conversation so you can use a few other tricks to give you the necessary breathing space while maintaining group momentum.

Confidence and assertiveness

The hardest thing for a novice dialogue mapper is the facilitation aspect of the craft. This is a key skill because good facilitation buys you the time you need to create a good map while also keeping a group engaged.

One of Paul's early experiences with mapping was for a large group on a complex problem in which he had minimal domain knowledge. Being new and not familiar with the decorum of the group, Paul erred on the side of politeness. Rather than being direct and steering or interrupting the group where necessary, he took a passive role, just mapping the conversation.

This is a common mistake that almost all budding mappers make. More than anything else, such an approach ultimately does a disservice to

351

the participants because the conversation is not mapped accurately. Paul's performance in this workshop was somewhat mixed. There were a few times where he mapped the conversation well, and the participants engaged with the argumentation as it unfolded on the screen before them, gesturing at the map to add additional points. However, at other times, when contentious issues were being debated, the conversation would fly with many participants wanting to voice their thoughts at the same time. This led to side conversations, drawing participants' attention away from the map.

As soon as this happens, the mapper has no hope of following the conversation. As a consequence, quality of rationale captured suffers. This is commonly characterised by lots of orphaned idea nodes on the map. The focussing power of the map is diminished and participants stop paying attention to it.

Thus, it is important to be confident and assertive from the very start: the first ten to twenty minutes set the tone for the rest of the session. This is where people will implicitly learn the decorum of your Dialogue Mapping session and know what to expect. Your actions during this period are critical to the overall quality of the session.

Jeff Conklin once told Paul that this facilitative process is like starting out with ten dollars in your pocket and playing the following game: you lose a dollar every time you interrupt or direct the conversation, but you win it back each time you successfully map and validate a contribution. The object of the game is to keep some money in your pocket throughout the session. So, although you lose a dollar when you interrupt someone to clarify a point, it is a good move because you improve your chances of mapping the rationale correctly. If someone else starts to interrupt when you do this, make it clear that you will get to them as soon as you are done.

Thus, it is fine to be assertive, but one has to mind those dollar bills! With IBIS firmly encoded into the mapper's brain, one can manage this process. Paul typically sets the tone by explaining that as a male of the species, he cannot multitask and is a mere two finger typist. Therefore, he can only concentrate on one person at a time. He also uses *reflection*—the art of paraphrasing what participants have said and asking them to validate it. This enables a mapper to keep track of the conversation while also validating the map as it is built.

Jeff Conklin (2007) also offers more detailed advice for dealing with the facilitation side in his book. But of course, in the heat of dialogue, all those advice may well go straight out the window as you struggle to keep up with the exchanges of dialogue. Therefore, one of the best ways to pick up facilitation skills is by watching an experienced facilitator or dialogue mapper practice the craft.

Observation

One of Paul's most enjoyable training experiences was to travel to the picturesque US town of Annapolis and learn Dialogue Mapping from Jeff Conklin himself. Up until then, he had been practicing the craft but after those two days, returned as a much better practitioner.

The single most important part of the course was an exercise in which each student dialogue mapped the others as they discussed a real-world issue. Every student sat in the hot seat for fifteen minutes or so, trying to map the discussion. The rest of the group were all being completely evil, deliberately starting side conversations, interrupting and interjecting, jumping all over the place and generally being as difficult as they could possibly be.

Unsurprisingly, all students struggled to create a coherent map in this situation. However, when Conklin took the floor, they saw what twenty years of practice can do. Conklin effortlessly brushed off attempts to trip him up, utilising some subtle tricks that went unnoticed until he told us afterwards. For example, Conklin always voices out loud what he is typing when he captures rationale. In doing so, he is able to keep control of the discourse. He also made a point of thanking all contributors as their rationale was added to the map which, apart from ensuring that each person felt they were being heard, ensured that Conklin's metaphorical wad of dollar bills remained healthy.

Shortcut questions

When mapping a live conversation, the practitioner has to paraphrase participants. A very useful technique to facilitate smooth and fast mapping is to use shortcut questions. Just as there are different question types, there is often a single word that can be used to represent the question. Common examples include:

- Really?
- Implication?
- Example?
- Mitigate?
- Precedent?
- Context?
- Aspects?
- Characteristics?

Obviously short cut questions will not work for root questions, but that is not their purpose. They are designed to be used to speed up the capture of rationale because the meaning of such a question can be inferred from the context provided by the surrounding nodes. However, after mapping the conversation, it is important to reword these questions more accurately. For example, "Mitigate?" should be replaced with a more contextual "What could we do to mitigate the issue of xxx"?

Start mapping live with your domain of knowledge

If one thinks of all the various things that need to be done simultaneously during Dialogue Mapping (listening, understanding, mapping and facilitating), it is amazing that anyone with a Y chromosome can manage it at all. As the stereotype goes, men cannot multitask. As a case in point, both Kailash and Paul admit that, when a cricket game is playing on the radio, they suffer from the problem of not being able to do anything else.

Nevertheless, there is hope: by working in a topic area you know well, you will be able to develop your IBIS and facilitation skills without the additional mental burden of mapping a topic outside your area of expertise. Among other things, you don't have to worry about the meaning of acronyms and much of the context will be familiar to you.

You do have to be careful though, because you run the risk of introducing your own biases into the map. Thus, it is absolutely critical that when a point is paraphrased, it is validated by the person who made it. That way you ensure that you are not introducing your own opinions based on your knowledge of the problem. As an example of the benefits that discipline expertise brings to the floor, consider this mini case study dealing with the immutable laws of IT department physics.

IT department physics and nerd law . . .

IT departments, like any other islands of humanity, have developed some characteristics, habits and norms that outsiders might find strange. Given this, non-IT folks need to understand the fundamental principles of how IT departments typically operate. These may be organised into the following near-immutable laws of IT departments. They are:

- The web site team usually dislikes the corporate marketing team because marketing can't seem to understand that the garish lime-green colours they have for their printed brochures won't translate to the online world of web sites;
- The IT infrastructure team tends to dislike the web team because they see them as a bunch of cowboys who mess with forces they do not understand and do not have to deal with the consequences of it;
- The web team tends to dislike the infrastructure team because they see them as a bunch of control freaks who won't even allow them to so much as break wind without filling in a change control form; and
- Nobody likes the misunderstood compliance/records management team at all. They, unfortunately, perpetuate this by droning on continually about whatever compliance standards the organisation has to adhere to.

Defying the laws of IT physics

One of Paul's earliest uses of Dialogue Mapping was to deal with a classic case of these laws at work. A project for developing a new IT system (which we will refer to as Product X) was underway. As it happened, no staff had any exposure to Product X. To make things even more interesting, the project was initiated by the web team. Based on our immutable laws mentioned above, we know that the following consequences are inevitable:

- The infrastructure team are automatically suspicious of the project because they don't want to be saddled with yet another, enterprise system to support and manage.
- The compliance management team, already scarred from trying to convince an uninterested workforce that their complex, unwieldy software does not suck, will now assume that this project is going to encroach into their area.

Each side will address the "obviously" out-of-bounds web team via the platitude (or methodological hammer) of "governance." Governance is mentioned in every second sentence, in a manner to bolster each party's base position, rather than steer to a useful solution.

In this project, Paul introduced Dialogue Mapping in the very first meeting with the web team. He started with a simple root question, "What are we going to do about Product X?" Paul knew this product well and being well aware of the destructive forces of the immutable laws of IT, he knew certain critical questions pertaining to broader buy-in needed to be asked, including:

- What are the goals of the project?
- What are the governance requirements of this project?
- What are the infrastructure requirements for Product X?
- What should we do about operational support for Product X?
- How will we develop the project?
- What else do we need to be aware of?

Figure 13.1 shows the basic map created. This project had a charter which explained, in some detail, the background to this project. Additionally, the organisation had just completed a large strategic review. The latter was a key document that pretty much set the direction of the organisation for the next four years. Both of these were linked into the IBIS map in Figure 13.1. Note that it is possible to attach documents into the IBIS map along with the argumentation.

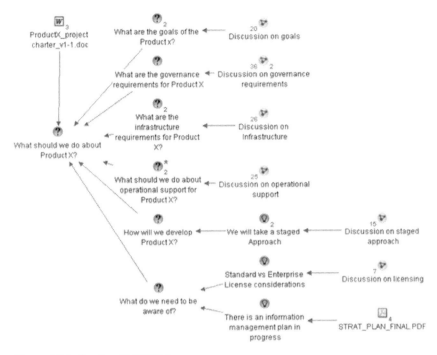

Figure 13.1: Product X IBIS Map

Adaptive requirements gathering . . .

Given that the product was completely new to the team, Paul combined interactive product training with Dialogue Mapping. Some questions could be answered or fleshed out by demonstrating the capabilities of the product and mapping would stop while this took place. As understanding of the new product capabilities grew from demonstrations and training, the map was refined as new knowledge, insights and understandings came to light.

While web teams are great at making awesome web sites, there are areas that they tend to be weak on, such as IT infrastructure, security and compliance—the very areas of the immutable laws. In this particular project, Paul had a dual role as dialogue mapper and consultant because he happened to be knowledgeable in technical areas relevant to Product X. Knowing those areas, he ensured that a lot of infrastructure and compliance considerations were captured and made explicit in the map *before* it was

357

taken to the other teams. Paul would deliberately ask questions, knowing full well that the web team could not answer without the input of the other teams. The important factor here though, was that those *questions were asked and made visible on the map.*

By making questions explicit in areas the web team were traditionally weak on, those involved were made aware that there was more to the problem than they originally thought. In doing this, Paul was able to move them from a state of "unknown unknowns" (known in training-speak as *unconscious incompetence*), to knowing more about what they *didn't know* (called *conscious incompetence*).

Fast forward a couple weeks of this iterative training and mapping approach, and the team had a very good understanding of not only the new product but also of what they *didn't know* about the scope of the project. Consequently, the web team called upon the other teams at various times to fill these gaps. These interactions answered those open questions and shared learning took place because the map painted a more complete picture than would have been possible had only one team been involved.

The ultimate test was when a department-wide meeting was called, involving all the opposing sides of the IT universe. There were a dozen people in all, including a few key decision makers who didn't always enjoy a particularly cosy relationship, crammed into a hot, tiny room with a portable projector.

The web team manager introduced the project via the charter and the entire group worked their way through the map. The discussion covered the goals of the project, how they related back to the strategic plan and how the phases were being structured to support those goals. Also discussed were the details of each phase: those deliverables that were in and those that were not.

At the end of the meeting everyone was on-side and excited about the project. Feedback indicated that such buy-in from the entire IT organisation was unheard of in this organisation. Moreover, it took just one meeting.

The success of this process boiled down to 3 major factors:

1. The participants in the Dialogue Mapping exercise were enthusiastic about the process. Dialogue Mapping was not "sold" with this engagement. In fact, no participants were told in

advance that it would be used. Instead, it was simply used from the very first workshop to support an open conversation. By the end of that meeting, participants were very impressed with the detail of what had been captured. They found it a highly efficient and engaging way to work and as a result, Dialogue Mapping became the standard way workshops and requirements meetings were conducted for this project.

2. The major concerns of the other (non-Web) teams were mitigated by the fact that the issues of importance to them were either addressed, or at the very least, were captured and made visible on the map. The web team had made *it clear that they did not know all the answers*. However, capturing those questions in the map, assured the other teams that the web folks were not running off and doing their own thing without consulting the others. This alone prevented traditional organisational defence mechanisms from being triggered.

3. As Paul was both a mapper and a trainer, it meant that fast-tracking of learning could take place. Conducting combined training/mapping workshops enabled team members to learn about the product and then apply that learning to improve their understanding of the problem in the map. This helped them to converge on a solution much faster than they would have been able to had they been learning about the product alone. As a specialist in this particular product, Paul was able to foresee problem areas and then use the map to steer the participants towards dealing with those more difficult issues.

All in all, this was a great example of the power of Dialogue Mapping in speeding up what would otherwise have been a laborious process of stakeholder consultation. However, the fact that Paul happened to be a subject matter expert, as well as a dialogue mapper, meant that he was able to exercise a fair degree of control over the conversational proceedings. He was able to answer questions, raise concerns and flag potential issues regarding the product while also capturing the essence of the dialogue in real-time.

In some situations, mappers will not be so lucky. Sometimes, a mapper has no domain knowledge of the subject being discussed. Accordingly, we will now discuss some techniques that will help novice mappers deal with conversations that traverse unfamiliar terrain.

Archetype conversations and mental models

The next step, perhaps the biggest step of all for a dialogue mapper, is to map in situations in which the mapper does not have subject matter expertise. This is a significant undertaking that shouldn't be taken lightly. Pulling this off requires three key Dialogue Mapping skills:

- The ability to form a mental "template" of what a map will look like in advance
- The ability to recognise patterns in conversation that can make use of these templates
- Facilitation skills that make the experience more enriching for participants

The first stage of Dialogue Mapping mastery is the ability to create a mental model of map structure. In Figure 9.5, we showed a basic example of this via maps based on the CATWOE mnemonic of Soft Systems Methodology and three principles of Breakthrough Thinking. Over time, a skilled mapper will start to find that most conversations follow recognisable patterns. Creating map templates to accommodate those patterns ensures that maps are clear, coherent and inviting for participants. Rather than create a transcriptive IBIS map, which reflects the meanderings that occur in conversation, a skilled mapper recognises the nature of the question or comment made and adds it to the appropriate section of his or her mental map before transcribing it on to the real map.

Figure 13.2 is an archetype dialogue map that is very common in *evaluation* problems, where participants need to choose a preferred option from number of competing options. You will notice that most question types, as Conklin described in Chapter 9, are catered for.

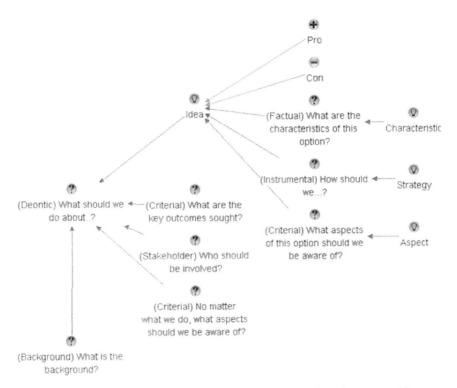

Figure 13.2: An example mental model for maps that deal with evaluation problems

Irrespective of the industry or make-up of the group, evaluation conversations typically start with a deontic (What should we do . . . ?) type question. Such a question usually elicits several ideas in response. Each idea will have supporting and opposing arguments, as well as instrumental, factual and criterial questions that flesh out various aspects of the idea (How do we implement it? What does it mean? What are the constraints?).

During the course of discussing an option or a course of action, a conversation will shift as knowledge and insights are exchanged. New opportunities, risks, constraints or outcomes will *emerge*. For example, consider a situation where a participant says "Well, no matter what happens, we need to . . ." The "no matter what" is a clear signal that the participant is about to articulate a criterion that applies to *all options*. Therefore, this should be attached to the root question, rather than the idea or argument that triggered the insight.

A skilled mapper will be able to identify these conversational signs and ensure that the resulting rationale is added to the correct section of the map. An inexperienced mapper is likely to capture the rationale in a transcriptive manner, adding contributions to the node that is being discussed at the time, instead of where it makes most logical sense.

The song beneath the words

Recognising patterns in conversations goes beyond recognising question types and mental models of maps. Among other things, it is about learning to recognise when a group is about to zero in on a key issue that may have been hidden up to that point. Heifetz & Linksy (2002) call this listening for the song beneath the words.

> "Learn from their stakes and fears. As social workers say, 'Start where people are at.' . . . After hearing their stories, you need to take the provocative step of making an interpretation that gets below the surface. You have to listen to the song beneath the words."

It is common in workshop scenarios for a group to be guarded at first. Consequently, a large chunk of the initial dialogue is more about participants "testing the barriers." The breakthrough moments come when a participant breaks through these barriers, thereby getting the group to *open dialogue*—the stuff that forges commitment.

Facilitators are trained to assist groups in achieving such breakthroughs. Paul considers himself fortunate to have been involved in Dialogue Mapping with different facilitators in varied situations. As is the case in many craft-based professions, facilitators tend to have their individual styles. Some adopt a divergent style, choosing not to push a group towards an outcome. Instead, they encourage the group to unpack the problem without constraining the conversation or restricting the group to a particular problem solving method. Others advocate an approach that is more structured and, accordingly push somewhat harder to get to a solution.

Paul often works with Dr Neil Preston, an organisational psychologist and facilitator with an uncanny sense for getting to the "song beneath the words." The more Paul worked with him, the better in-tune his own sense became.

A good example of this was when Neil and Paul where facilitating a discussion about a complex organisational issue outside of Paul's discipline area. At one point in the dialogue, a participant said something that Paul recognised as being very important. Although not knowing why, Paul sensed that something significant had changed in the conversation. He was about to interject to ensure he captured the point accurately, when Neil, sensing the same thing, honed on the point made and subsequently pushed the group to ask themselves deeper questions around that point. As it happened, this uncovered the key to the conversation and was a breakthrough for the group. This breakthrough led to a completely new way of looking at the situation and resulted in the group developing a new change strategy.

Later, when Paul asked Neil about that moment, Neil replied "You're starting to sense the patterns in group conversation. They were talking about *first order goals*, what you heard was someone getting to the *second order—or deeper goal.*"

Ever since that conversation where Neil put a name to what Paul picked up on, Paul has been able to sense the second order goals even before they emerge in the conversation. On one occasion, he was mapping a session at an educational institution, aimed at envisioning a new computer system for improving access to information for students. During the conversation he became acutely aware of what the success of the initiative would hinge on, although it was never mentioned explicitly. Through the conversation, the song beneath the words was that *teachers value the one-on-one relationships they build with their students.* After all, that is the essence of the vocation of teaching. Any computer system that devalued teachers, by giving the students an option to download class notes and thereby removing the need to attend class, was never going to work. The system, if it was to be successful at all, had to *support and enhance the student-teacher bond.* If an analyst created a perfect database driven system that enabled students to download notes (and thereby skip class), teachers would never commit to the solution.

This issue was brought to the surface and named for what it was. As a consequence "improving the student teacher experience" became one of five key focus areas of the project and one that was critical to its success.

Finding the groove

No two situations or groups are ever the same. In the usual course of a meeting or workshop, there will be times where a group works together in perfect harmony and others where one wrong word will upset the equilibrium requiring the group to stop, reset and restart. Over time, a pattern will emerge in the decorum of the sessions and the mapper will find that conducting the sessions in a particular way works well for the group. Mappers need to look out for such patterns or more correctly, cadences, in conversations.

One of Paul's early experiences with the craft of Dialogue Mapping was a baptism of fire. He had to map a meeting where stakeholders were discussing a problem that was completely unfamiliar to him. Not only had he no understanding of the problem, he also had no discipline knowledge, no background history of the project, no understanding of the group dynamics, or any idea of the positions of stakeholders on the issue.

Little did he know that this group had been meeting for 18 months and were still struggling to come to an agreement on what was a complex and polarising urban planning issue. Interestingly, the issue was not technically complicated. Anyone could have sat in the room and understood most of the dialogue (not the full context but enough to see what the problem was). What made this particular issue complex was the fact that the group members came from several different organisations and disciplines and, as a consequence, held diametrically opposing viewpoints.

To give a sense of the scale of the challenge, it is worth comparing it to the IT department example discussed earlier. In that example, it was hard enough just to get one IT department to agree on the parameters for a project that would be realised within 6 months. If you have ever complained about organisational silos and think it is hard to get a degree of consensus within an organisation, imagine what it would be like when over a dozen representatives from different organisations are involved, spanning a range of public and private sector concerns (with community representatives thrown into the mix). No wonder Rittel coined the term "wicked problem" from his experiences in urban planning!

There were simply so many stakeholders and interconnected issues that it was very hard to not get distracted by tangents and bogged down by repetition and frustration. Given that the group had been at it for eighteen months, it was no surprise that the atmosphere was tense.

The result was a little like the Precinct 5 case study of Chapter 11. Although Paul thought that the very first Dialogue Mapping session failed to cut through the complexity, the participants found it valuable enough to ask Paul back. The maps of the first session provided just enough structure to focus the conversation and reduce repetition. In the second workshop, participants were able to progress to a point where they were able to draw options on a topographic map of the area. This alone was a breakthrough because participants had never gotten to this point before. Indeed, photos were taken to capture the moment!

In a pattern reminiscent of the Precinct 5 study in Chapter 11, the group finally found its groove—an emergent cadence gave participants just enough momentum to negotiate previous roadblocks and flesh out a number of options that were acceptable to all.

Augmenting Dialogue Mapping

Earlier in the book, we argued that *visual reasoning techniques,* such as Dialogue and Argument Mapping, can help groups work towards a collective understanding of wicked issues. We then discussed how these techniques sometimes need to be augmented by *problem structuring methods* that help reframe complex problems through the use of focused questions. We then discussed how *novel governance structures,* like Alliancing, have the potential to address the imbalances created by unfair distribution of risk and thus create a more collaborative environment. These three elements are indeed the basis of a holding environment in which open dialogue (in the sense of how Habermas might define it) can occur.

That said, there are other ways to catalyse the creation of a holding environment. Trainers have long known that people learn best through activities that involve all the senses. Here are a few ways in which one can leverage this insight.

Sensory immersion

In our discussion of the Precinct 5 case study in Chapter 11, we discussed the "the magical mystery tour" in which a bus was hired and the residents taken to an area where a similar urban transformation had been made ten years before. They then walked around the area for an hour, soaking in the ambience and learning about the history of the area, how it was redeveloped and how certain planning challenges were overcome.

This enabled the Precinct 5 participants to get a real sense of the issues they needed to confront. Moreover, they felt it with multiple senses: sight, sound and touch, rather than through second-hand experiences related in with a room with a projected map on the wall. Later, when Paul dialogue mapped the session after the bus tour, the quality of the discussion and the resulting rationale was much richer, most likely due to the sensory immersion that took place before the mapping process began.

Information gathering for 40+ people

There are practical limits to how many people should be involved in a Dialogue Mapping session. However, the exact number varies as it depends on the wickedness of the problem being discussed, the past history of the group and the skill of the mapper.

One interesting case was when an organisation invited representatives from academia, charities and various public sector agencies to a half day workshop on social sustainability. There were 40-45 attendees, many of whom were there for the first time. It would have been difficult to cover the required topics using a standard Dialogue Mapping format of starting with a root question and letting things emerge. Among other things, it would have been impossible for all attendees to have a say in the allotted time, let alone set up the room to handle such a large number of people.

In the end, the solution was to run a pre-workshop session for a much smaller group drawn from the larger one. This subgroup had to create a series of "seed maps" for each of the sub-areas of social sustainability. By the end of this process, there were about a dozen maps on various subtopics, each with a few questions, ideas, pros and cons. Of course, these maps were not complete as they mapped only a part of the issue. However, they were well formed, easy-to-follow IBIS maps.

These maps were then *printed* out on large size paper and pinned to a display board. Attendees were then encouraged to wander from map to map and examine the argumentation in each of them while mingling and exchanging ideas with other attendees. Figure 13.3 is a photograph from the session.

Figure 13.3: Seed maps created prior to Dialogue Mapping for a large group

The table arrangements for the workshop were structured so that ten to twelve attendees were seated at one of four large tables. The workshop kicked off with a half-hour introduction to the purpose of the workshop. After the introduction, four of the maps were removed from the display and placed on *each table*. We explained to the group that each table had a unique map and each map was on a particular focus area. At this point, attendees had the opportunity to *move to a table where the topic was of most relevance or interest* to them.

Each table contained an ample supply of marker pens. Paul took the stage and explained the basics of IBIS grammar to the attendees and requested that they start adding ideas to the existing maps. He did not dwell on the grammar, nor did he expect participants to suddenly know how to map IBIS fluently. What he made clear instead, was that he was going to walk from table to table and *interrupt* if he felt the additions to the map made no sense or were ambiguous in some way.

The groups at each table had just under an hour to work on each map. At the end of the hour, the updated maps were removed and replaced with the next four from the display boards. The process was then repeated and

Paul walked from table to table, asking for clarification or pointing out where the rationale captured by participants was unclear.

Interestingly, these IBIS novices seemed to have little problems with the usage of ideas, pros and cons. However, participants would often forget to make the underlying question explicit. Paul would ask for the question being answered by a particular idea and would write the question into the map and redraw the lines.

After the workshop was completed, Paul took all the updated paper maps and added the additional rationale into the seed maps that had been created using the Compendium software. The process was surprisingly quick because the initial "seed rationale" on maps had made it easier for attendees to add more rationale. Although their additions weren't perfect IBIS, it was not a difficult task for Paul to "refactor" the additional information without losing any of the intent behind the participants' contributions.

For the record, additional workshops were conducted, but these reverted to standard Dialogue Mapping sessions with a subset of the attendees who had specialised skills and knowledge in the topic area. What this particular process demonstrated was that with a little planning, a single Dialogue Mapper can still manage to capture quality rationale from a very large group in a short time.

Dialogue Mapping with a facilitator

Dialogue Mapping a large group can also be done with a facilitator and mapper working in tandem. Paul performs many such sessions. For a large group, a facilitator can be very helpful because the mapper can concentrate on capturing the dialogue rather than directing the meeting. Equally though, a facilitator can, at times, make the process more difficult.

The key to a successful co-facilitation session is that the facilitator must know IBIS or have attended a number of Dialogue Mapping workshops. This is because, like the mapper, the facilitator is facing the group, asking probing questions, directing the course of conversation and therefore is not always looking at the map. Yet, the facilitator has the critical job of directing participants' attention to the map.

Furthermore, Dialogue Mapping requires a particular kind of facilitator who is willing to let the conversation explore varied terrain. Paul had experienced workshops where facilitators strive to keep the group on topic. In one particular example, the facilitator, conscious of the agenda slipping away, asked the group whether any of the options had any "fatal flaws" that enabled that option to be quickly discounted. It soon became apparent that one person's "fatal flaw" was diametrically opposed to another person's "fatal flaw." This attempt to shortcut deliberations actually backfired.

After this "fatal flaws" episode, Paul stopped mapping while the group resolved the fatal flaw issue and agreed to try a different approach. This subsequent approach proved to be much more successful. "No fatal flaws" became a bit of a mantra among this group—yet another example of how a group was able to find its "groove."

Benefits of Dialogue Mapping

The practice of Dialogue Mapping has some subtle benefits for a mapper beyond the satisfaction of seeing a group get great value out of the craft.

One of the greatest benefits is the ability to work with groups that you may be unlikely work with otherwise. Dialogue mappers get to reap the benefit of the wisdom of *many* crowds. Apart from improving a mapper's general knowledge, it teaches empathy and the ability to read the nuances of conversations. The value that the latter brings cannot be overstated.

One of the most important side benefits of Dialogue Mapping is that it captures decision rationale for posterity. As we mentioned in Chapter 7, it serves to *augment organisational memory*. It is perhaps worth elaborating on this point a bit: since the technique captures the essence of a discussion, the resulting map is a record of the *informal* knowledge exchanged in the course of the conversation (Conklin 2001). This is the knowledge that exists within peoples' heads as opposed to the documented processes and procedures that are the subject of best practices. These maps thus take us a step closer to capturing the actual knowledge that makes organisations tick, in a format that facilitates easy recall.

According to Ackoff (1994), organisations make two types of errors: errors of omission and errors of commission. Errors of commission occur when an action was taken, but in hindsight, was seen as a mistake or did not have the intended outcome. An error of omission is when an action was not taken when it should have been. Since it is usually easier to see what people do wrong than to see what they don't do at all, errors of commission are tracked and often punished whereas errors of omission are not. Making mistakes is a part of learning but in an environment where errors of commission are punished, it is safer not to try than to try and risk failure.

Dialogue Mapping provides an opportunity for a group to celebrate its wins. In delivering projects, it is common to find that teams tend to focus on the things they do not do so well. We don't know whether this is due to a cognitive bias or the realisation that project failure is a norm. Whatever the cause, one nice feature about Dialogue Mapping is that it has a better memory than those stakeholders who create the maps. In one particular workshop in the very complex area of mental health, stakeholders started by reviewing the progress of all the initiatives from the previous year. There was a realisation that words *had* been turned into actions and those actions had positive results. It enabled everyone a moment of self-congratulation: the opportunity to say "You know, we did do a pretty good job after all!" and this set the tone for a very productive two days of strategic planning work.

Seeing progress and goals being achieved is vital because it keeps you going. Unfortunately, as in the daily papers, negative news dominates the positive. Celebrating those wins cultivates a sense of purpose that binds people together and helps people see that the legacy they are creating is the one they have aspired to as they toiled.

Finally, IBIS maps are a great artefact for making knowledge more accessible. They are a rich exploration of a given problem and demonstrate, very effectively, the circumstances and understanding of a problem at a particular point in time. Errors of omission are noted through exploration of options when solving a problem. Dualistic, either/or decisions are further unpacked in a highly efficient and engaging way. Thus, with dialogue maps, gone are the days of looking at a process, policy or report years later and wondering "What the hell were they thinking?"

We think Ackoff would have loved it!

Coda

Reflections on Change,
Communication and Commitment

To freeze or to flee:
Change from a water dragon's perspective

In the summer of 2011, Sydney received more rain than it had in a long time. One weekend, taking advantage of a break in the rain, Kailash and his family went bushwalking in the Lane Cove National Park—a protected wilderness in suburban Sydney. The following narrative on change is based on something that he noticed during that walk. Paul will take a step back while Kailash relates the story from a first person perspective . . .

The track we chose was a bit slippery from the rain of the previous weeks but was drying out nicely in the morning sun. One of the consequences of sunny weather after a long spell of rain is that reptiles tend to seek open spaces to soak in some sun. With dense vegetation on either side, the open, rocky areas on the track provide inviting spots for reptiles looking to sunbathe. We thought we might see a snake or two but didn't. Instead, we walked into a number of Eastern Water Dragons—semi-aquatic lizards that are common in eastern Australia. Incidentally, fully-grown water dragons are a pretty impressive sight, growing up to a metre in length. They are also quite well camouflaged; black stripes over a grey-brown coat that merges nicely with the rock-and-mud colours of the track.

Figure 15.1: An Eastern Water Dragon

When a water dragon sunbathes, it stays still, rock-like, for long periods of time. This makes sense from a safety perspective since motion might attract the attention of predators, mainly omnivorous native birds such as currawongs and kookaburras. So the reptile remains statue-like, perfectly camouflaged by colours that merge with the ground it lies on—until a blundering bushwalker disturbs its repose, like we did many times that weekend.

At that point the creature has two options:

- freeze (maintain the status quo); or
- flee (turn tail and scuttle off)

The water dragon senses approaching bushwalkers by the disturbance caused by their footfalls along the trail, further amplified by the crackling of leaves and brush that come underfoot. To the water dragon, the approaching footfalls signify an unknown. It could be benign but could also be a predator on the prowl. It is safest to assume the latter because if the lizard chooses the former wrongly it could end up dead. However, even if it is a predator, it is quite possible that the lizard's superb camouflage will do its job and render it unnoticeable. Besides, it is comfortable out there in the sun, so there's an understandable reluctance to move. Consequently, the first reaction of the lizard is to continue its statue-like stance but remain alert to the danger. As the footsteps get closer it reassesses the situation continually, deciding whether to run for it or stay put. At some point, a threshold is reached and the lizard dashes off into the undergrowth (or a stream, if there's one handy—water dragons are good swimmers).

Now, if there were no blundering bushwalker, the dragon would presumably continue basking in the sun undisturbed. The bushwalker changes the lizard's environment and the lizard reacts to this change in one of the two ways it knows: it stays put (does nothing) or runs (takes evasive action). Both actions are aimed at self-preservation since we can take it as given that the lizard does not want to be a lizard-eater's lunch! The first action has the benefit of not expending energy unnecessarily but could lead to an unpleasant end. The second is a better guarantor of safety but involves some effort. There is a trade-off: not becoming lunch involves understanding that there is no such thing as a free lunch.

The interesting thing is that the threshold seems to vary from dragon to dragon. When I used the phrase "walking into" earlier, I meant it quite literally: many times we didn't notice a recumbent reptile until we were almost upon it. At other times, though, a startled slinker would speed off when we were several meters away. It seems some water dragons scare easily while others don't. In either case, the lizard makes an assessment of the situation based on the information gleaned through its senses and then decides on a course of action. Then, "decision" made, the little critter will freeze or flee.

Marbles lost

Most organisational initiatives, whether projects or business restructures, involve change of some kind. Although such changes are rarely life threatening, they can be unsettling. It is interesting that typical first reactions to workplace change are much like those of a water dragon to approaching footsteps. People will either attempt to maintain the status quo or move fairly quickly to a perceived safer place.

This is perfectly normal reaction considering our evolutionary heritage. Most creatures, be they water dragons or humans, prefer the familiar and will do what they can to avoid change. It is no surprise, then, that the most common gut reactions to change are:

- Pretend it hasn't occurred; or
- Run away from it.

In terms of the marble-board metaphor discussed in the introduction, when people see that their "wellbeing marbles" are headed in the wrong direction, they'll think themselves as being unable to influence the course of the game—and therefore remain as passive players or leave the game altogether.

Both courses of action are forms of running away . . . one psychological, the other literal. The only real option is to stay in the game as an active player. The key to doing this is through building relationships based on mutual understanding, which—as we have discussed in this book—boils down to communication. While this is a pretty trite statement (let's face it, many management and leadership books talk about the importance of effective communication), we hope this book has offered you some practical methods and examples which go beyond the mere platitude of "effective communication."

Marbles regained—
organisations as networks of commitments

In the world of organisations, communication is generally seen as a means to let people know what is going on. This is a limited view of communication because it is essentially a one way affair. The message recipients are merely passive consumers of information. This blinkered notion of communication is even enshrined in "best practice" guides. For example, quoting from the PMBOK® Guide (Project Management Institute, 2009):

> "Effective communication creates a bridge between diverse stakeholders involved in a project, connecting various organisational and cultural backgrounds, different levels of expertise, and various perspective and interests in the project execution or outcome."

This is fine as it goes but bridges do not make commitments, and commitments are critical in managing organisational initiatives. There is a bridge between North and South Korea, but you would not say that a lot of commitment stems from it being there.

Individuals or groups can commit to something only after they understand it and feel that their contributions have been taken seriously. Communication therefore plays a deeper, less appreciated role in organisations: building shared understanding and commitment to action via collective deliberation. This is the main point we have attempted to make in this book. To that end, we hope we have been successful in providing you with some practical tools that can help you facilitate rational dialogue and commitment in your workplace.

In their deeply philosophical book on computers and cognition, Winograd and Flores (1987) used the metaphor of *organisations as networks of commitments*. We believe this phrase spells out an ideal of what organisations ought to be: a group of people working towards common, mutually agreed goals, via commitments that are made based on a shared understanding. It is idealistic but we hope, after reading this book, you will not think that it is hopelessly so.

While the fanboys argue . . .

It is worth noting that our notion of the holding environment and the tools to achieve it do not prescribe any particular methodology. Instead, we have focused on what it takes to get the relationships between stakeholders right. This forms the basis for a holding environment in which individuals can reach a shared understanding based on which they can make commitments that are achievable and that they intend to fulfil. We conjecture that once this is done, it matters little which methodology is used to manage the project.

The endless debates among the fanboys over the efficacies of particular methodologies serve only to distract us from the real work of delivering projects, which is finding effective ways to achieve and manage individual commitments.

A statement regarding efficacy of a particular methodology is essentially a claim regarding cause and effect. When someone states, "our project success rate has increased by 50% since we implemented Methodology X," it implies that the use of the methodology was in some way responsible for the improvement. Such a statement can be called into question because it does not tell us how the alleged success of Methodology X is a consequence of individual intentions and actions. In contrast, the approaches we have described in this book, which focus on achieving shared understanding project objectives, directly facilitates individual commitment to achieving those goals. We suggest this commitment, when expressed in a tangible form, is the causal link between a particular methodology and the outcomes produced from it.

Beyond best practices

When we started writing this book, we had a hard time agreeing on a title. Some of the possibilities we tossed about included:

- "How to deprogram your manager"
- "The heretics guide to how organisations work and what to do about it"
- "The BOHICA experiment"
- "Beyond Best Practices"

. . . and many others. Finally, we settled on "The Heretic's Guide to Best Practice" because, even though the book was just an idea at the time, the phrase seemed to capture the essence of what we wanted to say and conveyed a sense of trepidation that we felt in saying it. Looking back now, we see that it also worked to remind us of the "big picture" when we lost our way in mazes of ideas which seemed to go nowhere (which, we should admit, happened a number of times).

We realise there is more than a little irony in presenting practices and techniques in a book that purports to be a heretic's guide to going beyond them. Moreover, in the event that this book gains enough attention to be treated seriously, we are caught in a bind since a new "heretics guide" memeplex would be spawned and we'd have to defend our methods using similar arguments to those we have taken to task. Yet, we have a defence . . .

We haven't labelled any of the techniques we talk about "best." We haven't even called them "good." Our point is that practices ought not to be taken at anyone else's word regardless of their authority or guru-status. Ideas should be evaluated critically on the basis of their relevance for you in your particular organisation and context. The other important point is that organisational initiatives are collective efforts—and shared understanding and commitment to action must precede them.

These two points are the essence of what we have attempted to convey in this book. We hope we have succeeded in doing so.

References

1. Ackoff, R. (1981), The Art and Science of Mess Management, *Interfaces*, Vol 11, pp. 20-26.
2. Ackoff, R. (1986), Management in Small Doses, New York, NY: John Wiley and Sons.
3. Ackoff, R. L. (1987), Mission Statements, *Strategy and Leadership*, Vol. 15, pp. 30-31.
4. Adams, C. (1995), Whatever happened to the metric system in the USA, *The Straight Dope*, available online at http://www.straightdope.com/columns/read/947/whatever-happened-to-adoption-of-the-metric-system-in-the-u-s (Accessed: July 2011).
5. AgileCollab (2008), Interview with Ken Schwaber, Available online at: http://www.agilecollab.com/interview-with-ken-schwaber (Accessed July 2011).
6. Ariely, D (2008), Predictably Irrational: The Hidden Forces That Shape Our Decisions, New York, NY: Harper Collins.
7. Art of Hosting (2011), Available online at: http://www.artofhosting.org/home (Accessed June 2011)
8. Awati, K. M. and Howes, T (1996), Stationary waves on cylindrical fluid jets, *American Journal of Physics*, Vol. 64, pp. 808-811.
9. Awati, K. (2011), Mapping project dialogues using IBIS:A case study and some reflections, *International Journal of Managing Projects in Business*, Vol.4, pp. 498-511.
10. Barabba V., Pourdehnad, J. and Ackoff, R. L. (2002), On misdirecting management, *Strategy and Leadership*, Vol. 30, pp. 5-9.
11. Bennett, P., Bryant, J. and Howard, N. (2001), "Drama Theory and Confrontation Analysis" in Rosenhead, J. and Mingers, J. (Eds), *Rational Analysis for a Problematic World Revisited: Problem Structuring Methods for Complexity, Uncertainty and Conflict*, Chichester: John Wiley & Sons.

12. Brooks, F. (1987), No Silver Bullet—Essence and Accidents of Software Engineering. *IEEE Computer*, Vol. 20, pp. 10-19.

13. Checkland, P. (1985), From Optimizing to Learning: A Development of Systems Thinking for the 1990s. *Journal of the Operational Research Society*, Vol 39, pp. 757-767

14. Checkland, P. (1999), Systems Thinking, Systems Practice, Chichester: John Wiley & Sons.

15. Checkland, P. (2001), "Soft Systems Methodology" in Rosenhead, J. and Mingers, J. (Eds), *Rational Analysis for a Problematic World Revisited: Problem Structuring Methods for Complexity, Uncertainty and Conflict*, Chichester: John Wiley & Sons.

16. Cicmil, S., Hodgson, D., Lindgren, M. and Packendorff, J. (2009), Project management behind the façade, *Ephemera*, Vol. 9, pp. 78-92.

17. COAG Reform Council (2010), National Affordable Housing Agreement: Baseline performance report for 2008-09, *COAG Reform Council*. p. 17

18. Cohn, N. T. (2005), A Cognitive Approach to Graphic Signs and Writing, Available online at: http://www.emaki.net/essays/visualsigns.pdf (Accessed July 2011).

19. Conklin, J. (2001), Designing Organisational Memory: Preserving Intellectual Assets in a Knowledge Economy, *Cognexus Institute Whitepaper*. Available online at: http://cognexus.org/dom.pdf (Accessed August 2011).

20. Conklin, J. (2003), "Dialog mapping: reflections on an industrial strength case study," in Kirschner, P., Shum, S.J.B. and Carr, C.S. (Eds), *Visualizing Argumentation: Software Tools for Collaborative and Educational Sense-making*, London: Springer, pp. 117-35.

21. Conklin, J (2005), Dialogue Mapping: Building Shared Understanding of Wicked Problems. Chichester: John Wiley & Sons.

22. Connell, J. and Waring, P. (2002). The BOHICA syndrome: a symptom of cynicism towards change initiatives, *Strategic Change*, Vol. 11, pp. 347-356.

23. Culmsee, P. and Awati, K. (2012). Towards a holding environment:building shared understanding and commitment in projects, *International Journal of Managing Projects in Business*, Vol. 5, pp. 528-548.

24.   Dahl, R. (2007-Puffin Edition), Charlie and the Chocolate Factory, New York, NY: Puffin Books.

25.   Dawkins, R. (2006), The Selfish Gene (30ᵗʰh Anniversary Edition), New York, NY: Oxford University Press.

26.   DeGrace, P. and Stahl, L. (1990), Wicked Problems, Righteous Solutions: A Catalog of Modern Engineering Paradigms, New York, NY: Prentice-Hall.

27.   Duff, G. (1994), Current Practices in Strategic Partnerships, *Australian Journal of Public Administration*, Vol.53, pp. 29-35.

28.   Dutoit, A. H., McCall, R., Mistrik, I. and Paech, B. (2006), Rationale Management in Software Engineering, Secaucus: NJ, Springer-Verlag.

29.   Eden, C and Ackermann, F. (1998), Making Strategy: The Journey of Strategic Management, Thousand Oaks, CA: Sage Publications

30.   Euler, E., Jolly, S. and Curtis, H. (2001), The Failures of the Mars Climate Orbiter and Mars Polar Lander: A Perspective From the People Involved, *Proceedings of the Annual AAS Rocky Mountain Guidance and Control Conference* (January 31-February 4, 2001), pp. 2-23.

31.   Finlayson, J (2005), Habermas: A Very Short Introduction, Oxford: Oxford University Press, pp. 28-46.

32.   Finucane, M., Alhakami, A,.Slovic, P. and Johnson, S. (2000), The Affect Heuristic in Judgements of Risks and Benefits, *Journal of Behavioral Decision Making*, Vol. 13, pp. 1-17.

33.   Flybjerg, B. (1998), Habermas and Foucault: Thinkers for a civil society, *British. Journal of Sociology*, Vol. 49, pp. 210-233.

34.   Flyvbjerg, B. and Richardson, T. (2002), "Planning and Foucault: In Search of the Dark Side of Planning Theory," in Allemendinger, P. and Tewdwr-Jones, M. (Eds), *Planning Futures: New Directions for Planning Theory*. London and New York: Routledge, pp. 44-62.

35.   Frey, B. and Bohnet, I. (1997), Identification in democratic society, *Journal of Socio-Economics*, Vol. 26, pp. 25-38.

36.   Friend, J. (2001), "The Strategic Choice Approach" in Rosenhead, J. and Mingers, J. (Eds), *Rational Analysis for a Problematic World Revisited: Problem Structuring Methods for Complexity, Uncertainty and Conflict*, Chichester: John Wiley & Sons.

37. Galway, L. (2004), Quantitative Risk Analysis for Project Management, RAND Working Paper—WR-112-RC, Santa Monica. Available online at: http://www.rand.org/pubs/working_papers/2004/RAND_WR112.pdf (Accessed July 2011).

38. Glass, R. (2003), Facts and Fallacies of Software Engineering, Boston, MA: Addison-Wesley Professional.

39. Goldkuhl, G. (2000), The validity of validity claims: An inquiry into communication rationality, *Proceedings of the Fifth International Workshop on the Language-Action Perspective on Communication Modelling (LAP 2000),* Aachen, Germany, p. 171

40. Goldkuhl, G. (2001), Communicative vs material Actions: Instrumentality, sociality and comprehensibility, *CMTO Research Paper No. 2001:06,* Centre for Studies of Humans, Technology and Organization, Linköping University, Linköping, Sweden.

41. Gray, J. (2000), Meta-risks, *Journal of Portfolio Management,* Vol. 26, pp. 18-25.

42. Gutting, G. (2005), Foucault: A Very Short Introduction, Oxford: Oxford University Press.

43. Haidt, J (2005), The Happiness Hypothesis: Finding Modern Truth in Ancient Wisdom, New York, NY: Basic Books.

44. Heifetz, R. A. (1994), Leadership without easy answers, Cambridge MA: Harvard Business Press.

45. Heifetz, R. A. (1998), "Mobilizing Adaptive Work: Beyond Visionary Leadership" in Jay A Conger, Gretchen M Spreitzer and Edward Lawler (Eds), *The Leader's Change Handbook: An Essential Guide to Setting Direction and Taking Action,* San Francisco, CA: Jossey-Bass.

46. Heifetz, R. A, Grashow, A and Linsky M (2009), The practice of adaptive leadership: tools and tactics for changing your organisation and the world," Cambridge, MA: Harvard Business Press

47. Hodgson, D.E. (2004), Project Work: The Legacy of Bureaucratic Control in the Post-Bureaucratic Organisation, *Organisation,* Vol. 11, pp. 81-100.

48. Horner, J. and Atwood, M. E. (2006), "Effective Design Rationale: Understanding the Barriers," in Dutoit, A.H.; McCall, R.;

Mistrík, I and Paech, B. (Eds), *Rationale Management in Software Engineering*, Berlin: Springer Verlag, pp. 73-90.

49. Hubbard, D. (2007), How to Measure Anything: Finding the Value of "Intangibles" in Business, New York, NY: John Wiley and Sons Inc.

50. Hubbard, D. (2009), The Failure of Risk Management: Why It's Broken and How to Fix it, New York, NY: John Wiley and Sons Inc.

51. Jackson MC. (1991), The origins and nature of critical systems thinking, *Systemic Practice and Action Research*, Vol 4: 131-149.

52. Johnson, B. (1992), Polarity Management: Identifying and Managing Unsolvable Problems, Amherst MA: HRD Press.

53. Kahneman D. (2002), Nobel Prize Lecture, Available online at: http://nobelprize.org/nobel_prizes/economics/laureates/2002/kahneman-lecture.html (Accessed July 2011)

54. Kahneman, D. (2003), Maps of Bounded Rationality: Psychology for Behavioral Economics,

55. *American Economic Review*, Vol. 93, pp. 1449-1475.

56. Kahneman, D. (2007), A short course in thinking about thinking (Edge Master Class 2007), Auberge du Soleil, Rutherford, CA, July 20-22, 2007. Available online at: http://www.edge.org/3rd_culture/kahneman07/kahneman07_index.html.

57. Kahneman, D. and Frederick, S (2002). Representativeness Revisited: Attribute Substitution in Intuitive Judgment, in Thomas Gilovich, Dale Griffinn, and Daniel Kahneman (Eds), *Heuristics and biases: The psychology of intuitive thought*. New York: NY, Cambridge University Press, pp. 49-81.

58. Kahneman, D. and Renshon, J. (2007). Why Hawks Win : A look at why the tough guys win more than they should, *Foreign Policy*, 158, pp. 34-39.

59. Kahneman, D. and Tversky, A. (1974), Judgment under Uncertainty: Heuristics and Biases, *Science*, Vol. 185, No. 4157, pp. 1124-1131.

60. Kapitola, M. (2011). *The Key Elements of Alliancing*. [email] (Personal communication).

61. Keating, T. (2009), Divine Therapy and Addiction, Brooklyn, NY: Lantern Books, p.5.

62. King, D. L., Case, C. J., & Premo, K. M. (2010). Current Mission Statement Emphasis: Be Ethical and Go Global. *Academy of Strategic Management Journal*, Vol 9, no. 2: pp. 73-89

63. Krug, S. Don't Make Me Think! A Common Sense Approach to Web Usability, Berkeley, CA: New Riders, 2nd Ed. (2005).

64. Lakoff, G. and Johnson, M. (2003), Metaphors We Live By, Chicago, IL: University Of Chicago Press; 2nd edition.

65. Larman, C (2003), Agile and Iterative Development: A Manager's Guide, Boston, MA: Pearson Education, pp. 102-104.

66. Larman, C. and Basili, V. (2003), Iterative and Incremental Development: A Brief History, *IEEE Computer*, Vol. 36, pp. 47-56.

67. Lee, J. (1989), Decision Representation Language (DRL) and its Support Environment, MIT AI Lab, Working Paper No. 325.

68. Lee, J. and Lai, K. (1991), What's in design rationale? *Human-Computer Interaction*, Vol. 6, pp. 251-280.

69. Lengel, R. amd Daft, R. (1989), The Selection of Communication as an Executive Skill," *Academy of Management Executive*, Vol. 2, pp. 225-232.

70. Lennertz, B, Lutzenhiser, A. and Failor, T. (2008) "An Introduction to Charrettes," *Planning Commissioner's Journal*, No. 78, pp.1-3.

71. Levitt, S. and Dubner, S. (2005), Freakonomics: A Rogue Economist Explores the Hidden Side of Everything, New York, NY: Harper Collins.

72. MacLean, A., Young, R. M., Bellotti, V. & Moran, T. (1991), Questions, options, and criteria: Elements of design space analysis, *Human-Computer Interaction*, Vol. 6, pp. 201-250.

73. Maskell, P. and Malmberg, A. (1999), Localised learning and industrial competitiveness, *Cambridge Journal of Economics*, Vol. 23, pp. 167-185.

74. Merchant, N. (2009) The New How: Creating Business Solutions Through Collaborative Strategy, Sebastopol, CA: O'Reilly Media.

75. Microsoft. About Microsoft: Your Potential. Our Passion (2011) http://www.microsoft.com/about/en/us/default.aspx (Accessed July 26 2011)

76. Murphy, M. Book Review Polaris. Available online at: http://www.cadmus.ca/bookreviewpolaris.htm(Accessed July 2010).

77.   Nadler, G. and Hibono, S. (1998), Breakthrough Thinking: The Seven Principles of Creative Problem Solving, Roseville CA: Prima Lifestyles.

78.   New South Wales Treasury (2004), "Value Management Guideline," Document No. TAM04-14. Available online at: http://www.treasury.nsw.gov.au/__data/assets/pdf_file/0009/5112/value_management.pdf (Accessed July 2011).

79.   Nicholas, J and Steyn, H. (2008), Project Management for Business, Engineering and Technology, Burlington MA: Butterworth-Heinemann.

80.   Nonaka, I. and Konno, N. (1998), "The concept of "Ba": Building a Foundation for Knowledge Creation," *California Management Review*, Vol. 40, pp. 40-54.

81.   Ostrom, E. (1998), A Behavioural Approach to the Rational Choice Theory of Collective Action, *American Political Science Review*, Vol. 92, pp. 1-22.

82.   Patching, A. (1994). Partnering and Personal Skills for Project Management Mastery. Sydney, Alan Patching and Associates. Available online at: http://www.alanpatching.com/content/project-management/partnering-for-project-management-mastery/ (Accessed July 2011).

83.   Polanyi, M. (1966), The Tacit Dimension, Chicago, IL: The University of Chicago Press.

84.   Project Management Institute (2008). A guide to the project management body of knowledge—Fourth Edition, Newtown Square, PA: Project Management Institute.

85.   Queensland Governnment (2008), Relational Procurement Options—Alliance and Early Contractor Involvement Contracts, Queensland Government Chief Procurement Office—Procurement Guidance Series. p. 17.

86.   Rathbun, G. (2007). Silenced by a Mission Statement: An Organisation's Cloak of Ambiguity." *Human Communication*, Vol. 10, 547-556.

87.   Roam, D. (2008), The Back of the Napkin: Solving Problems and Selling Ideas with Pictures, London: Penguin Books.

88.   Rittel, H. W and Kunz, W. (1970), Issues as Elements of Information Systems, *Working Paper 131, The Institute of Urban and Regional Development*, University of California, Berkeley

89. Rittel, H.W.J. (1972), On the Planning Crisis: Systems Analysis of the First and Second Generations, *Bedriftsokonomen*, No. 8, pp. 390-396.

90. Rittel, H. W. J & Webber, M. (1973), Dilemmas in a General Theory of Planning, *Policy Sciences*, Vol. 4, pp. 155-169.

91. Rosenhead, J. (2001) "Robustness Analysis: Keeping Your options Open" in Rosenhead, J. and Mingers, J. (Eds), *Rational Analysis for a Problematic World Revisited: Problem Structuring Methods for Complexity, Uncertainty and Conflict,* Chichester: John Wiley & Sons.

92. Rosenhead, J. and Mingers, J. (Eds) (2001), Rational Analysis for a Problematic World Revisited: Problem Structuring Methods for Complexity, Uncertainty and Conflict, Chichester: John Wiley & Sons.

93. Ross, J.. (2003). "An Introduction to Project Alliancing (on engineering and construction projects)". Alliance Contracting Conference, Sydney, 30 April 2003. Available at: http://www.pci-aus.com/files/resources/Alliancing_30Apr03_F.pdf

94. Royce, W. (1970), Managing the development of large software systems: Concepts and techniques, *Proceedings IEEE Wescon,* pp 1-9.

95. Sapolsky, H. (1972), The Polaris System Development: Bureaucratic and Programmatic Success in Government, Cambridge MA: Harvard Business Press.

96. Savage, S. (2009), The Flaw of Averages: Why We Underestimate Risk in the Face of Uncertainty, New York, NY: Wiley.

97. Scharmer, C. S. (2009), Theory U: Learning from the Future as It Emerges, San Francisco, CA: Berrett-Koehler Publishers.

98. Schwaber, K. (2004), Agile Project Management with Scrum, Redmond, WA: Microsoft Press.

99. Schwaber, K. and Sutherland, J. (2010), Scrum, scrum.org, Available online at: http://www.scrum.org/storage/scrumguides/Scrum%20Guide.pdf (Accessed July 2011)

100. Senge, P (1994), The Fifth Discipline: The Art & Practice of the Learning Organisation, New York, NY: Doubleday Business Publishing.

101. Shore, B. (2009), Systematic Biases and Culture in Project Failure, *Journal of Project Management*, Vol. 39, pp. 5-16.

102. Shum, S. B. and Hammond, N. (1994), Argumentation based Design Rationale: What use at what cost? *International Journal of Human-Computer Studies*, Vol. 40, pp. 603-652.

103. Simon, H. (1977), The New Science of Management Decision, Saddle River NJ: Prentice Hall PTR.

104. Stern, D. (1998), Mothers' Emotional Needs, *Paediatrics*, Vol. 102, pp. 1250-1252.

105. Stewart, N. (2009), The Cost of Anchoring on Credit Card Minimum Payments, *Psychological Science*, Vol. 20, pp. 39-41.

106. Stiles, R. and Oliver J. (1998), Anecdotes from Alliancing, Paper presented at the 1998 New Zealand Petroleum Conference. Available online at: http://www.nzpam.govt.nz/cms/petroleum/conferences/conference-proceedings-1998/anecdotes-from-alliancing (Accessed July 2011).

107. *Stirling City Centre Alliance "Environemtal Health" Area of Strategic Focus*, digital image, Stirling Alliance Web Site, http://www.stirlingcitycentre.com.au/our-vision/environmental-health. (accessed 13 March 2011)

108. Sunstein, C. (2006). Deliberating Groups vs. Prediction Markets (or Hayek's Challenge to Habermas), *Episteme: A Journal of Social Epistemology*, Vol. 3, pp. 192-213

109. Swartz, L. (2003), Why People Hate the Paperclip: Labels, Appearance, Behaviour and Social Responses to User interface Agents, Bachelor thesis—Stanford University (Unpublished).

110. Takeuchi, H. and Nonaka, I. (1986), The new product development game: Stop running the relay race and take up rugby, *Harvard Business Review,* Jan/Feb issue, pp. 137-146

111. Thorp, J. (1999), The Information Paradox, Whitby, ON: McGraw Hill Ryerson.

112. Tolman, E. C. (1948), Cognitive maps in rats and men, *Psychological Review*, Vol. 55, pp. 189-208.

113. Ulrich, W. (2001a), A Philosophical Staircase for Information Systems Definition, Design and Development: A Discursive Approach to Reflective Practice in ISD (Part 1), *Journal of Information Technology Theory and Application (JITTA)*, Vol.3, pp. 55-84.

114. Ulrich, W. (2001b), Critically Systemic Discourse: A Discursive Approach to Reflective Practice in ISD (Part 2), *Journal of*

Information Technology Theory and Application (JITTA), Vol. 3, pp. 85-106.

115. Underwood, J., 1(996). Models for change: soft systems methodology. Business Process Transformation, University of Technology, Sydney (Unpublished Lecture Notes)

116. Van Gelder, T. (2002), Argument Mapping with Reason!able, *The American Philosophical Association Newsletter on Philosophy and Computers*, pp. 85-90.

117. Van Gelder, T. (2003). "Enhancing Deliberation Through Computer Supported Argument Mapping," in Kirschner, P. A., Shum, S. J. B. and Carr, C. S. (Eds.), *Visualizing Argumentation: Software Tools for Collaborative and Educational Sense-making*, London: Springer-Verlag, pp. 97-115.

118. Wareham, J. and Cerrits, H. (1999), "De-contextualising Competence: Can Business Best Practice be Bundled and Sold?" *European Management Journal*, Vol. 17, pp. 39-49.

119. Whiteley, D. (2004), Project Alliancing, An investigation into the benefits and attributes of the project alliance contracting strategy, MSc Thesis—Curtin University of Technology (Unpublished).

120. Whiteley, D. (2011). *The Key Elements of Alliancing*. [email] (Personal communication).

121. Whitty, S. J. (2005), A Memetic Paradigm of Project Management, *International Journal of Project Management*, Vol. 23, pp. 575-583.

122. Wilson, A. (1994), Cognitive Factors Affecting Subjective Probability Assessments, Institute for Statistics and Decision Sciences, *Institute of Statistics and Decision Sciences Discussion Paper #94-02*, Durham, NC: Duke University.

123. Winnicott, D.W. (1960). The Theory of the Parent-Infant Relationship. *International Journal of Psychoanalysis*, Vol. 41, pp. 585-595.

124. Winograd, T. and Flores, F. (1987), *Understanding Computers and Cognition*, Norwood NJ: Ablex Publishing Corporation, p.150.

Index

About the Authors

Paul Culmsee (twitter: @paulculmsee) is currently an IT professional, facilitator and sense-maker and has a bachelor's degree in Information Science from Edith Cowan University. He co-founded Seven Sigma Business Solutions (www.sevensigma.com.au) and is a Microsoft Certified Systems Engineer, Microsoft Certified Technology Specialist, Microsoft Certified Trainer, Certified Information Systems Security Professional, one of only three Cognexus Certified Dialogue Mappers in the world. He and his wife have the best two children in the world and live in Perth, Australia.

Outside of CogNexus trainers, Paul is the only authorised trainer of Issue Mapping world-wide and conducts two-day classes in Issue Mapping around the world. Details of the class and training locations and dates can be found at www.issuemappingclass.com

Paul also is the author and principal instructor of the two-day SharePoint Governance and Information Architecture Master Class run around the world. Much of the material in this class was inspired from this book. Details of the class and training locations and dates can be found at www.spgovia.com

Kailash Awati (twitter: @kailashawati) is Head of Service Development, Asia-Pacific at a pharmaceutical multinational. He holds Ph.D.s in physics and chemical engineering along with assorted certifications in project and data management. His professional interests include IT strategy, business intelligence, knowledge management, risk analysis and decision-making in organizations. He writes about these and related topics on his blog, "Eight to Late" (http://eight2late.wordpress.com).

Kailash has worked in various consulting, technology and research roles in Europe, U.S.A, India, Australia and Singapore (where he resides currently). He and his wife, Arati, have two wonderful children.

CPSIA information can be obtained at www.ICGtesting.com
Printed in the USA
LVOW07s0842250914

405832LV00002B/533/P